THE HAMLET SYNDROME

—

OVERTHINKERS WHO UNDERACHIEVE

Adrienne Miller and Andrew Goldblatt

WILLIAM MORROW
AND COMPANY, INC.
NEW YORK

Miller, Adrienne.
    The Hamlet syndrome : overthinkers who underachieve / Adrienne
Miller and Andrew Goldblatt.
        p.   cm.
    Bibliography: p.
    Includes index.
    ISBN 0-688-07851-6
    1. Underachievement.   2. Money—Psychological aspects.
3. Decision making (Psychology)   4. Civilization, Occidental—Psychological aspects.   I. Goldblatt, Andrew.   II. Title.
    BF637.U53M55   1989
    155.2'32—dc19   88-30866
                                                                         CIP

Printed in the United States of America

First Edition

1 2 3 4 5 6 7 8 9 10

BOOK DESIGN BY RICHARD ORIOLO

Acknowledgments

We would like to thank, first and foremost, the dozens of Hamlets who overcame their doubt and indecision long enough to spill their guts into a tape recorder held by people they hardly knew and weren't sure they should trust. We hope we've given you reason to feel good about your leap of faith. We are also grateful to the many Hamlets from all over the country who filled out our lengthy questionnaires. Deserving of special thanks is Glen McClish, who gave us invaluable suggestions for improving the manuscript.

Adrienne would like to express her appreciation to Dr. Bates Huffaker. She would also like to thank her father, whose Polonius complex reinforced her admiration for Shakespeare's understanding of human nature.

Andy would like to dedicate this book to his parents, who would have been proud. He would also like to thank Lisa Goldblatt, Janice Schachter and Leon Nehmad, Mr. Sam, Sue McKibbin, and, above all, Christa Matty, without whose patience, support, and understanding this book could never have been written.

Contents

V

SOLILOQUIES: HAMLET SPEAKS HIS MIND 187

VI

COPING WITH THE HAMLET SYNDROME 223

SOURCES 255

THE
HAMLET
SYNDROME

I

EVEN IF YOU WIN THE RAT RACE, YOU'RE STILL JUST A RAT: THE HAMLET SYNDROME EXPLAINED

An' can you by no drift of circumstance
Get from him why he puts on this confusion,
Grating so harshly all his days of quiet
With turbulent and dangerous lunacy?

He does confess he feels himself distracted,
But from what cause 'a will by no means speak.

Hamlet, ACT III, SCENE i

To look at Mike you'd swear he was a winner. Dressed casually but not carelessly, he moves with the dignity of a man at peace with himself. He speaks in mild tones, and the gleam in his eye adds a hint of detachment and amusement to his otherwise thoughtful mien. He's starting to show his age—crow's-feet gather about his eyes as he laughs, and his hair is flecked with gray—but the touch of maturity complements his otherwise youthful features and suggests he's entering the prime of his life.

Talking to him only deepens the good impression. He can speak intelligently about almost anything—politics, relationships, the arts—and he has that special ability to connect seemingly random events into coherent patterns. He tells fascinating stories about the people and places he's known. Often there's a message behind his stories, but he's hardly a holier-than-thou type or egghead. He talks just as passionately about his favorite TV show (a sitcom you've described to other friends as implausible and stupid) as he does about the state of the world, and he absolutely loves to gossip—the nastier the better. When you tell him how impressed you are with his knowledge and eloquence, he works feverishly to suppress an embarrassed smile. He belittles himself, calls you easily fooled, in fact does anything but tell you the truth, which is that he's thrilled there's someone besides himself who thinks his head is screwed on straight. Talking to Mike is always refreshing, and you come to rely on him for penetrating, frequently amusing insights into the life the two of you have in common.

Over time you get to know him better. He's extraordinarily sensitive to himself and others. He's tolerant, curious, and a Doubting Thomas of the highest order. And sometimes he comes out with the most outrageous statements! Take, for example, the conversation you had with him about the last election; if the FBI had been around, surely he'd have been arrested for what he was saying. "We think we're so much better than the Russians because we're a democracy and they're not," he said, "but how can we call ourselves a free people when the Republicans and Democrats are so alike? Big money runs them both, just like the state runs the Communist party in Russia. And as for our system being more open, it's obvious to me that Gorbachev hides fewer skeletons in his closet than George Bush does in his." Whether you agree with him or not, it's clear to you that Mike is one of a vanishing breed: someone who thinks for himself.

Mike has ambivalent feelings about his family. On the one hand he's grateful for their loyalty, generosity, and affection, but on the other he suspects they don't know who he *really* is. Except for a younger brother who shares his love for baseball—how can a guy of Mike's intelligence live and die over the exploits of twenty-four muscleheads named the *Orioles*?—he maintains only fitful contact with anyone in the family besides his parents. Mike prefers friends to relatives. "You can choose your friends," he says. But you soon learn that he doesn't have very many friends, either. In a crisis he'd have only a handful of people to call on, so you're not surprised when Mike confesses that he feels lonely a lot of the time.

He was anything *but* lonely in college. Though hardly the big man on campus, he had lots of friends. He earned a degree in English with honors and considered going to graduate school, but decided against it because he didn't want to become a critic or, worse still, a bore. As the years rolled by, he lost contact with most of his college buddies, and now his opportunities for making new friends are practically nil. He's not a joiner; he'd rather spend a night in jail than sit through a club meeting with a bunch of people he finds boring. His only hobby, writing short stories, is essentially solitary. He reads for hours on end. About the only time he's consistently around people is at work, but with all the jealousy and backbiting going on at the office that's the last place he's likely to make friends.

You notice that Mike is pretty down on his work life. When you first ask him what he does for a living, he smiles puckishly and says, "I'm a garbage man." You don't buy it, and you tell him so. "All right, I'm not a garbage man," he admits, but he doesn't tell you what he *is*. Instead he tries to change the subject. You have to pry to the point of rudeness before he gives you the truth: "I work in a hotel." "Doing what," you ask, "accounting?" "Some of that," he acknowledges. "I do a little bit of everything. I even cleaned the rooms once when all the maids called in sick." He laughs at that, then moves on to another topic. Whatever he does for a living, he's obviously not proud of it.

Only after you've known him awhile and he feels totally comfortable around you does he give you the straight story about his job. He's a hotel desk attendant. He checks guests in and out of rooms, vacillating between envy and contempt for his customers, especially when they pay their bills with gold cards or C-notes. He'll never be like those people, he says, but deep down he's not sure whether he's happy or sad about that. When he first started working at the hotel he figured on staying only a few months, until something better came along. But that something never came—in good part because he didn't make much effort to find it—and so two years later he still devotes eight hours a day to ringing for bellhops.

Ask why a smart, articulate, affable guy like him is doing dead-end work and his face curls into a grimace. "Lots of reasons," he explains. "The main one is that there aren't any good jobs out there for English majors, unless you count the ones in publishing that pay less than what I make as a clerk. Another is that I just don't see myself as the corporate type, riding the train to work in a suit and carrying a briefcase full of memos I don't have time to read. I'm not cut out for that kind of stuff." He gets animated now. "I can't be cruel like you have to be in business. And face it, most business is just the art of ripping people off. At least at the hotel we give people a clean bed and a television for the night.

Even that's a rip-off when you consider how much we charge. The whole country's built on a system of civilized theft we refer to as free enterprise. Call me a wimp or whatever, but I can't handle that sort of thing. Not me. I just can't be a part of it."

The grimace slowly dissolves. The gleam returns to his eyes. "Maybe someday I'll sell out and get myself a real job," he confides, smiling. "But I'm not ready for that just yet."

Mike is thirty-six years old. If he's not ready for a real job at this age, you say to yourself, the odds are good that he'll *never* be ready.

Like Mike, Linda is outwardly thoughtful and amusing, inwardly fretful and defensive. She has a bachelor's degree in resource management, but now that she's approaching her thirtieth birthday she can feel the discipline and direction of her college years slipping away. A secretary for a nonprofit organization, she intended to stay at her job only until she decided what she really wanted to do with her life, but she never did figure that out. So instead of leaving she's taken on additional responsibilities. This way, she says, she isn't going stale, she's expanding her skills. Too bad she's never gotten a salary that matches her contribution to the office—and too bad also that she's never had the courage to insist on a raise.

Despite her many duties, she makes the job look easy. In fact, everyone in the office tells her that if she ever left, the organization would have to hire two people to replace her. She's an ideal co-worker not just because she's extremely competent, but because she has an irrepressible sense of fun. Whenever her fellow staff members look too serious, Linda ambushes them with a hail of paper clips and rubber bands. And she always has a moment or two to chat. She seems to know something about everyone and can conduct a conversation on any topic, even if her contribution is limited to asking questions. She talks about the Super Bowl with the football fans (and always participates in the office pool, even though she doesn't know a halfback from a humpback whale), the latest Broadway hit with the drama buffs, and politics with the folks who get their news from *The New York Times*. She likes to listen to other people talk about their interests, and that too endears her to her colleagues; a sincere listener is a rare treasure.

Linda's own passion is gardening. She lives in an apartment, so she keeps her fingers in the dirt by designing gardens for friends who have houses. Her gardening serves as a testament to her fine aesthetic sense and her commitment to the environment. She makes sure every plant gets the right amount of light and that the entire plot is pleasing to the eye. She does such good work that several friends regularly encourage her to start her own landscaping business. Her creativity, they tell her, paired with her encyclopedic knowledge of plants and local growing conditions, would make her an instant success. At times Linda's really tempted by the idea. After all, these are the eighties; women routinely start their own businesses. She'd like to be her own boss, set her own hours, and make money at something she enjoys rather than type memo after memo in a stuffy office. Then, too, she has this nagging feeling that she's wasting her potential. The sooner she gets on to a challenge equal to her abilities, the better she'll feel about herself.

But after Linda imagines how nice life would be if she were her own boss and gardening for a living, she thinks of the problems business people have to put up with. She'd have to incorporate, which would mean finding a lawyer she could trust. She'd have to attend to all the petty practical things that go with running a business: bookkeeping, scheduling appointments, finding quality wholesalers, collecting debts. She'd have to convince total strangers she was competent, more competent than the host of gardeners and landscape consultants who've been listed in the Yellow Pages for years. Fights with unhappy customers would be inevitable. And where on earth would she come up with the capital for this enterprise? Except for a couple of months when she couldn't pay off her Visa bill, Linda has never been in debt. She's proud that she doesn't owe anybody anything, and the prospect of begging for a loan and making payments every month leaves her feeling more than a little bit sick. Compared to the office routine she's accustomed to, running a business sounds risky, too much of an ordeal. It would be a lot simpler just going on as before, designing gardens for her friends in her spare time.

This whole cycle of thought, which Linda seems to repeat ten times a day, leaves her feeling disappointed in herself and life in general. She wonders whether the choices opened up by the women's movement have merely created more opportunities for failure. Unable to choose among the countless options available to her, she sticks with the risk-free situation she's in. After all, as one of her resource management professors used to tell her, if you haven't done anything, you haven't done anything wrong.

Then there's Linda's boyfriend, Roy. While everyone else encourages her to go into business for herself, he dismisses the notion with a sarcastic laugh. "You can't do that. You know you can't follow through on any plan," he says. And, of course, he's right—the creep. Roy knows her, and to his credit he doesn't coddle her by joining in on her pie-in-the-sky fantasies. That's why she loves him; his realistic world view anchors her more securely to terra firma.

In that respect Roy is different from Bill, her first serious boyfriend. Bill had been much more easygoing. He thought Linda was terrific no matter what she did. Indeed, her friends were shocked when she broke up with him. Linda agreed that Bill was charming and easy to be with. His fatal flaw, in her eyes, was that he wasn't honorable. He was a landlord, and if for some reason he didn't like a tenant, he said he wanted to move his mother into the tenant's apartment by the end of the month. But Bill's mother had died years before he bought the apartment building. Bill also violated state laws—his building would fail an inspection on a zillion counts. In winter, Bill would turn the heat on only three hours a day, and when the tenants complained he'd lie and say the heat was on at least twice that long. Whenever Linda voiced her concerns about his behavior, Bill ran a guilt trip on her: "Hey, honey, I don't hassle you for wasting away at that dead-end job of yours, do I?" The last straw was when she heard him bragging about his dishonorable tactics. She couldn't bear to associate with a man who took joy in exploiting other human beings, and so more out of principle than anything else she dumped him.

Looking at Roy, who for all his brutal honesty makes only $5.25 an hour, Linda wonders whether breaking up with Bill was a smart move after all. Bill would have been happy to lend, maybe even *give,* her some of his ill-gotten money so she could start her landscaping business. And then there's the matter of starting a family. If she's going to have a child it has to be soon, but she can't see raising one on the paltry salaries she and Roy bring in. She sighs. She's screwed up her personal life almost as badly as she's screwed up her career. She came out of college a bright young woman with a ton of potential, but she's squandered that potential on clerical work and second-rate men. If she had to choose one word to describe her life and her future, that word would be *bleak.*

But this is a Linda hardly anyone sees. To the outside world she's a competent, savvy woman. The people in her office would never guess that beneath the classy, contented façade Linda is wracked by doubt, indecision, and frustration.

Even If You Win the Rat Race, You're Still Just a Rat

* * *

Mike and Linda are composites—but there are millions of real Americans like them. Thoughtful, inquisitive, lovingly raised, these twenty-one- to forty-year-old men and women are long on potential and fascinating thoughts but short on concrete achievement. Were there but a few of them, we could easily dismiss them as wimps or mental cases. But they're everywhere, driving delivery vans, sorting mail, waiting tables—and their numbers promise to increase. In many ways these people hold the key to America's future, yet they remove themselves to the periphery of society, there to brood year after year. They cripple themselves, vex their families and friends, and deprive the nation of sorely needed intellectual resources. Just what's wrong with these young people?

Mike and Linda, along with the millions of Americans like them, have the Hamlet Syndrome. (Although we'll refer to Hamlet throughout this book as *he,* we do it for the sake of easier reading—to avoid the awkwardness of the *he/she* type of grammatical construction—not because female Hamlets are unusual. Indeed, since women are schooled from birth in many of the values associated with the Hamlet Syndrome, they may be *more* susceptible to the syndrome than men. Please keep in mind, then, that unless we refer specifically to the *male* Hamlet or *female* Hamlet, the traits we ascribe to Hamlets in this book apply to both sexes equally.)

1

Defining the Hamlet Syndrome

The Hamlet Syndrome is characterized by an inability to decide between the heart and the dollar. To Hamlet, the heart represents principle, conscience, consideration for others—all those intangibles that make someone morally good; the dollar represents wealth, power, and inclusion in the mainstream—the standards by which we measure ourselves against others. Hamlets are bright, sensitive, well-educated, middle-class young people aged twenty-one to forty. More than anything else they want to preserve their purity of heart, but they also feel the need to succeed and earn lots of money and esteem. Torn between their dual desires, they can't decide what to do, and so they do nothing. While inaction effectively preserves their purity of heart, it puts the dollar further and further out of reach. As the years roll by and Hamlets grow tired of making just enough money to survive, their bitterness toward themselves and the system increases, leading to frustration, cynicism, and a dramatic loss of self-esteem.

Almost every Hamlet has at least one personality trait that predisposes him to the syndrome. He may never have developed the taste for risk required for success in a free market economy. He may have been humiliated by defeat once too often to engage in competition. He may have little patience for details or knotty problems. He may lack self-confidence. He may hate work. He may be a procrastinator, figuring that he'll get around to a career sometime in the future. Or he may be passive by nature, counting himself a victim of forces beyond his control. Whatever the personality trait, it provides psychological underpinning for the Hamlet Syndrome and makes the heart-or-dollar conflict more than just a philosophical conundrum.

The Hamlet Syndrome is named after William Shakespeare's most famous character. Hamlet, the prince of Denmark, is known to all as the speaker of the immortal line "To be or not to be." He's witty, well-educated, from one of the best families in Europe—and, for a thirty-year-old, pathetically indecisive. When an uncle murders Hamlet's father and marries Hamlet's mother, in the process usurping Hamlet's throne, the brooding prince simply *has* to act. After all, if that's no cause for action, nothing is! Yet Hamlet protests, procrastinates, and intellectually perambulates through the entire play before he finally makes the move he was supposed to make at the beginning. For all his insight he simply cannot take control, and so over the years his name has become synonymous with indecision and inaction.

Modern Hamlets come in five general types, each of which comes to the heart-or-dollar dilemma from a different direction. The first and most common variety of Hamlet is the *I-have-not-yet-begun-to-fight* type. The not-yet-begun-to-fight Hamlet has never even tried to chase after the dollar. His personality and his commitment to the heart stick up like nails through the heels of his shoes, and so he sees any attempt at racing after money as downright injurious. Most of the time he's content with where he is and sees no pressing *need* to chase the dollar. Sooner or later, however, he feels the temptation to show the world he can succeed if he really wants to. But before he can chase the dollar he has to decide what he's going to do about the nails in his shoes. They're so firmly lodged he has to struggle to pull them out. He hates struggling, so the not-yet-begun-to-fight Hamlet drops the whole idea of chasing the dollar, telling himself he's not a very swift runner anyway.

We'll follow two not-yet-begun-to-fight Hamlets through the course of this book. The first is Martin, a thirty-three-year-old New Englander. The youngest child in a typical suburban family, he's had plenty of successful examples to follow: his father worked for the same company for more than a quarter of a century; his oldest brother is a veterinarian; his middle brother, who holds a doctorate in virology, programs computers. Yet for the last ten years Martin has been sorting and delivering mail for a large nonprofit organization, earning well under $20,000 annually despite working full-time. Laconic and self-effacing, Martin illustrates how the Hamlet Syndrome can combine with individual personality traits to make the heart-or-dollar dilemma hard to resolve. He believes that "people are scum," that the petty machinations of humankind perpetuate misery. He also suffers from an irrational lack of self-confidence. Thus he not only sees the pursuit of success as morally wrong, but sees his *chance* for success as extremely remote—*two* good reasons not to fight.

Our second not-yet-begun-to-fight Hamlet is Maxine, a twenty-eight-year-old from Philadelphia's cozy Roxborough section. An honor student throughout her academic career, Maxine has the brainpower and discipline to succeed in whatever field she chooses. Since graduating from college summa cum laude, however, she's bounced from one clerical job to another. "Work is a prison, day care for adults," she says acerbically. She currently puts in twenty hours a week as coordinator of volunteers in a hospital while she attends graduate school in library science. Like many Hamlets, she hopes she'll someday solve the heart-or-dollar dilemma by finding a job that's *both* righteous and remunerative. Not much chance for big bucks in the library business, but the work's more meaningful than typing memos. "If I'm going to spend eight hours a day at a job, I want to work at something I *believe* in. The only institution I believe in at this point is the public library, so that's why I'm going to library school," she explains.

The second variety of Hamlet is the *hippie*. Whether he came of age in the 1960s or merely wishes he did, the hippie Hamlet hearkens back to the time when interpersonal barriers like competition and suspicion were junked in favor of cooperation and love. The hippie Hamlet doesn't necessarily dress or look like someone out of the sixties, but attitudinally he's never left the Woodstock Nation. He's dumbfounded by the cynicism and competitiveness of the seventies and eighties, and feels himself part of an ever-shrinking minority that doesn't snicker at the mention of words like *love, peace,* and *understanding.* In his mind those old principles still apply, and he'll be damned if he starts kowtowing to the Establishment now after all these years on the fringe.

"I'm not an old hippie," protests thirty-seven-year-old Jeff, whose ponytailed hair extended halfway down his back until he finally cut it in 1986. To a large extent he's right. Most old hippies, as the yuppie phenomenon proves, participated in the countercultural movement because it was popular, not because they wholeheartedly believed in it. They were afraid of going to war, they liked the clothes and music, the drugs made them feel good, and the sex was easy. When conformity and conventional success came back into style they readily traded their tie-dyes and bell-bottoms for business suits, marching with yipster-turned-networker Jerry Rubin into the American mainstream.

But a core of old hippies—Abbie Hoffman comes readily to mind—truly believed in those sixties ideals, and didn't just go along with the crowd. That's the sort of hippie we're referring to when we speak of the hippie Hamlet: someone whose principles and life-style remain rooted in the sixties. An affable, gentle fellow with a sophisticated world view, Jeff came of age in the late 1960s and early 1970s. He graduated from the University of Kansas highly skeptical of conventional society, and he's resolutely held himself apart from the mainstream all these years. With all due apologies, then, we're going to make him our hippie Hamlet in spite of his objections.

The third type of Hamlet is the *perpetual student.* The perpetual student has figured out that he can avoid the heart-or-dollar question indefinitely just by doing what he's always done: going to school. After four or five years of undergraduate work, he enrolls in graduate school, taking three or four years to earn a master's degree and upward of half a dozen more to receive a doctorate. By the time he gets out of school his only career option is teaching. Unfortunately, no one's likely to offer him a tenure-track position after he's taken so long to produce his dissertation. Forced in his late thirties to make his way in the world, the perpetual student may wind up driving a taxi or tending bar, his years of study good for little more than psychic comfort.

Born, raised, and educated in Wisconsin, Jessica epitomizes the perpetual-student Hamlet. Now thirty-seven years old, she spent a *decade* pursuing her doctorate. An indifferent high school and college student, she took such an interest in Chinese literature that, although she had virtually no background in the subject, she wormed her way into a graduate program. She spent all those years in school partly because she couldn't bear dealing with the workaday world. "I've done office work as a temporary," she says, "but I always knew it was temporary. The thought of a permanent nine-to-five job, where I'd always have to be in one place . . ." Her voice trails off, and she shakes her head. "I couldn't stand it. I've had the luxury of being able to set my own schedule for so long that I could never deal with being on someone else's schedule."

The fourth variety of Hamlet is the *artist*. By artist we mean someone blessed from childhood with the talent and discipline to excel at an art or a craft. In adulthood virtually all Hamlets express themselves through art—in good part because they can't express themselves on the job—but that doesn't make them artist Hamlets. The artist Hamlet has known from a very early age that he has a special ability to make music or write or paint, and he has chosen to develop his gift to its fullest rather than embark on a safer, more conventional career. The typical artist Hamlet takes a poorly paid, uninvolving day job and spends his nights and weekends toiling at his true calling, dreaming of the day the world recognizes his talent.

For our artist Hamlet we've chosen a remarkable forty-year-old named Antonio. Antonio's mother was a Panamanian singer and musician who fell in love with an American soldier. She left little Antonio with her parents and followed her soldier husband to California, and thus Antonio spent the first dozen years of his life in Panama, in the modest but loving environs of his grandparents' house. "In the living room was my mother's nine-foot concert Steinway," he recalls. "It had a padlock on it, and never once in my entire childhood was it ever opened. My grandfather was an accomplished violinist, and whenever he would invite friends over to play music, my grandmother would take me out for a Coke or an ice cream cone. They wanted so hard to keep me away from music. Music and entertainment were regarded as the wrong kind of society."

But despite his grandparents' best efforts, Antonio became a musician. Upon joining his mother in the United States he started diddling at the piano. "But then I heard the harpsichord," he says, "and I knew I *had* to be a musician, because this instrument was my voice." He's since evolved into a concert-level player. So strong is his devotion to his art that he's walked away from a promising career as an accountant to further his musicianship.

The fifth and final type of Hamlet is the *dropout.* The dropout has actually taken on the real world and enjoyed his share of conventional success, but he's grown disillusioned with the chase for the dollar and has opted for the noncompetitive life-style characteristic of Hamlets. The dropout Hamlet often goes straight from college to a promising entry-level position, but somewhere on his way up the success ladder the pressure gets too much for him. He spends too many hours at the office, takes too much abuse from his boss, or realizes he's never had a chance to kick back and do his own thing. The dropout is more secure than other Hamlets, principally because he's braved the real-world hazards the others are afraid of, and he's also more zealous about preserving his low-pressure life-style.

Brent, now thirty-four, is a lawyer. So zealous is he about protecting his Hamlethood that he's remained unemployed for the last two years, living on the money he saved from his last job. He's excelled at virtually everything he's tried. A National Merit Scholar, he graduated magna cum laude from an Ivy League university. From there he went to work as an economic analyst, but found the work so boring he quit after one year. He roamed through the Rocky Mountains and Alaska for a while, went to law school—where he finished in the top 10 percent of his class—and then took a position with a well-regarded law firm, making what he calls an "unconscionable" amount of money. But the money and prestige couldn't compensate for the stress. "I had the capacity to survive and succeed in the rat race," he says, "but like the graffiti I saw in a law school bathroom said, 'Even if you win the rat race, you're still just a rat.'" So rather than live like a rodent Brent dropped out. He resigned from the firm, picked up the banjo his parents gave him for a graduation present, and joined a country and western band.

Most Hamlets are a mixture of these general types. By going back to school for a degree in a poorly paid field, not-yet-begun-to-fight type Maxine acts a bit like a perpetual student. Jeff, our hippie, and Jessica, our perpetual student, have a lot of not-yet-begun-to-fight in them. Antonio, our artist, worked for a while as an accountant, meaning he's also a dropout. Regardless of background, all Hamlets are caught between the need to live by their ideals and the need to get along in mainstream society. That dilemma forms the core of the Hamlet Syndrome.

One of the biggest reasons for the enduring popularity of Shakespeare's Hamlet is the universal nature of his plight: Each of us has at one time or another faced a situation that paralyzes all but our thoughts. The English poet Samuel Taylor Coleridge saw Hamlet as a sort of Everyman: "Hamlet's character is the prevalence of the abstracting and generalizing habit over the practical. He does not want courage, skill, will or opportunity, but every incident sets him thinking. . . . I have a smack of Hamlet myself, if I may say so." Although modern literary critic Frank Kermode disagrees that Hamlet is an Everyman, he concedes, "In the perplexed figure of Hamlet, just because of our sense that his mind lacks definite boundaries, we find ourselves." At one time or another, then, we all exhibit characteristics of the Hamlet Syndrome. But that doesn't mean we all *have* the syndrome. Many Americans who fit within the demographic framework—aged twenty-one to forty, from a middle-class background, well-educated, sensitive, bright, poorly paid—nevertheless are *not* Hamlets. Let's clarify a little further whom we're talking about in this book by defining the Hamlet Syndrome in negative terms, i.e., describing who *isn't* a Hamlet.

Most children from lower socioeconomic backgrounds are free of the Hamlet Syndrome because their underprivileged circumstances motivate them to make money. Unlike little Hamlet, they didn't grow up in a split-level house or tool around the neighborhood on a shiny new bike. They grew up wanting, and so in adulthood they strive, as poor people in our society often do, for a piece of the American dream. To them Hamlet is spoiled and effete, a whiner who's never known what it's like to go without. If Hamlet thinks he has it bad, they scoff, let him try raising a family on peanuts the way their parents did.

People in public service professions are not Hamlets. Teachers, social workers, librarians, and the like are hideously underpaid, often paid less than Hamlet gets for menial labor, but they have both direction and a profession. No one just *falls* into being a social worker, for instance—you have to go to graduate school and do fieldwork for at least two years. Working in public service also requires a tremendous commitment to people and a tolerance for failure in both humans and institutions. Hamlet has neither quality in such abundance that he could handle, say, teaching tenth-graders. (Although Maxine is willing to give librarianship a try.) Public service professionals are the unsung heroes of American society, taking on some of the hardest work around and getting few material rewards. They're much too dedicated to be compared with diffident, brooding Hamlets.

Social activists are too ambitious to be Hamlets, for they aspire to nothing less than transforming society. We define social activists as people devoted to an idea or cause more than money. Clergypeople are social activists, as are grass-roots organizers and other campaigners for a cause. They've decided that what they believe in is more important than a big house or a wide-screen TV, so they transfer their ambitions from themselves to the movement they serve. When the movement advances, they do too. Although they may not have a profession per se, they're usually so loyal to their cause that they spend as much time at it as any doctor or lawyer—in contrast to Hamlet, who normally has to be strapped to his chair before he stays at his job more than the prescribed number of hours per week.

Speaking of doctors and lawyers, in the course of our research we came across a number of professionals who claimed that they too have the Hamlet Syndrome. Subject to bouts of indecision and disillusion, these high-salaried, middle- to upper-middle-class success stories often feel just as alienated from the mainstream as any Hamlet. They're like Brent before he dropped out, winning the rat race but feeling like rats. Real as their suffering may be, though, it's obvious they're not Hamlets. They have plenty of drive, discipline, and tenacity. They're eminently capable of making decisions that affect not only themselves but many other people. And, of course, they've got the dollar. Uncomfortable as their situation may be, they're hardly crippled by the heart-or-dollar dilemma the way Hamlet is.

2

The Social Causes of the Hamlet Syndrome

Nobody *wants* to be a failure. Nobody wants to be rejected and scorned by the community. Some people *act* like they prefer failure and rejection, but they're quitting before they're fired, dropping out of the mainstream because they can never hope to receive the rewards they desire. Offer them those rewards—acceptance, security, and riches—and they're likely to step right back into society; in the vernacular of the outcast, that's called *selling out.* Even those who remain on the fringe, uttering none but the most contemptuous remarks about the mainstream, would rather coexist with society than continually battle against it. Going against the mainstream is as self-destructive as running headlong into a stampede of cattle.

Which makes it all the more remarkable that Hamlet, unassertive, quiet Hamlet, insists on following a contrary path.

For Hamlet understands that in exchange for its rewards, society expects us to yield up the better part of our autonomy. Sure, sure, it's a free country, we're allowed to do anything we want that's not specifically prohibited by law. But in reality we have *two* sets of laws: the written law established by government, and the social law established by the public at large. The social law, which includes custom, tradition, and manners, covers behavior unregulated by written law. It tells us what's *normal,* what's expected of us attitudinally and behaviorally, in every situation. Social law prohibits us from wearing blue jeans to our sister's wedding; the federal, state, and municipal codes have nothing to say on the matter. The problem is, social law gets so intrusive it borders on tyranny. Out of a pendulum's swing of possibilities, it restricts us to a narrow arc of acceptable options. As soon as we stray outside that narrow arc, we open ourselves to censure and run the risk of ostracism—and, as we said at the start, no one wants to be rejected and scorned by the community. So when it comes to dealing with society, Hamlet has a grim choice. He can either subsume his independence and fit in with the mainstream, or he can hold on to his independence and stand apart.

The mainstream, he sees easily enough, values money above all. Money, even when it's gained shadily or by some fluke, confers prestige. Closely following money is power—not just political power, but social, religious, philosophical, economic, emotional, sexual, and even aesthetic power. In this society money and power go hand in glove, indeed, are so closely linked they're often thought of as the same thing. Together they constitute the conventional definition of success. After that it helps to have an attractive spouse, a spacious, well-appointed home, and a shiny, late-model car. The mainstream is a realm of surfaces, where appearance counts more than substance. As long as you *look* right you fit in, you're a success, and it doesn't matter that underneath you're a rotten human being—or have less money than someone deemed a failure.

Hamlet has a great deal of trouble with the mainstream's definition of success. He wants enough money to live comfortably, but excessive wealth scares him. Power, in his view, corrupts. And he looks for *substance* in addition to appearance. He regards life not as an interminable series of tests to be passed or failed, but as a continual learning process that, taken as a whole, leads on to wisdom. You "succeed" each time you arrive at a more comprehensive insight into existence. You "fail" only by learning nothing. Integrity and conscience count for more than money and power. The *quality* of life means more than the appearance of success or failure. Hamlet genuinely believes that it's not whether you win or lose, but how you play the game.

In one very important respect, however, Hamlet's values match up with the mainstream's: He wants to stay on the right side of the social law and fit in. He desires the safety that comes with conformity. But in every other respect his values and the mainstream's *directly conflict.* Under those circumstances he finds it nearly impossible to conform, and so after much hesitation and regret he gives first priority to the values of his heart. He'd *prefer* to be part of the crowd; like any normal person he doesn't want to be an outsider, ostracized and scorned. But so long as he feels as strongly as he does that money isn't everything, that power corrupts, and that quality counts more than appearance, his heart takes precedence over his hunger for the dollar.

Mainstreamers recognize pretty quickly that Hamlet's a deviant. There's that hesitant look in his eye every time they talk about their latest triumph at work or their new revolving charge account. They may not know or care *why* he gets that look, but they understand it amounts to something less than agreement. And when they think on it, they realize Hamlet doesn't go along with them in a lot of respects. He doesn't know the first thing about making his way in the world—and he doesn't seem to care. He doesn't have a good job. He doesn't go to church every Sunday. He lives in a ratty apartment in a run-down part of the city. He takes every little thing seriously, to the point where he thinks himself to death. What kind of a life is that, anyway? He can't get his act together. He's afraid of making a move. He is, when you put it all together, nothing but *a failure.*

So society creates Hamlets when it values money, power, appearance, and conformity above all else. But over the last decade it has also created Hamlets a second way: through a general decline in the economy. During the Reagan era, Americans went on a buying spree unprecedented in the nation's history. Both the national debt and the trade deficit soared to previously inconceivable heights. Surrounded by personal computers and VCRs, compact disk players and brand-new cars, Americans could be forgiven for thinking their economy was booming. But the booming economies belonged to Japan, Korea, Taiwan, and Singapore—ours sagged as we shook empty the national piggy bank. A study issued in December 1986 by the Joint Economic Committee of Congress belied the boast that Reaganomics created more opportunities than any economic policy since the 1960s. More than half the eight million new jobs created between 1979 and 1984 paid less than *$7,000* per year—opportunities to live in poverty, maybe, but not much more than that. The number of jobs paying $28,000 or more per annum over that same five-year period actually *dropped*. The share of new jobs falling in the middle-income category (between $7,000 and $28,000, an awfully wide spread, especially on the low side) decreased to 47.5 percent in the early 1980s—down from 64.2 percent of all jobs created in the recession- and inflation-riddled 1970s. No wonder in this great era of prosperity it takes two incomes to maintain the same standard of living we could afford on one income twenty years ago.

The study by the Joint Economic Committee reveals that most new jobs are part-time or require few skills, and that there are fewer and fewer challenging, well-paying positions for the hundreds of thousands of young people who graduate from college each year. With the pool of qualified workers waxing and the number of good jobs waning, competition for employment becomes an increasingly masochistic exercise. Check out your nearest college campus. Those students are *grim*, especially compared to their counterparts from a decade or more ago. The pressure to succeed has them so gnarled up inside they're committing suicide and seeing therapists in record numbers. They can either devote themselves totally to the pursuit of gainful employment, neglecting most every other aspect of their development, or they can drop out and bear, perhaps for the first time, the stigma of failure. Those who choose the latter course are economy-caused Hamlets, and their numbers will increase when the American economy spirals down into recession—as inevitably it will.

A survey of 1984–85 graduates of the University of California, Berkeley, suggests that economic conditions may now rival value conflict as the primary social cause of the Hamlet Syndrome. Forty percent of the students expected a career in either business, engineering, law, or medicine. Almost all the rest envisioned themselves as executives, administrators, salespeople, or marketers. Less than 5 percent listed as career goals such public-minded vocations as teaching high schoolers, serving in the military or foreign service, doing social work, or working in the arts, and hardly any listed government or politics as a desired career. "These students are aiming to fill slots in a system," commented Tom Hayden, the ex-hippie who now represents the city of Santa Monica in the California State Assembly. But of the twenty-three hundred–plus graduates responding to the survey (representing more than *half* the class), 30 percent are in downwardly mobile jobs that don't even require a college education! Another 8 percent are unemployed. These are students from Berkeley, one of the top ten colleges in the country. If 38 percent of *them* stumble out of the gate, winding up on the dole or in dead-end jobs, the numbers can't be much better at other universities.

How do these people feel when, in spite of their qualifications, they can't get the slot in the system they want? How do they feel when they turn on the television and watch commercials for the good life, a life they want but can't have? They feel, in a word, like *failures*— much the same as Hamlets whose values conflict with the mainstream's. And they may in fact adopt the values of the heart, even though they started out embracing the dollar. For nothing sets true believers doubting faster than a lack of reward for their faith. As the system swells the ranks of Hamlets in the years ahead, watch out; millions of intelligent, underutilized people taunted with homages to money, power, and conformity may discover their common resentment of the mainstream, and their collective energy could manifest itself in a countercultural movement that challenges prevailing values in a way we haven't seen since the 1960s.

The mainstream's perception of Hamlet as a failure has particularly onerous implications for the Hamlet who happens to be female or a member of a minority group. Long after there's any excuse for stereotyping, it's still acceptable in many circles to harbor demeaning notions about a woman's place or the characteristics of various minorities. Even where it's *not* acceptable, many Americans still hold unconsciously sexist or racist attitudes. On top of the hazards of nonconformity, then, the female or minority Hamlet has to cope with prejudice.

Twenty years after the rebirth of the feminist movement, America remains terribly confused about what it expects from a woman. By and large we play it safe and expect *everything* from her: the traditionally demure housewife and the go-getter woman of the world. This forces a woman to make a choice that few men ever have to face: whether to forsake home life for a career, a career for home life, or go crazy and try to have both at the same time. In a national workplace that's long discounted female prowess, educated, advantaged women represent their entire sex. They are the cutting edge of the women's movement, and their choices will determine the future of women's influence on the nation's larger agenda. If they leave politics and business to men, the gains of the last twenty years may well be lost. If enough of them pursue careers, they'll eventually force America to address such issues as sexual harassment, child care, maternity leave, and comparable worth. What this means to a female Hamlet is that any flinching from career goals is not just a personal failure but a betrayal of the sex. Less enlightened Americans will view her as more proof that the "typical" woman is hopelessly indecisive and deserving of her second-class status.

The black or Hispanic Hamlet bears the same burden as female Hamlets: His people have been down so long that his success (or lack of it) reflects on the entire group. His disdain for competitive society becomes, to meaner spirits, reinforcement for the ugly stereotypes that have developed over many years. Blacks are shiftless and lazy; Hispanics have a mañana complex. Adding to the burden is the fact that the black and Hispanic middle classes—from which Hamlets spring—have the best chance of integrating into the larger society. Each black and Hispanic Hamlet, therefore, diminishes by one the already short-handed vanguard trying to bring the minority into the mainstream.

Asian and Jewish Hamlets are burdened by the perception of their groups' historic success. Because of their ethnic background they're expected to be big-time achievers, so their failure means they must be especially lazy or inept. Their lack of achievement also gives comfort to unenlightened citizens who perceive the rise of Asians and Jews as some sort of threat to America. To these prejudiced Americans, Hamlets named Wong and Rosenberg are casualties of an inhuman dedication to achievement, and lend credence to the suspicion that there must be something wrong about Asian and Jewish cultures.

Then we come to gay and lesbian Hamlets. These two groups already suffer such widespread condemnation that their economic failure can hardly make things worse. Most Americans have never known a successful person who's openly homosexual, so as far as they know Hamlethood may be the homosexual norm. But denizens of San Francisco, Manhattan, and other communities with proudly gay and lesbian communities know differently. They've met enough successful homosexual businesspeople and professionals to know that the gay or lesbian Hamlet has *two* problems vis-à-vis mainstream society, the first being sexual orientation, the second being the inability to choose between the heart and the dollar.

3
Live by the Mind...

U nable to identify with the prevailing social norms, Hamlet must turn inward and build an independent value system. He rests his value system on three mighty pillars: tolerance, curiosity, and skepticism.

Hamlet's belief in tolerance may spring as much from self-defense as heartfelt principle. Being something of an outsider, he *needs* just as much tolerance as he's willing to grant. And grant tolerance he does, for he believes implicitly in *live-and-let-live*. Several Hamlets we interviewed or surveyed, when asked to sum up how they deal with other people, cited the negative version of the Golden Rule: Do *not* do unto others as you would *not* have them do unto you. They objected to the more popular positive version of the rule (*Do* unto others . . .) because it tacitly endorses the imposition of values on others—an imposition that may not be welcome. Hamlet doesn't want anyone telling him how to live, and he's not about to go preaching to others.

One very important point: Hamlet's tolerance must never be interpreted as acceptance or agreement. Although he grants that the Ku Klux Klan has a right to rally and speak out, he does so grudgingly, regarding Klansmen as white trash possessed of room-temperature IQs. If they were to disappear tomorrow he'd cheer their demise. Nor does his tolerance extend to actions that strike him as hurtful to others. His heart hardens against harm-doers, and though he's hardly the sort to jump up and protest any callous behavior, he'll sometimes exact revenge in little ways: boycotting the products of unethical companies, avoiding manipulative or aggressive individuals, trashing offenders in conversation.

Hamlet understands that there are a million different ways to bake bread, worship God, or do anything, and only social law makes one way more right than another. Wandering outside the arc of acceptable options, he seeks to know as many of those different ways as possible. He's a searcher, insatiably curious about matters large and small. It's not enough that he know the Judeo-Christian concept of God. He also wants to know how the Buddhists see God, how the American Indians see God, and why the atheists see no God at all. Only by acquainting himself with the full range of ideas on a subject can he formulate a firm opinion of his own. And he doesn't confine his curiosity to the serious questions. He's a stimulus junkie, always on the lookout for exotic information and ideas. Don't ever bet against him in a game of Trivial Pursuit; his head is full of little facts about Sky King, the periodic table, and Pacific atolls. Many Hamlets find daily satisfaction doing crossword puzzles, poring over the box scores of baseball games, and reading everything they can get their hands on, from *People* magazine to epic poetry.

Hamlet's hunger for mental stimulation explains, in good part, why he's likely to live in a city or college town. He quickly outgrows the limited variety of the suburbs and villages. Why should he settle for Wonder bread when he can have pita, tortillas, injera, chapati? There's a whole world to discover, and he's just amazed at all the people who can be satisfied on so little brain food day after day after day. The suburbs and small towns, to him, represent America's intellectual Siberia, a cultural wasteland where minds go to starve. Give him the city, where there's more to see, more to do, people from different back-

grounds—an intellectual feast table. In his opinion, curiosity doesn't kill
anything at all except the taste for provincialism.

Perhaps the most important pillar in Hamlet's value system, however, is his skepticism. He takes on faith the value of tolerance, curiosity,
and skepticism itself, but *everything else* he zero-bases, continually questioning authority and conventional wisdom. He just can't unconditionally
accept the traditional values handed him by his family, friends, teachers,
and leaders. This is not to say that he *never* accepts traditional values,
just that he insists on thinking them over first. Most of the time he
concludes that there's no rational basis for mainstream beliefs. That's
when he sets his own standards—and incurs the wrath of a majority that
equates popular values with truth.

Such a skeptic is Hamlet that he regularly questions *himself.* Especially once he reaches his mid-thirties, everything he stands for—even
tolerance, curiosity, and skepticism—falls subject to scrutiny, and down
go values he may have cherished since college. For the ultimate purpose
of his skepticism is not to establish his own rigid system of right and
wrong, nor is it to sublimate through logic his hostility toward the
mainstream. Rather, it is to assure that he takes nothing for granted, that
he recognizes the fallibility of all things, including himself, and doesn't
unwittingly get sucked into something he doesn't believe in or doesn't
want to do. He's wise enough to know that truth changes with time and
experience. Let others protect their peace of mind by clinging to unbend-
ing beliefs; Hamlet will protect his with doubt and flexibility.

Most Hamlets would recoil if you called them intellectuals. True,
many of them, especially perpetual students, devote themselves to the
life of the mind and adopt a scholar's perspective toward everything. But
Hamlet is a *free* thinker, not necessarily a profound thinker, and we
shouldn't confuse his independent thought with genius. If he seems
smarter than the average human, it's because he *uses* his brain more—
and because he augments the power of his thoughts with two neat twists
of mind: a knack for association, and the capacity to project the consequences of actions.

By association we mean the ability to connect seemingly discrete
facts or events to each other and to greater phenomena. Hamlet need
only see a handful of trees, in other words, to perceive he's in a forest.
This tendency to fit bits of data into larger truths runs counter to the

prevailing mind-set, which seeks to break the whole down into little pieces—specialization. Hamlet wants to see a greater significance in everything. He frequently has trouble dealing with detail unless he understands how each detail relates to the whole. At first we were surprised by the number of Hamlets who enjoy scientific work and other technical pursuits, thinking their associative tendencies would incline them toward the liberal arts and holistic endeavors. But to a one they see their work as part of a larger framework. They reject the temptation to look upon their isolated tasks as ends in themselves. They see a whole, not the sum of many parts, and in that respect they're identical to their more traditionally holistic, liberal-arts-loving brethren.

The need to infuse every jot and tittle with meaning occasionally provokes Hamlet to dubious leaps of logic—in many ways he makes an ideal conspiracy theorist—but more often it gives him sweeping insight into whatever he examines. Shakespeare's Hamlet, beholding the skull of long-dead court jester Yorick, could turn to his friend Horatio and muse "To what base uses we return, Horatio!/Why may not imagination trace the noble dust of/Alexander, 'til we find it stopping a bunghole?" (Act V, Scene i). Although modern Hamlets may not be nearly as morbid, their power of association can be just as far-reaching. They're expert at synthesizing immediate experience into generality: people are scum, work is a prison, even if you win the rat race you're still just a rat.

Then there's Hamlet's ability to foresee the consequences of actions—regardless of how minor those actions may be. For example, when he walks into the corner deli and orders a cup of coffee to go, an innocuous act by almost anyone's standard, he realizes that he's endorsing with his wallet the activities of a whole host of people: the worker who serves him; the owner of the deli; the producer of the coffee; and the producer of the cup. In fact, he's endorsing the entire capitalist system. This in itself may not bother him. He may like the counter clerk and the owner of the deli, and he may well figure that capitalism works better than any other economic system. But what about that cup the coffee comes in? It's made of Styrofoam. Styrofoam is a chlorofluorocarbon (CFC), the compound responsible for blowing a hole in the ozone layer. Less ozone means more ultraviolet radiation, which means more cancer and blindness plus a raft of environmental ills. When that cup gets thrown out, it'll be burned at the city incinerator, freeing the CFCs so they can float into the stratosphere and destroy yet another few molecules of ozone. Thus Hamlet realizes that by purchasing coffee that

comes in a Styrofoam cup he's furthering what may be *the* great disaster
of the twenty-first century.

Taken together, Hamlet's associative thinking and ability to see
consequences show a propensity for logic uncommon in our society.
Nowadays we appeal to one another on a visceral level—*do it because it
feels good*—with little consideration for implication or consequence.
We'd rather be instantly gratified, thank you. Hamlet's far-ranging
thought rarely translates into action—that Big Mac tastes too good to
make a stink about the acres of Amazon jungle burned down to produce
it—but in the main he understands the greater significance of everything
he does, whereas the rest of us wander from one titillation to the next,
conscious of little beyond the superficial and immediate. That's probably
why Hamlet strikes so many of us as intellectual—he thinks things
through. But again, it's not as if he's been naturally endowed with
superior intelligence; it's just that he *uses* his intelligence in a manner
the rest of us have largely abandoned.

There's one more key to the power of Hamlet's thought, and that's
honesty. Most human beings use their power of reason to rationalize, i.e.,
clothe in noble intention, the actions they take out of base desire. They're
trying to justify, to themselves and the world, deeds that might otherwise
be seen as nefarious. Because he's so skeptical, Hamlet often catches
himself rationalizing. He doesn't like lying to himself, so he dedicates
his powers of reason to getting at the truth behind the excuses. Sometimes he succeeds, arriving at brilliant but frightening revelations about
himself. Other times he succeeds only in creating more subtle deceptions.
Whatever the result, he's alert to the fact that he *does* rationalize, and
that forces him to be more honest intellectually. Is this what I really
feel? he asks himself, or is this just a rationalization for something
deeper and meaner? Although he'll never eliminate his internal lies
completely—in fact, as we'll see in the following pages, he relies on
rationalization just as much as anyone—he'll nevertheless come closer
than most people to understanding the real motives behind his thoughts
and deeds.

4

... Die by the Mind

Now whether it be
Bestial oblivion, or some craven scruple
Of thinking too precisely on th' event–
A thought which quarter'd hath but one part wisdom,
And ever three parts coward–I do not know
Why yet I live to say 'This thing's to do,'
Sith I have cause and will and strength and means
To do 't.

Hamlet, ACT IV, SCENE iv

Hamlet's greatest asset—his thoughtfulness—is also his greatest weakness. For every bit of wisdom his speculations bring him, they also seem to bring three bits of cowardice that discourage him from acting. No matter how hard he tries to root out his rationalizations, his thoughts often create excuses to justify his deep-seated reluctance to seize the initiative. All three pillars of his value system are riddled with debilitating cracks: Because he's so tolerant, fewer things outrage him to the point of fighting; because he's so curious, he seeks more information even though he already has enough to make a decision; and because his skepticism reveals flaws in everything he inspects, he despairs of finding a course he can defend one hundred percent.

Even Hamlet's associative thinking and ability to see consequences discourage him from acting. Let's look again at Brent's pronouncement that "even if you win the rat race, you're still just a rat." It gives him perspective on the way his work as a lawyer fits in with the larger scheme of things, and that's good. But look at the terms he's chosen! Successful competitor equals *rat*, the world's most repulsive rodent. Not the sort of association that would inspire someone to greater achievement. Brent could have associated the free enterprise system with something a bit nicer, looking at it not as a rat race but as the means by which cream rises to the top. Then when he succeeded he'd be the cream of the crop. But by comparing capitalism to something as low as a rat race he gives himself an excuse not to compete. Similarly, when Hamlet considers the implications of his actions—even the most minor actions, such as buying coffee that's packaged in a Styrofoam cup—he's bound to find a consequence somewhere along the line that has a negative impact. He can then build that negative consequence into something so monstrous he can't possibly take the action that causes it.

Less-refined motives lurk beneath all rationalizations, including Hamlet's. Earlier we cataloged some of the psychological traits that predispose a person to the Hamlet Syndrome: reluctance to take risks, a loathing for competition, a low threshold of frustration, lack of self-confidence, a distaste for work, procrastination, passivity. There's no need to go into detail about these traits, since they're familiar to all of us either through personal experience or observation of other people. They have two common elements, however, that we should explore a bit more closely: an aversion to responsibility, and good old-fashioned fear.

"I think I can handle a certain amount of responsibility well, but only so long as it's at a slow pace," says Maxine, the not-yet-begun-to-fight Hamlet. Hamlet has enough trouble taking care of *himself;* the last thing he wants to do is take responsibility for something or somebody else. He equates the acceptance of responsibility with initiation into adulthood—and he'd rather stay a kid. Maxine, in spite of her distaste for responsibility, took care of her mother's business while her mother spent half a year overseas. "I looked after everything for her as well as my own stuff. I was very responsible, and it was very tiring." The experience, she says, made her "feel grown-up." Dropout Brent would also prefer to remain as carefree as a child—and acknowledges that for him the Hamlet Syndrome stems in part from arrested development. "One relative of mine has a theory about me," he adds. "He thinks I have a fear of commitment. I think that makes some sense."

Then, too, Hamlet is *afraid,* especially of confrontations. Rare is the Hamlet honest enough to proclaim, "Yeah, that's right, I'm scared to death most of the time." But he says as much indirectly when he talks about compromise, the ultimate entanglement with the outside world. Given the choice among fight, flight, and negotiation, he flees. As Maxine puts it, "My form of compromise is to move someplace else. I'm not a fighter. Instead I think, I'll go over here and remove myself from all this conflict." Jeff, our hippie, has some issues he's willing to compromise on, others he's not. Either way, he steers clear of confrontation. "At work it doesn't bother me at all to compromise. I don't go home and think to myself, shit, I gave in to that asshole, my integrity has dropped a notch. Then, when it comes to the larger issues, I *don't* compromise. I resist the impulse to fully participate in what goes on out there—there's just too much garbage." Hamlet, in sum, would rather run away than expose himself to the dangers inherent in dealing closely with others.

This fear of engaging the world helps to explain why Hamlet's so quiet. He's afraid of offending us, of exposing his nonconformity, and especially of putting himself in a position where he has to either fight or argue. Even when his audience promises to be sympathetic, Hamlet fears to put himself forward. Both Jessica and Brent agreed to appear in this book only after receiving assurances their identities would be obscured. (We've taken the precaution of protecting the identities of *all* Hamlets quoted in this book. Their names are false, and in most cases specific background information, such as the town they grew up in or the college they attended, has been changed, omitted, or left vague.) One of many Hamlets who refused the authors' request for an interview said, "I may be a Hamlet, but I don't want to be a famous one." He feared that by opening his life-style to examination he'd lose the peace he's protected through silence for more than a dozen years.

Beyond his penchant for turning empowering thoughts into paralyzing rationalizations, Hamlet has another way of dissuading himself from moving forward: He portrays his options as either *black and white* (one or the other) or *shades of gray* (so multitudinous he can never sort them out). Since his purpose is to excuse himself from action, Hamlet will use the black-and-white and shades-of-gray perspectives interchangeably, depending on which one makes the more compelling case for passivity.

The heart-or-dollar dilemma at the core of the Hamlet Syndrome is itself a black-and-white construct. Hamlet can be either a morally bankrupt success or a virtuous pauper, because successful people can't be good, and good people can't be successful. There's little in between; it's basically an all-or-nothing proposition. If he goes after the dollar, he's got to put his integrity aside. If he opts for the heart, he can kiss good-bye his dreams of owning a little house by the shore. Both options stink— good reason, in his mind, to do nothing.

By invoking shades-of-gray logic, Hamlet creates so many in-between possibilities that he needs forever to sort them all out. He's bewildered by too *much* choice, like the little kid in the candy store who can only have one sweet. Not-yet-begun-to-fight type Martin recounts his first and only search for work this way: "They throw out a billion choices, whether you want to be a flight attendant, a garbage collector, whatever. There are just so many choices I couldn't decide. So I took what fell my way." The shades-of-gray thinker intent on finding excuses for inaction utilizes to the fullest his ability to associate and foresee consequences of actions, playing out every scenario as far as he can take it—dressing his bedraggled indecision in the more acceptable garb of circumspection. The shades-of-gray rationalization also serves as a handy excuse for failure. Why did I wind up in such a rotten job? Because I was forced to make a move before I looked at all my options; if I'd had the time to study the possibilities more thoroughly, I'd have made a better choice.

Whether he invokes a black-and-white or shades-of-gray excuse for his inaction, what Hamlet's really saying is that he won't move until he strikes upon the *perfect* choice. He doesn't want any negative side to his actions. On the surface that's wonderfully ambitious and idealistic—he's going to hold out until he gets precisely what he wants. But that's also incredibly unrealistic, and way down inside even Hamlet knows that the perfect choice doesn't exist. In this world good and bad are inextricably intertwined. Every act has both positive and negative consequences. The best we can hope for is that the choice we make leads to more good than bad, and ultimately does less damage than the choices we decide against. By portraying his options in stark black and white or infinite shades of gray, all Hamlet does is give himself a superficially plausible reason for delaying a move he doesn't want to make.

When pushed to the wall and forced to make a choice, Hamlet almost always opts for the path of least resistance, the one that requires the least expense of energy and commitment. He tries as much as possible to achieve his goals through inaction. And just what are his goals? Mainly to preserve the purity of his heart and not drop out of society completely. For the most part he can keep his heart clean through *no effort at all.* He merely has to maintain his distance from the corrupting influences of the material world. Thus he hangs out on the fringe of the economic mainstream, at an easy, dead-end job, earning enough to remain independent but not so much that he feels he's a part of the system. A hard bed, all in all, but one that Hamlet can lie in without losing too much sleep.

Unfortunately for Hamlet, we live in a what-have-you-done-for-me-lately society, and if you haven't done much lately, people conclude that there must be something *wrong* with you. Although Hamlet does indeed have a mind-set that works against his succeeding in conventional terms, he's no more neurotic or psychologically hobbled than anyone else. The Hamlet Syndrome is *not* a mental illness or imbalance. Rather, it is a state of mind, a pervading sense that one would lose one's integrity by blindly adopting the values of the mainstream. As we've noted, that state of mind *does* stem in part from psychological traits that impede action: reluctance to take risks, fear of competition, aversion to work, etc. But if we choose to call those traits *neuroses* (a dubious call, to say the least) and treat the Hamlet Syndrome as a psychological problem, we'd only obtain a partial cure for Hamlet. We'd turn him into someone willing to take a risk, or compete, or go to work. But he'd *still* object to prevailing values and would *still* find it nearly impossible to integrate into society. He'd still think the American workplace degrades employees, still think materialism stinks, still think an ounce of skepticism outweighs ten pounds of loyalty. Psychology has enough to do treating mental illness; it has little place in the arena of values.

5

There Is Nothing New Under the Sun

There's ample evidence that the Hamlet-type personality has existed from the beginning of recorded history. Back when reading and writing were rare skills, only kings, conquerors, priests, and philosophers would inscribe their thoughts for posterity. The kings and conquerors were men of action, so naturally their stories reveal little evidence of the Hamlet Syndrome. But among the religious and philosophical orders there existed a few people who meditated deeply on the value of wealth, power, and action. Their reflections, written on animal skins and crudely made paper, provide a philosophical framework for much of modern *civilization,* not to mention the Hamlet Syndrome.

The Indian prince Siddhartha Gautama lived twenty-five hundred years ago. He was a highly privileged, well-educated young man, yet for all his wealth and comfort he felt terribly unfulfilled. After years of musing on his unhappiness he realized that life is painful no matter what one's station, so at the age of twenty-nine he renounced his high place and dropped out of the mainstream. An itinerant preacher the rest of his days, he became known as the Buddha, or Enlightened One. *Life is suffering* is the first of his Four Noble Truths, and is today the cornerstone of the religion named after him and observed by nearly a billion people. According to the Buddha, the only way to stop suffering is to follow the Eightfold Path, a discipline that consists of attaining right view, right intention, right speech, right action, right livelihood, right effort, right mindfulness, and right concentration—the values of the heart.

The Chinese philosopher and priest Lao-tzu lived at roughly the same time as the Buddha. The father of Taoism, we know him best for the saying "The journey of a thousand miles begins with a single step." His book of eighty-one epigrams, the *Tao-te-Ching (The Way and Its Power)* has had a profound influence on Jessica, our perpetual student, as well as a number of other Hamlets. It is the work of a man thoroughly disgusted by humanity's obsession with money, power, and aggression. To Lao-tzu,

> *The best man is like water.*
> *Water is good; it benefits all things and*
>   *does not compete with them.*

His book abounds with Hamlet-type wisdom: "Wealth and place breed insolence that brings ruin in its train"; "Banish skill, discard profit, and thieves and robbers will disappear"; "That there can be teaching without words, value in action that is actionless, few indeed can understand."

In the Western tradition, the Athenian philosopher Socrates stands out as having much in common with modern Hamlets. He left no writings of his own, but Plato and other Greek thinkers quoted him liberally in their works. "Bad men live that they may eat and drink, whereas good men eat and drink that they may live," he said, rejecting the materialistic impulse that prevailed twenty-five hundred years ago just as it does today. Socrates extolled the value of knowledge over ignorance and skepticism over belief. Unlike modern Hamlets, however, he had no fear of confrontation. He would argue with anybody, and in the end he was put to death by the people of Athens as much for being a nuisance as for breaking the law.

The best-known Hamlet in the Bible is the author of Ecclesiastes.

Writing sometime around the year 200 B.C., he was, according to biblical scholars, a well-to-do Palestinian Jew. Yet he took little comfort in his wealth, as indicated by the opening lines of his testament: "Vanity of vanities, saith the Preacher, vanity of vanities; all is vanity. What profit hath a man of all his labour which he taketh under the sun?" He clearly saw that conventional success is ephemeral and leads to corruption of the soul. The fulfillment of worldly desire breeds not contentment, but greater desire: "He that loveth silver shall not be satisfied with silver." Orthodox Jews and Christians often have a hard time with the hard-boiled, skeptical viewpoint of Ecclesiastes; the book was one of the last accepted into the biblical canon. Secular experts speculate that the few conventionally pious sections of the book of Ecclesiastes were added after the author's death in an effort to make the work more palatable to the mainstream.

In using the Buddha and the author of Ecclesiastes as examples of early Hamlets, we don't mean to imply that the Hamlet Syndrome has a spiritual or religious base. Many modern Hamlets, in following their hearts, live according to a fairly strict set of principles. But they don't necessarily derive those principles from religion. They're just as likely to be agnostics or atheists as believers. In ancient times few commoners had the ability, inclination, and means to leave a record of their lives for future generations. Thus we cannot assume that secular Hamlets didn't exist. They undoubtedly did—but were probably just as skeptical about inscribing their thoughts for posterity as they were of the prevailing values of their culture.

Prior to the Renaissance there were proportionally fewer Hamlets in society because three factors necessary for their development were scarce to the point of nonexistence. The first factor was affluence. Only a very few individuals had the time to indulge in sociological speculation. The overwhelming majority of humanity was too poor and burdened by physical labor to ponder much of anything beyond survival. The second factor was freedom of inquiry. The brave spirit that dared to question the values handed down by the prevailing culture did so at his own peril; anyone even *suspected* of doubting the accepted verities risked condemnation as a heretic and subsequent acquaintance with the gruesome tortures of the times. The third factor was social mobility. No matter how talented or ambitious, children were fated by the rigidities of feudal society to remain in the socioeconomic niche of their parents. The son of a cobbler became a cobbler, the son of a lord inherited the estate, and the dilatory oaf born to the lord had power of life and death over the enterprising genius born to the cobbler.

But as civilization evolved, affluence, freedom of inquiry, and social mobility slowly increased, and so did the proportion of Hamlets. The story William Shakespeare adapted for *Hamlet* comes from Norse legends of the twelfth century. In those legends, Hamlet is a man of action, raping the Ophelia character, boiling the Polonius character and feeding the remains to pigs, killing the throne-usurping uncle in hand-to-hand combat, and, in a grand finale, burning down the palace. The fact that Shakespeare turned the story on its head and transformed the hero into a man of *in*action proves that by the reign of Elizabeth I, audiences were sufficiently familiar with the overthinking, underachieving type to accept one as a hero.

Shakespeare died in 1616. Over the next two hundred years the growth of capitalism, along with the spread of democracy and the arrival of the Industrial Revolution, led to a sharp rise in the number of Hamlets. Whereas earlier societies were so stratified that children had no destiny other than the one into which they were born, children in the rapidly industrializing nations of Europe and America grew up in a world of social mobility—and insecurity. Particularly in early America, which lacked the traditions, ethnic homogeneity, and population density necessary for a strong social law, the individual (unless a slave or woman) was master of his fate to a degree unheard of in the past. But that freedom had a double edge: A person could just as easily go from high to low as from low to high. To stay on the high side, a person had to be ready to fight tenaciously, and not everyone could do that and still sleep at night.

By the nineteenth century the innovations of the Industrial Revolution relegated most Americans to the lower class. Their poorly paid, seemingly pointless jobs offered little opportunity for upward mobility, and as early as the 1840s many of the nation's more sensitive citizens were rebelling against the dollar-hungry forces of big capitalism. In "The Transcendentalist," a famous lecture he delivered in Boston in 1841, Ralph Waldo Emerson focused his attention on one particularly interesting group of people who turned their backs on a rapidly mechanizing, urbanizing America:

It is a sign of our times, conspicuous to the coarsest observer, that many intelligent and religious persons withdraw themselves from the common labors and competitions of the market and the caucus, and betake themselves to a certain solitary and critical way of living, from which no solid fruit has yet appeared to justify their separation. They hold themselves aloof: they feel the disproportion between their faculties and the work offered them, and they prefer to ramble in the country and perish of ennui, to the degradation of such charities and such ambitions as the city can propose to them.

That sounds exactly like the symptoms of the Hamlet Syndrome, doesn't it! Emerson goes on to render early-American Hamlets in greater detail:

They shun general society. . . . Meantime, this retirement does not proceed from any whim on the part of these separators; but if any one will take pains to talk with them, he will find that this part is chosen both from temperament and from principle; with some unwillingness, too, and as a choice of the less of two evils; for these persons are not by nature melancholy, sour, and unsocial . . . but joyous, susceptible, affectionate; they have even more than others a great wish to be loved.

A wordy fellow, Emerson, but dead on target when it comes to describing the Hamlet Syndrome, right down to his ascription of the phenomenon to both temperament and principle. The main reason his insight into the Hamlet personality still rings true after 150 years is that the conditions responsible for creating Hamlets haven't changed since the Alamo fell—except to become more pronounced. By the beginning of the twentieth century, America had so thoroughly industrialized and citified that the rural milieu in which Emerson's Hamlets rambled was practically gone. There was no escape from the values of big capitalism. Laborers slaved upward of seventy hours a week in sweat shops, earning peon wages—and most people expressed more reprehension at the workers' attempts to unionize than at the rapacious conditions of employment. Mainstream Americans, when they recognized the disillusioned but quiet Hamlet at all, regarded him as either an anachronism or some sort of Bolshevik.

But many philosophers pitied Hamlet, seeing him as a passive but principled holdout for the values of the heart at a time when everyone else was taking a disastrous turn toward brutality. Friedrich Nietzsche, the renowned German philosopher, defended Hamlets' inaction with these words from *The Birth of Tragedy:*

[They] have *gained knowledge*, and nausea inhibits action; for their action could not change anything in the eternal nature of things; they feel it to be ridiculous or humiliating that they should be asked to set right a world that is out of joint. Knowledge kills action; action requires the veils of illusion: that is the doctrine of Hamlet, not that cheap wisdom of Jack the Dreamer who reflects too much and, as it were, from an excess of possibilities does not get around to action. Not reflection, no—true knowledge, an insight into the horrible truth, outweighs any motive for action. [Italics Nietzsche's.]

Nietzsche discounts the psychological underpinnings of the Hamlet Syndrome, attributing Hamlet's inaction instead to an all-too-clear understanding of the world's immutable corruption. Hamlet's paralysis stems from knowledge and principle, not fear. Within a few decades a generation of French thinkers would use Nietzsche's philosophy in their formulation of *existentialism*, the most influential philosophical movement of the twentieth century. The starting point of existentialism is that once we see the world for what it is, without the illusion of God or some other omnipotent authority, we have to supply our own meaning for action. If we can't supply that meaning—and many existentialists can't—we have no basis for action. The early existentialists dwelt so heavily on the meaninglessness of action that many were left in a lurching state the philosopher Jean-Paul Sartre described as *nausea*—the very same term by which Nietzsche characterized Hamlet's inaction.

The flattering portrayal of the Hamlet personality by the philosophers may have been a reaction to the sudden popularity of psychoanalysis in the late nineteenth and early twentieth centuries. The revelations of Freud, Jung, and their followers spread quickly to the general culture. No one had personality quirks anymore, they had *neuroses* and *psychoses*, both of which could be cured by a few years of therapy. In *Civilization and Its Discontents*, which probes the relationship between the individual and society, Sigmund Freud analyzes the plight of people like the modern Hamlet. "The problem before us is how to get rid of the greatest hindrance to civilization—namely, the constitutional inclination of human beings to be aggressive towards one another," he writes. We try to solve the problem through *ethics*, the superego's check against our basic desires. Freud seizes on "Love thy neighbor as thyself" as a perfect example of *cultural superego*, or mass ethics:

Anyone who follows such a precept in present-day civilization only puts himself at a disadvantage *vis-a-vis* the person who disregards it. What a potent obstacle to civilization aggressiveness must be, if the defense against it can cause as much unhappiness as aggressiveness itself!

Adherence to the values of the heart puts Hamlet at a disadvantage against society's competitive element, Freud says, and moreover leaves Hamlet no happier than people who care not a whit for principle, dignity, conscience, and the welfare of others. A lamentable situation, but one for which the pioneering psychoanalyst offers no practical solution.

The end of the Great Depression and World War II brought affluence, freedom of inquiry (in the form of higher education), and social mobility to America on an unprecedented scale, leading to an explosion in the population of Hamlets. Today everyone seems to know at least one person who fits the profile set forth in this introduction. Hamlets have an importance well in excess of their numbers. They possess intellect, talent, and character the nation sorely needs in its scramble to maintain prosperity and democracy. If we are to avoid economic and political decay we cannot overlook our Hamlets any longer. When does the Hamlet Syndrome start showing itself? Why do some young people become Hamlets when others just like them become achievers? What can we do about the syndrome? In the following pages we'll tell the story of the six Hamlets we introduced earlier. We'll occasionally supplement their accounts with testimony from other Hamlets. Part Two explores the modern developments that predispose so many of today's young people to the Hamlet Syndrome. In Part Three we'll follow Hamlet to college, where the syndrome sprouts, and in Part Four we'll cover Hamlet's adulthood. In Part Five we'll hear how Hamlet feels about the big issues. Finally, we'll look at ways that Hamlet can handle his heart-or-dollar dilemma, and we'll also explore some of the Hamlet Syndrome's implications for the nation as a whole.

II

MELANCHOLY BABY: HAMLET'S CHILDHOOD CIRCUMSTANCES

'Tis meet that some more audience than a mother,
Since nature makes them partial, should o'hear
the speech. . . .

Hamlet, ACT III, SCENE iii

Survival—the first imperative. For hundreds of thousands of years, small, roving bands of human beings fought hyenas and other humans for access to limited supplies of food and water. Predators lurked everywhere: snakes, bears, cats, wolves. Life was a moment-to-moment proposition, and humans responded to the constant life-or-death pressure with strategies designed to maximize their chance of survival. They grouped together, intuitively understanding that there's safety in numbers, and they developed technology to make themselves equal, if not superior, to their competitors. The first technological inventions were weapons. Weapons expanded the food supply, enabling humans to bring down animals larger and faster than themselves. Weapons also increased their bearers' chance of emerging alive from a tangle with competitors. The arms race, in other words, started more than a million years ago. With all that impetus behind it, no wonder it's shown no signs of abating.

And that's the point. We no longer live under the primitive conditions of the African savannah, with death breathing down our necks every minute of the day—yet we act as if we do. Our food and water supplies are more or less assured. Except for a few grizzlies in the national parks we've killed off our predators. Our arsenal is powerful enough to obliterate the world. But we can't undo more than a million years of evolution. We're still obsessed with survival, and we still use technology—on a level our cave-dwelling ancestors could never have imagined—to maximize our security.

The greatest threat to our security comes from our fellow human beings. Whether we've known them for years or have never met them before, we can never predict with absolute certainty the behavior of the people around us. We must always be on our guard against others, for they hold in their hands the power to maim or kill. In a civilized society like ours (and despite what often seems like overwhelming evidence to the contrary, ours *is* a civilized society) we're pretty safe in assuming that our neighbors will respect our physical well-being—*but we can never be absolutely sure.* The newspapers are full of stories about random encounters, misunderstandings, and arguments that end in murder. So we hide pistols under our pillows, study the martial arts, and take care to avoid unstable people, volatile situations, and bad neighborhoods. And always we try to keep our cool in public; we devote substantial energy to reducing hostility in our personal relations—an effort that contributes mightily to stress, the universal malady of our time.

National agendas, especially in democratic societies like ours, reflect the concerns of the citizenry. For most of our history the two vast oceans separating North America from the Eurasian landmass kept us safely remote from the bad guys *over there,* so we didn't worry much about foreign affairs. But around the turn of the century multinational corporations began to tie our economy to the rest of the world's, and soon after that air travel brought the continents within hours of each other. Geographical barriers no longer protected us from other peoples. Excepting our year-and-a-half involvement in World War I, through the first three decades of this century we successfully ignored the rest of the world and its problems. But isolationism proved no buffer against the catastrophes of the next two decades. An entire generation grew up reeling from the horrors of the Great Depression and World War II. When those terrible days ended, the American people, especially those born in the 1920s and 1930s, vowed never to go through such agonies again. So starting in the late 1940s and continuing to this day, they sought security from others with an intensity worthy of our spear-bearing ancestors.

No ten-year span in American history, with the exception of the years bracketing the Civil War, saw a more dramatic transformation in the way Americans lived than the decade from 1945 to 1955. Because Americans had developed new and powerful technological capabilities during the war, they had the ability to bring about the safer life they wanted in short order. But to create that safer life they needed capital, so they went at commerce with a singular zeal, taking full advantage of the fact that the rest of the world's economic base was in shambles. Whole enterprises sprang up where none had existed before. Small and mid-size corporations grew into globe-girdling giants. Millions of Americans joined the middle class, for the first time in their lives earning more money than they needed to survive. Endowed with bulging savings accounts and programs like the GI Bill, they made up for years of deprivation and insecurity by removing themselves en masse from the threat of violence.

The atomic bomb—and, from 1953, the hydrogen bomb—made the United States invulnerable to all foreign threats except the Russians, and we labored with paranoiac intensity to secure ourselves from them. On a subconscious level, we realized that domestic security increased as chance contacts with other humans decreased. So we looked to escape the glowering hordes of the city. That led to a slew of major changes in the way we lived, the biggest being the exodus to suburbia. Most of us fail to realize how swiftly the suburbs arose—hardly any existed before the Second World War, yet a full 40 percent of us live in suburbia today. Suburbanites commuted to work—between 1945 and 1950 public transit ridership fell 30 percent—prompting a boom in the automobile and road-building industries. To satisfy the suburban denizens' desire for material goods (and keep the wife and kids out of the dangerous city) developers constructed shopping malls. Once television arrived in the early 1950s the decentralization of American life was essentially complete. Except for the father who worked in the city, middle-class Americans no longer had to risk indiscriminate, daily contact with masses of other people.

Before long the changes in society made children of the Depression feel safe enough to have kids—the Baby Boom generation. Reflecting on the terrible experiences they'd endured, the new parents resolved to provide their kids with every trifle, and to protect the little tykes from the sort of miseries that forced Mom and Dad to grow up before their time. Parents starting families in the 1960s vowed the same thing. Perhaps no generation in the planet's history was as safe and well provided for as the middle-class American children of the 1950s and 1960s.

But as with every success story, there's a down side. In securing themselves so thoroughly from dangers domestic and foreign, the parents of the Baby Boom generation also shut off the flow of ideas, values, and life-styles from outside. They demanded—and got—a self-reflecting, self-exalting culture. Their breadth of experience narrowed, and with it their tolerance for deviation. As a result, the social law grew to suffocating proportions. Here and there occurred rebellions—the beatniks, rock and roll, *Playboy*—but those reactions took years to mature into cultural forces. In the main, Americans shut themselves off in their tract homes (bomb shelter optional) and raised their children in antiseptic safety.

No better evidence for the mass preoccupation with security exists than the musical theater of the time. Born in the 1920s, musical theater celebrated in song and dance the fulfillment of the American dream, and through the first half of this century was in many ways the ultimate cultural reflection of the middle-class mind. Through the ominous Depression and war years musicals had an innocent, hopeful, expansive air. But in 1947 Lerner and Loewe presented *Brigadoon,* the story of a town that escapes danger by existing only one day every century. The plot concerns a young New Yorker who stumbles on Brigadoon the one day it's awake and falls in love with one of its women. Although he leaves, he so longs for his girlfriend that he returns to the site of the town, which miraculously comes back to life and grants him permanent refuge from the complexities of the postwar world. *Brigadoon* became one of the biggest Broadway hits of the late 1940s and 1950s, outlasting Rogers and Hammerstein's *Allegro* and E. Y. Harburg's *Finian's Rainbow,* socially conscious productions that made their debut the same year.

Contemporary Hamlets grew up in the security-obsessed environment of post–World War II America. More than 90 percent of the Hamlets we interviewed or surveyed grew up in middle-class circumstances or better. The great majority hail from suburbia or less densely populated urban areas like Bayside in New York City or Pacific Heights in San Francisco. All Hamlets, even those raised in small towns, rural areas, or the inner city, have in common a stable upbringing that made them feel secure. And that sense of security is the key factor in their early development. Unlike their parents, who knew the miseries and insecurities of depression and war, Hamlets grew up with no idea the world is a dangerous place. So completely sheltered were they by their nurturing families and homogenized neighborhoods that many common misfortunes were mysteries to them. As Martin says, "I didn't even know anyone with divorced parents until high school."

Nor were Hamlets encouraged to find out about the world beyond their neighborhood. Privation, violence, and dissent were abstract concepts, seen occasionally in TV news snippets but otherwise unreal. Maxine's parents, whom she fondly refers to as "beatniks," took her to Washington, D.C., on anti-Vietnam War demonstrations. What she remembers most about the protests were the "goofy" T-shirts her folks wore. Despite her parents' political orientation, "I was never encouraged to be political or activist," she says. "I knew I should follow current events, and I tried to, but it bored me to read the papers." Few Hamlets were allowed even *that* much exposure to troubling issues. Their parents had embraced the *Brigadoon* ethic, running away from anything that might lead to trouble, and Mom and Dad weren't about to reverse course and face monsters for the sake of educating junior.

We don't mean to blame the parents of Hamlets for their children's problems. Mom and Dad, in providing all that security, were merely responding to the survival imperative ingrained in their genes and given urgency by the horrors of the times. By and large the parents of Hamlets are good people. With one exception, none of the Hamlets we interviewed were physically abused. Nor did our interviewees report much in the way of parental alcoholism, depression, or abandonment. Hamlets whose parents divorced were well cared for during the breakup and seemed relatively unimpaired by the split. Clearly, the mothers and fathers of Hamlets placed their children's welfare above every other consideration. The results show: To a one, Hamlets are cordial, accommodating, and generous individuals.

Mom and Dad's only mistake—if we can call it that—was in giving their children too much protection. The obsession with safety, doing for baby lest he hurt himself, sheltering him from the workaday hazards of life, deprived Hamlet of the chance to learn responsibility. Rues Martin, who nevertheless regards his folks warmly, "My parents get an F when it comes to preparing me for adult life. They could have let me arrange my own dentist or doctor appointments in high school or something, but they did even that for me until I left home, so I never had to do anything for myself." Children so coddled have a hard time making the transition to the pitiless world of adulthood. Some kids overcome the handicap. Hamlets don't. In getting the best of everything from Mom and Dad, they get the worst preparation for life on their own.

6

The Trivialization of Survival

It's one thing to hold a child an arm's length from life's unhappier aspects. It's quite another to imply that those unhappy aspects *don't exist*. Yet judging by the content of our favorite mass medium—television—Americans sought not only to keep their children a safe distance from danger, but to lull them into thinking danger wasn't really *dangerous*. The casual treatment television accorded to threatening situations even extended to matters of life and death. Thus to the great American security blanket television added the comforting illusion that lethal circumstances could be overcome with minimal sweat or panic—an ironic outgrowth of America's fear-fueled obsession with safety.

Television was one of the new technologies that contributed to the sweeping changes in American society between 1945 and 1955. As late as 1952 it was a minor industry, owing largely to a freeze on channel assignments by the Federal Communications Commission

(FCC). When the freeze was lifted that year, the industry exploded. Within three years television supplanted radio as the nation's favorite broadcast medium, and soon after that it surpassed the popularity of newspapers as well. Every Hamlet grew up with television. Many confess to having watched hours and hours of it each day, sometimes doing their homework at the same time. They were part of a national phenomenon; as early as 1961 pollsters and rating services were reporting that the average TV stayed on five hours per day. In less than a decade, watching television had gone from a novelty to America's number one leisure-time activity.

The arrival of television presented the United States with a golden opportunity to raise the collective consciousness. Reporters could instantly relay important events to news-hungry citizens, well before the newspapers put the story on the street. Scholars could transmit their knowledge to millions of people rather than to the few students who could fit into a classroom. Cultural events once reserved for those who could afford a seat in the auditorium could be beamed into the living room of every American. The people had the power to make television into anything they wanted, for they owned the airwaves. The FCC granted broadcast licenses to individuals and corporations under the provision that programming serve the public interest. If the people didn't like what was being broadcast, they could complain to the FCC—or more effectively, not watch the shows they didn't like.

We all know what happened: TV turned into huckster heaven. The holders of broadcast licenses discovered they could make money—lots and lots of money—selling airtime to advertisers. Because they could charge the advertisers more as audience size increased, they sought the most broadly appealing programs they could find. They didn't need social scientists to tell them that the prevailing mood of the time favored programs with escapist themes. Right from the beginning, television devoted about 10 percent of its programming to public services such as the news, another 10 percent to highbrow cultural offerings, and a whopping 80 percent to entertainment. Some Americans protested (and still do) that TV shows were too violent or sexual, but hardly any protested that TV was too entertaining. In contrast to the citizens of other countries (and we're talking about Western democracies here, not the Soviet Union), whose TV networks offered a more balanced proportion of information, culture, and entertainment, Americans demanded noth-

ing more from the new medium than lukewarm comedy and melodramatic fluff—the better to stick their heads in the ground.

But television's unforgivable crime, at least with respect to the
Hamlet Syndrome, is that it went one step past adding a layer to the great
American security blanket. The heavily escapist fare that dominated the
movies and radio in the thirties and forties couldn't fool kids into taking
survival as a given—depression and war touched them too closely. But
television so conscientiously sanitized messy situations—and so relent-
lessly candy-coated everyday life—that the more protected children of
the fifties and sixties could easily get the impression that survival was
a cinch. Adults, especially those who've been through a war, know that
bodies bleed when pierced by bullets. Children, after watching their ten
thousandth bloodless, now-for-a-station-break murder on TV, can hardly
comprehend the gore and trauma involved in a real-life shooting. Sure,
there's some blood, they think, but it isn't *that* bad. And casual murder
is one of television's grosser distortions of reality. How many subtler
distortions sneak past the barely developed critical faculties of preadoles-
cents to form a warped but indelible sense of reality on their minds? For
that matter, how many of those subtle distortions get past the critical
faculties of adults, too? But we're talking about kids here, young Hamlets. To see how the one-eyed monster, television, entices the little
juniors into taking survival as a given, let's look at two types of programming the children enjoy.

Situation comedies usually revolve around family life. *I Love Lucy,*
Ozzie and Harriet, and *Father Knows Best* in the fifties; *Leave It to Beaver,*
My Three Sons, and *Dennis the Menace* in the early sixties; and *Bewitched,*
The Brady Bunch, and *Family Affair* in the late sixties and early seventies (this is hardly an exhaustive list of shows in the genre) all feature
innocuous families in a middle-class setting. Dad obviously makes a
pretty good living because the family can afford a big house, a late-model
car, and lots of playthings for the precocious kids. But except for band-
leading Desi Arnaz in *I Love Lucy* we have only the vaguest notion of
what Dad does. Work, without which the family can't afford the big
house and flashy goods, is irrelevant! Moreover, Dad never comes home
late, never chews out the wife and kids after a bad day, and never
monopolizes dinner conversation with complaints about his boss. You get
the impression that the office is someplace Dad goes to get cheered up
while the kids attend school or annoy Mom. Nowhere does an eight-year-

old Hamlet watching *Leave It to Beaver* get the message that Beaver starves if Mr. Cleaver loses his job, or that Mr. Cleaver might endure forty hours of hell each week to keep that split-level roof over his little brat's head.

Maybe the scriptwriters of family sitcoms, drawing from the realities of *their* work, found few humorous possibilities in plots revolving around Dad's job. But surely these shows could have been enriched by having the kids spend a day at the office with Dad or by having Dad bring home a co-worker and the co-worker's kid. One can object that after watching episode after episode clever little Hamlet would notice discrepancies between real and TV families and peg the latter as fake. But often the reverse occurs. Children in situations different from the televised ideal feel disappointed that their parents and siblings fall short. *TV*, not life with Mom and Dad, is the norm. Then, too, some Hamlets' families *do* resemble their television counterparts. Martin describes his parents as "a couple you'd see in a TV commercial. I never heard them argue about anything. They knew their roles, and they accepted them."

From the mid-sixties on, the subject matter of situation comedies broadened—and survival was trivialized even further. Consider a pair of shows so popular they still run in syndication: *Gilligan's Island* and *Hogan's Heroes*. The very idea that the settings of these shows could be humorous betrays an almost unparalleled contempt for reality. In *Gilligan's Island* a bunch of tourists on a pleasure cruise get caught in a storm and wind up stranded on an uncharted tropical island. Even a child recognizes this as a life-and-death situation. The castaways need water, food, shelter, and warmth. Without technological aids, real Robinson Crusoes would have to spend the better part of each day engaged in the struggle to survive. Yet Gilligan and his acquaintances have plenty of time. Their thatched shacks (doors and windows in perfect plumb), not to mention water and food, are provided not by any effort of their own but through the "magic" of television. Gilligan never expresses to Ginger the fear that the mangoes might run out—and perish the thought that he suggest they get together in his shack for a coconut cocktail!

Even more appallingly, *Hogan's Heroes* is set in a German prisoner of war camp during World War II. Colonel Klink and Sergeant Schultz, the Nazi officers, are bumptious but good-hearted buffoons who never once drag one of the American prisoners to execution—or worse. The Americans, for their part, appear well-fed and clean. Nothing in their manner suggests they're languishing in desperate circumstances. Per-

haps a responsible adult, on viewing *Hogan's Heroes*, would explain to
a child that the Nazis weren't really like that. But could that adult fully
communicate the horror of life in a prisoner of war compound? He'd
better; for watching this show, a child might think life in a stalag no
worse than life in summer camp.

In the early seventies Norman Lear proved that family-centered
situation comedies could be improved by realism. His *All in the Family*
featured a vulgar father who worked on a loading dock and treated his
family capriciously. The wife was easily flustered and the newlywed
children had trouble adjusting to married life. The show zoomed to
number one in the Nielsen ratings and remained there several years,
permanently broadening the scope of the situation comedy. But it was
too late for Hamlet. Whether born in 1947 or 1967, he grew up on
old-style sitcoms. Despite *All in the Family*'s success, the networks
continued to churn out atavistic new diversions like *Happy Days* and
Laverne and Shirley for young Hamlet's viewing pleasure.

The other type of programming that influenced young Hamlet is the
action/adventure series. This format encompasses a range of genres: cop
shows (*Dragnet, Adam-12*); detective shows (*The FBI, The Avengers*);
spy shows (*The Man from U.N.C.L.E., Mission: Impossible*); war shows
(*The Gallant Men, Combat!*); westerns (*Gunsmoke, Bonanza*); medical
potboilers (*Ben Casey, Dr. Kildare*); even science fiction (*Time Tunnel,
Star Trek*). Action/adventure shows pretend to more realism because
they routinely place their protagonists in life-threatening situations. But
this attention to realism makes action/adventure stories even more pernicious than situation comedies. As we noted when discussing bloodless
murders, TV skirts the powerful emotions associated with life-threatening situations. Indeed, when strong emotions come out at all in action/
adventure shows, they're usually overplayed by female characters whose
main purpose is to scream as they're chased or killed. Of the shows
mentioned above, only *The Avengers* features a woman in a central role.
But rather than convey realistically the emotions associated with intrigue
and violence, Emma Peel reacts with the same insouciance as her male
partner. Thus young Hamlet hardly ever gets an honest depiction of the
roiling emotions intrinsic to life-threatening situations. Although he may
recognize that the account is only a story, the broad message imprinted
on his unconscious is that one can survive life-and-death ordeals without
any strain on the pysche.

The serial nature of action/adventure shows also cushions Hamlet from anxiety. The hero, with whom Hamlet is encouraged to identify, returns week after week. That means no matter how much danger the hero may be in during the current episode, it's a sure thing he'll get out of it. Grievous injury and death are for guest stars and bit players. When *Star Trek*'s Kirk, Spock, and McCoy bring along an anonymous ensign on a visit to a strange new world, you know which one the alien monster will attack first. It's hard to feel any loss when the ensign gets zapped, because we barely even know his name; he's plot fodder, nothing more. To a Hamlet snuggled deeply in the suburban cocoon, death, the ultimate threat, happens only to extras.

As with situation comedies, the pat formulas of the action/adventure show were exposed as inadequate in the 1970s. *M*A*S*H*, ostensibly a comedy, crossed barriers to realism that previous medical and war dramas never approached. The central characters, doctors, regularly steeped themselves in blood. They suffered the fears, horrors, and privations of soldiers on the front, and they showed plenty of emotional scars, lapsing into bouts of depression and alcoholism. At one point one of the main characters even died. Shows like *Hill Street Blues* took cues from *M*A*S*H*'s award-winning format and gave the American people more realistic, less comforting views of life. But again, the changes came too late for Hamlets, who grew up on the old fare. The shows of their youth echoed the message of parents and neighborhood: don't worry, you're safe here, you'll be fine.

That boob-tube–induced sense of security would betray Hamlet once he outgrew the protections of his childhood.

7
Thought as a Subversive Activity

Our public schools serve two functions. The first is to instruct the young in basic skills: reading, writing, mathematics, and science. The second is to socialize children into the larger society. Inevitably the two functions intertwine. In teaching children how to read, for instance, we need to supply them with a text to read *from*. The choice of texts is subjective, entirely dependent on what we want to expose our children to. Take for example Mark Twain's *The Adventures of Huckleberry Finn*. None can deny Twain's status as one of the best writers the nation has produced, and more than one literary critic has dubbed *Huck Finn* the Great American Novel. The book is readily understandable to most seventh-graders: It's humorous, it's written from a child's standpoint, and it's a rip-roaring adventure story. From historical, literary, and psychological vantages it's a remarkable work, and many school districts are proud to include it in their curriculum. But then, look more closely at the subject matter of *Huck Finn:* There's slavery, child abuse, running away from home, and (compliments of Tom Sawyer at book's end) sadism. Some parents, upon reviewing the story, conclude that their children can learn to read just as well from another text—and they lobby their school board to ban *Huck Finn* from the school district's bookshelves.

Problems arise when a community cannot agree on what values to convey to its schoolchildren. A text may be a wonderful teaching tool that deals with issues most parents want their children to know about, but if other parents revile the text and are willing to resist its use in school, we come to some sticky questions about First Amendment rights. May schools promote the discussion of values and issues some parents disagree with? If so, do the schools have an obligation to present the minority's opinion, too? Lawsuits have been filed over less weighty matters. Cognizant of that, school boards and education officials generally go out of their way to avoid controversy in the classroom. They prefer—here's that idea again—*safety* to good pedagogy. To appease the Left, they buy social studies texts that feature children from various ethnic groups playing happily together. To appease the Right, they purchase scientific texts that soft-pedal the theory of evolution. In just the same manner Victorian prudes censored (or *bowdlerized,* after Thomas Bowdler, the prime culprit) Shakespeare's plays, including *Hamlet.* Reality gets short-changed and the kids get only half the story, but there isn't any controversy.

But controversy is a valuable teaching device. Kids get interested when they see sparks fly. The public schools are paid for by the people of the United States of America. As such, the schools ought to further the values of the nation, and the first and greatest value of the nation is democracy. Yet by glossing over controversial issues rather than examining them closely, the public schools, particularly our high schools, drain the very lifeblood of democracy—disagreement and debate—from the classroom. How can people decide among conflicting ideas without hearing them all in detail? Democracy is more than a daily recital of the Pledge of Allegiance. It requires the free flow of a variety of arguments and the ability on the part of the people to make an educated choice from among those arguments. By purging controversy from our public schools we wrap our children in yet another layer of ignorance and security. Worse still, we deny them the opportunity to learn the most valuable basic skill of all: critical thinking.

Critical thought is the ability to evaluate the assumptions and arguments underlying any proposition. Beliefs are embraced not on the basis of who holds them but on whether they stand up to logical scrutiny. Once a critical thinker, an individual truly becomes his own person, for he makes up his *own* mind about what he believes in. Adolescents learn critical thinking more readily than anyone else, owing to their newfound sense of possibility; even without formal training, they have a knack for detecting hypocrisy in individuals and institutions. High school is the time to engage them. Yet by and large we leave it to the universities to teach critical thought—a big mistake. Too many children never get to college. Of those who do, many avoid the courses (such as logic and expository writing) that enhance their critical-thinking ability. Instead of asking high schoolers to memorize a litany of facts, then, why not demand that they link the facts in some meaningful way? Instead of sheltering them from arguments over how they should be educated, why not *involve them directly*? Why not have them evaluate the arguments for and against, say, teaching creationism alongside evolution? Let *them* present the pro and con arguments to the school board. The adults would still make the decision, but the children would frame the discussion. Not only would the children learn about the subject matter, but they'd learn how to structure and defend their position on a major issue. They'd learn the basic principles of logic, which they could apply to *any* field or question later in life.

We keep hearing that worker productivity or lower interest rates or quality circles will keep the United States economically competitive, but new *products* give the economy its strength, and new products originate in minds, logical, *thinking* minds that link technologies to applications and solve problems through methodical analysis. Yet we are discouraging our children from thinking logically and methodically. We're whispering *don't worry, don't worry* and locking them into intellectual closets. Then we wonder why they can't compete with their European and Japanese counterparts. Let's expose them to sensitive issues and dissenting viewpoints, get their budding intellects accustomed to a challenge. Not only would such an exercise serve the long-term economic interests of the United States, but it would give the children a lasting lesson in democracy, an exercise in Americanism that will stay in their minds far longer than any ten-page reading assignment out of a presweetened history text.

Now, to tie all this to the Hamlet Syndrome. The avoidance of controversy and critical thought expands the coziness of Hamlet's home life to the hours he spends in school. Because he's not challenged, he hardly has to work to get good grades. This furthers the illusion that life is easy. But there's a second, equally damaging consequence to the public schools' failure to encourage critical thinking. Especially in high school, Hamlet gets *bored.* He possesses a natural inclination to think critically—which leads to the full-blown skepticism of adulthood—but little if anything is done in school to nurture it. He's asked only to regurgitate memorized facts. As a result Hamlet is not intellectually challenged, and he develops none of the mental discipline vital to professional success later in life. So bored of school does Hamlet become that he often finds more pleasure and wisdom in his own reading (and by the time he leaves high school he may be reading literary classics and scholarly texts) than he does in his homework assignments. In spite of that, most Hamlets take school seriously and finish in the top 10 percent of their class. Those who don't are usually so bored by their classes that they just don't give a damn.

"High school was terribly, terribly boring," recalls Jeff, our hippie Hamlet. "It was just something to get through. Things were happening out there in the world, and there was this burgeoning sense of being part of a generation of purpose and destiny. But no one was discussing the things that were of interest to us back then. There were a couple of teachers who were very entertaining, and I enjoyed them a lot. But how do you study trigonometry when there's a war going on? And the history they taught!" He sighs. "There was *nothing,* no ideas. It was just a lot of events held together by these big titles, you know, the Civil War, the Revolutionary War." Although he hardly ever studied, Jeff made the honor roll several times. He read Ayn Rand ("Great stuff—at that age it's really easy to latch onto dogmatic and hard-edged ideas") and played guitar in a band formed by his friends. In short, he had a more stimulating life outside school than he did in.

A few Hamlets are so turned off by their secondary education that they presume college will be more of the same—and they decide not to go. But most go straight from high school to college. Their parents want them to go, their friends are all going, so they figure they might as well join the crowd. They're not thinking for themselves yet, owing to their lack of training in critical thought, the protectiveness of their parents, and their own willingness to submit to the dictates of social law—the one lesson high school teaches them very well. Consequently, Hamlet arrives on campus with but a pittance of real-life experience, completely unprepared for the social and academic bumps he'll have to ride out in the next few years.

8

The Four Warning Signs of Hamlethood

Millions of children born in the 1950s and 1960s grew up with security-obsessed parents, television, and public education. What turns some middle-class, suburban, TV-watching kids into Hamlets while others just like them go on to "normal" lives and careers? How early can we distinguish Hamlets from their conventionally successful peers? Are there some childhood experiences peculiar to Hamlets? Are there some personality traits endemic to Hamlets alone?

Within the broad parameters of terms like *middle class, suburban,* and *TV-watching* there are millions of gradations. No two childhoods are exactly alike, even those of identical twins. And, of course, no two *children* are exactly alike; the same parents can produce offspring light-years apart temperamentally and intellectually. For these reasons it's impossible to identify traits that are always present in Hamlets and never present in other kids. For example, as we've shown, Hamlets are smart and usually good in school. But so are plenty of other children who are easily assimilated into the mainstream.

Nor are there any environmental factors that *definitely* lead to the Hamlet Syndrome. Trendy theories of behavior based on factors such as birth order tell us nothing about the Hamlet Syndrome. Hamlets can be the eldest or youngest of their siblings, and in families of more than two kids plenty of Hamlets come from the middle of the pack. None of this is to say that traits characteristic of Hamlet in adulthood—wide-ranging intellect, sensitivity, respectful demeanor, lack of direction—aren't present in childhood. It's just that we know of no foolproof basis for predicting whether a child with those attributes will become a Hamlet or vice president of a Fortune 500 corporation.

Even though they may not become Hamlets, children who *do* exhibit wide-ranging intellect, sensitivity, respect for authority, and lack of direction nevertheless possess a *predisposition* toward the Hamlet Syndrome, and so it's important that we take a closer look at these "warning signs" of impending Hamlethood.

We'll start with wide-ranging intelligence, which provides the foundation for Hamlet's later tolerance, curiosity, and skepticism. Mom and Dad almost always stress the importance of doing well in school, and Hamlet strives to please them. As a result, early in life, when grades are the principal yardstick of accomplishment, Hamlet is considered quite an achiever—perhaps the only time in his life he's thought of that way. He's quick to link his identity with his superiority in the classroom. "I loved school," Maxine recalls fondly. "I liked everything about it. I liked stationery supplies, I liked eating in a cafeteria, I liked the new pair of shoes every year. I was always, always one of the smart kids in class. I liked that role."

Perhaps an even more significant sign of Hamlet's intellectual curiosity is the great deal of reading he does on his own. Maxine, like almost everyone else her age, watched plenty of television as a youngster—but she also read voraciously. "The Oz books were real big when I was a kid. We had thirty-eight of them," she says. Brent, Jeff, and Martin also report spending hours alone with books. "I would sit and read all day from the age of seven," says Brent, who religiously read *The New Yorker* magazine cover-to-cover starting in eighth grade. Jeff's reading consisted mostly of baseball books—but he also read novels and "current stuff." "My seventh-grade teacher was great," he says wistfully. "He read to us in class. There's nothing like being read to, I think. He read us *To Kill a Mockingbird,* the whole thing. Not only that, but he took all the voices and made them sound different." Martin's love of books began before he even went to school. "I got hooked on dinosaurs when I was four years old," he says, recalling his earliest experience with reading. "I still have the very same comic book which got me interested in them. I saw it in a store and probably whined and cried and said 'I want that' until my parents got it for me. I learned all the dinosaurs' names, and decided right then I was going to become a paleontologist."

We spoke earlier of television's role in lulling Hamlets into an exaggerated sense of security, but we didn't mention the role television plays in inculcating thought patterns. Marshall McLuhan's landmark work in media criticism established that when it comes to television, the medium is the message—that is, the *means* of communication is more important than the content. Television communicates primarily through moving pictures. To hold the viewer's attention, the pictures are selected for maximum visual impact. Thus a televised presentation need not be rational, only provocative or emotionally compelling. Consider commercials. When is the last time you saw a commercial that patiently, quietly, and logically explained why you needed to purchase the sponsor's product? That kind of commercial would likely bore you into a stupor. So what you get instead is a stark, often sex-tinged series of images meant to stir up anxieties only the advertised product can relieve. Because it's so intensely visual, television conditions us to respond to appearances and emotions rather than logical discourse.

Print does almost the opposite. Its sole visual elements, letters, are symbols for words, nothing more. Anything you "see" when you read comes from your imagination. But you can't imagine anything if the words you read don't make sense, so print has to be a logical medium. Each word has to lead to the next if you're to make sense of the sentence. Each sentence must connect with the sentence that follows if you're to understand the idea of the paragraph. If that doesn't happen, you can't form a picture in your mind of what the author is trying to say. There's a break in understanding—and communication falters. Print therefore conditions us to respond logically rather than emotionally.

Good reader that you are, you're probably wondering how all this relates to what we're supposed to be talking about, the early manifestations of Hamlet's intelligence. It relates this way: Hamlet generally does a lot of reading as a child. Reading teaches him how to think logically.

When his reasoning abilities fully mature he applies his logical thinking patterns to everything around him. That's the critical thought we were talking about—a major component of full-fledged Hamlethood. The source of the Hamlet Syndrome, then, can be traced to Hamlet's joy in reading.

But there's more to young Hamlet's curiosity than his passion for reading. He finds he can apply his intelligence to any number of endeavors. Jeff took up chess in sixth grade. "Some friends of mine were trying to get together a chess club. They had an odd number of people one weekend, so my friend Bob taught me to play chess on Saturday and I was in the chess tournament on Sunday. I was just cannon fodder for the rest of the guys. But I got good at it." Laughs he with satisfaction, "I discovered how much fun it was taking advantage of people who didn't know how to play the game."

Some Hamlets, in addition to intelligence, exhibit early flashes of talent. "I found out I could draw really well in first or second grade," says Martin. "I'd draw pictures of dinosaurs and my classmates would say 'That's great! Draw me one!' I'd end up drawing three or four of these things in a row—same picture. My folks encouraged my art. In third grade they sent me up the street to this guy who gave oil painting lessons. I wouldn't call them lessons, actually. He didn't tell you how to do anything. You just paid him so you could paint there for two hours. I didn't learn anything, but I had fun. It always smelled good—you know, turpentine."

Hamlet's parents can usually tell he's a gifted child. They're pleased, but for various reasons some parents are reluctant to heap praise on their prodigy. A few are threatened by Hamlet's intelligence. One particularly bright Hamlet, on showing her father a test on which she'd scored a 99, the highest grade in the class, was asked why she didn't get a perfect 100. This same Hamlet performed so well on her Scholastic Aptitude Test that she qualified for a National Merit Scholarship and could have gone to the college of her choice—but her jealous father insisted that she go to her state's inferior public university. Other parents have more benign reasons for their indifference, but whatever the cause, the lack of appreciation for his curiosity and intelligence makes Hamlet modest about his precocity. He may even apologize to family and friends for his superior aptitude. This discounting of his greatest asset robs Hamlet of confidence. It gives him the impression that raw wit doesn't count for much, an impression that, carried into adulthood, is as self-defeating as a gladiator's throwing down his sword before entering the arena.

Most of us refer to people as *sensitive* in condescending tones generally reserved for the slightly retarded: *Why, you'd hardly suspect that he isn't quite normal.* The word implies delicacy, excessive emotion, perhaps even a touch of instability. We're more comfortable around people who keep their lips stiff and their eyes dry in adversity. This standard for stoicism pertains especially to men. Think of our more successful male movie heroes: John Wayne, Clint Eastwood, Arnold Schwartzenegger, Sylvester Stallone. Even Stallone, whose Italian forebears could weep without worrying for their masculinity, plays the invulnerable he-man flick after flick. Don't stop to admire the jungle scenery, Rambo, some black-pajamaed, subhuman sniper might get a chance to fix you in his sights! We see the same trend in popular music, where rock stars from Mick Jagger to Michael Jackson cultivate a too-cool-for-it-all image. Feelings are for wimps like Alan Alda and Jackson Browne. Real men keep their emotional distance.

On women we force the sort of double standard that has enraged feminists for a century. The traditional American woman is expected to feel more than she thinks; it's her duty to divine the wishes of others and place those wishes before her own. But then we routinely condemn her for being too emotional! Few women relish the bind, but even women in equal relationships feel the tug of the old sexist pattern, thinking of their husbands and children before themselves even when they know hubby and kids don't reciprocate. They resent having the discounted role of emoter heaped upon them, but then, *someone's* got to feel and express genuine emotions. Since men have too much at stake to show sensitivity, women resign themselves to pulling double duty.

Fortunately those stereotypes largely don't apply to Hamlets. Male or female, they can be sensitive without sinking into sentimentalism. They often display acute self-awareness and sensitivity to others from the moment they start school. The classroom is the first place they make their own niche in a social context, their place in the family having been predetermined, and despite the esteem they derive from good grades, many Hamlets worry that they don't fit in with their peers. Maxine, a top student who loved school, confesses that "I felt different. I thought of myself as a misfit kid. I don't know from what, I just felt like an oddball." She ponders a moment. "I dressed differently, because I wore a lot of hand-me-downs and offbeat things. I'd have green pepper sandwiches for lunch and things the other kids laughed at. I heard remarks behind me in the hallways once or twice, about me being stuck up. By the time I got to high school I was pretty shy."

To her credit, Maxine tried to fit in by taking small parts in school plays, even though performing made her nervous. Most Hamlets don't go that far. Very few become cheerleaders, jocks, or class presidents. They either find a niche for themselves with a small group of friends or make early acquaintance with the role of outsider.

Self-awareness alone doesn't distinguish a child as the feeling type—every kid is sensitive to his own needs. True sensitivity lies in the child's consideration of others. When he first overcomes the natural temptation to be cruel and considers the needs of another before acting, he takes a giant step toward maturity. When he puts his own needs aside so another might realize an even greater benefit, he's reached a level of civilized behavior many politicians and Wall Street connivers never attain. Hamlets can be capable of this deference for others from an astonishingly early age.

Says one male Hamlet, now thirty-four years old, "I was always conscious of other kids' feelings. There was this one kid that people used to pick on all the time. We used to call him Spaghetti Eddie. I picked on Spaghetti Eddie up until a certain point. I can even picture the point; it was when somebody had just teased me about something, and all of a sudden, it was like a flash of illumination, I realized that was what I was doing to Spaghetti Eddie. I never did that to him anymore." He had this revelation in third grade, at the age of eight.

Parents, of course, play a big part in instilling sensitivity in their children. Their efforts plus Hamlet's safe environment lead him to believe, if only on a subconscious level, that life should be fair—and no one should be hurt, least of all by him. Out of this compassionate impulse develops Hamlet's conscience and consideration for others. Combined with the respect for authority we'll discuss next, that sensitivity also forms the basis for his idealism and strongly held ethical convictions.

* * *

Melancholy Baby: Hamlet's Childhood Circumstances

*I pledge allegiance to the flag of the United States of America and to
the republic for which it stands: one nation, under God, indivisible,
with liberty and justice for all.*

From Bangor to San Diego grammar school children recite these words
every day before they begin their lessons. Often the chant is followed
by a patriotic song. The daily ritual is meant to teach the children love
of country. But how many seven-year-olds ever *think* about the Pledge
of Allegiance? To them it's just another part of the September-to-June
ritual, like washing their faces and getting dressed in the morning. The
few who *do* apply their child's logic to the pledge may come up with some
disturbing questions. What does allegiance mean? Why do we pledge it
to a colored cloth hanging from a stick? The adults to whom such queries
are brought often thank their stars the little upstart doesn't have the
background to ask about God, the Civil War, and the criminal justice
system.

Some children attend parochial schools, where in addition to the
Pledge of Allegiance they recite prayers and verses from the Bible. A
goodly number of public school kids receive religious instruction every
Sunday, either in church with Mom and Dad or in special classes. But
to a child still possessed of milk teeth the notion of God is nebulous, even
a little frightening. He sees *everything*? He knows what I'm thinking,
too? Does that mean I'm going to hell because yesterday I wished my
baby sister would break her nose? A child can know none of the nuances
of religious belief. Therefore, adults intent on imbuing their offspring
with religious values must do it the same way the public schools teach
patriotism—through indoctrination—and hope the message sinks in so
deeply the child will never be able to uproot it.

When pointed at adult minds, indoctrination goes by other names:
brainwashing, propaganda, advertising. Depending on the subtlety of the
technique used and the individual's capacity for critical thought, an adult
can see through such manipulation. But little kids aren't sophisticated
enough to recognize the manipulative aspects of indoctrination. When
employed on them in a wholesale manner indoctrination has a pernicious
effect: They learn that in this land of freedom and justice for all, the most
important social relationships function as dictatorships—and their role
is to unconditionally obey.

Of course, home life is a dictatorship, too. The first and ultimate
authorities in a child's life are mother and father. Parents have such

complete control of their child, even in the midst of a tantrum, that the youngster has no choice but to eventually comply with what they expect of him. Out of love, fear, or both, he learns to submit to the will of his parents, hoping thereby to earn their approval. But that's as it should be. We're not arguing against indoctrination at home—we're arguing against *institutional* indoctrination. Once the authoritarian pattern is established at home, the nation's major institutions socialize children through the same autocratic mechanisms—and that's too pervasive. Children get accustomed to taking orders they can't understand, to letting others do their thinking for them. Are we so insecure about our national and religious values that we have to *brainwash* our little children into adopting them? In the name of state and church must we indoctrinate our children into the kind of thinking that leads to fascism?

Sadly, the answer to both questions is yes, and little Hamlet, intelligent and sensitive as he is, readily picks up on the authoritarian realities of his environment. Consequently, his demeanor is almost always respectful: quiet, mannerly, and well within the behavioral bounds set by mother and father. But as he grows up, this submission to authority will cut a second way, exacerbating Hamlet's conflict over whether to follow the heart or the dollar. He'll develop his own internal dictator. Accustomed to giving or taking—mostly taking—orders, with no middle ground for negotiation, the young adult Hamlet will tend to regard himself and his world in absolutist terms. The internal dictator will expect only the highest standards of behavior from others—and from Hamlet himself. I've *got* to be me, he'll think in adulthood, and he'll follow the innermost yearnings of his heart no matter how much conventional (and sometimes greater) wisdom contradicts. Inasmuch as he owes what few decision-making powers he possesses to that dogmatic voice inside his head, the internal dictator is actually good.

But even as he turns respect for authority to his own ends, Hamlet's childhood need to fulfill others' expectations remains strong. The early indoctrination in obedience makes Hamlet *want* to follow the social law, makes him long for the rewards of the dollar, and there's practically no chance he'll follow the dictates of his heart so far that he becomes a revolutionary. He'll always want *in,* to be accepted. He's been told since earliest childhood that doing what others want of him is his primary duty, and the indoctrination is so thorough he simply cannot overcome it.

Martin was a most well-behaved child. So well behaved was he that he vividly remembers the two times he wasn't. "A friend of mine taught me all these swear words in third grade. I was fascinated by them. I used them constantly, but not at home, of course. One day this friend, my older brother, and I were shooting a basketball in the driveway, and my friend starts telling my brother, 'Yeah, Martin's got the filthiest mouth in the school.' I said, 'What are you doing? You're signing my death warrant!' So what happens? My brother goes in and tells Mom, and she comes out later and asks, 'Is this true?' What could I say? I never was a good liar. I said, 'Yeah, it is true,' and she burst into tears and ran into the house. I felt like shit—or, maybe I should say, dung. I stopped cursing real quick after that. Didn't use a four-letter word for years.

"Then, in high school, I did another stupid thing. It was a blatant act of disobedience. We drove out, two cars, my parents and myself in one car, this other couple and their son in the other, to this abandoned quarry. They were hunting for flowers in the woods around there. Nearby were these big tires all over the place. We had to climb up this hill to get to the woods, so we left the cars down at the bottom and hiked up. This other kid and I, we weren't too interested in looking for flowers, so we started rolling tires down the hill. I found this big monster tire. I stand it up, and the other kid is down the hill going 'Go ahead!' I'm all ready to let it go when my mother comes out of the woods and says, 'Don't you roll that!' I look at my mother, I look at this kid—and I roll the tire down the hill.

"It started heading straight for the friends' car. The kid sees where it's going, so he runs in front of the car. The tire's coming, it's coming, and as it bounds up near him he tries to push it out of the way but *whack!* it smashes into the side of the car and leaves a big black smear. My mother didn't hit me or anything. She just looked like the world had come to an end. There was deadly silence all the way home." Martin might have felt less guilt about his disobedience, perhaps even forgotten about it by now, if his mother had simply yelled at him. By showing hurt rather than rage, she filled young Martin with the kind of guilt anyone finds hard to outgrow. (For the record, Martin and his family took home the other couple's car and cleaned off the black smear.)

Just because little Hamlet follows rules, however, doesn't mean he knows which way he's going. An adult stuck with somebody else's kid for a long period of time can always kill at least thirty seconds asking the child what he wants to be when he grows up. It's one of the routine questions of childhood, and by the time a kid reaches ten he's usually got his response memorized. He's going to be a doctor, a lawyer, an engineer, maybe a fireman, because someone he admires is one or because he read a book about it, and the work seems pretty neat. The child has no idea what it takes to actually *become* a doctor or lawyer, though, and the adult asking the question is often too bemused to give the kid a clue. "That's nice," the adult says, and the conversation turns to another subject. Since the child has an answer for the stock question, he's thought to have direction, and so long as he does well in school Mom and Dad—and other adults—assume he will amount to something.

But that's a hasty assumption, at least in the case of little Hamlet. Nothing in his background is preparing him for the rigors of pursuing a profession. The shelter of his middle-class neighborhood, the distortions of television, and the zealous care of his parents are giving him the impression that as long as he holds up his end of the deal, i.e., gets good grades and behaves, he'll get whatever he wants. He's not told that he'll have to *work* if he wants to live as well as his parents—or if he is told, the message doesn't sink in. Thus we find two possible misunderstandings between parents and little Hamlet when it comes to his future direction. In the first, Hamlet says he knows what he wants to do when he grows up, but the adults in his life don't encourage concrete steps toward his goal. In the second, Mom and Dad show a great deal of concern for Hamlet's professional future, but Hamlet doesn't take the matter seriously.

Martin's experience illustrates the first situation. From age four he wanted to become a paleontologist, because he loved dinosaurs. His parents "accepted paleontology. It was an interesting science, and I probably could get a good job." But in practical terms his mother and father did little to ready him for the difficult science courses he'd have to pass to major in the field. (They did send him to art school to develop his talent for drawing, but they made it clear to him that art should be an avocation rather than a meal ticket.)

Martin's parents further handicapped him through coddling. We've already heard him give his folks an F because they did everything for him. They also protected him from his older brother, who in the best tradition of sibling rivalry pummeled Martin regularly. "What they should have said was, 'Okay, no dinner for you until you go over there and beat your brother's face in.' That was what I had to do. I had to start fighting him back, at least make him know he wasn't going to get away with it so easily every time." But Martin didn't fight back. He was already getting hit, so it wasn't fear of pain that deterred him. Rather, his sensitivity and his desire to obey his parents prevented him from mixing it up with his brother. Looking back, he feels that this early passivity explains in good part why he has not yet begun to fight for himself in adulthood.

Jeff's experience followed the second pattern: His parents were very concerned about his future, but he didn't much care. "My father wanted me to follow in the business," he recounts. "He had a couple of different things going. Early on he had a couple of fabric stores. Then he joined my uncle in this custom tailoring and uniform business. He would have preferred that I join him there. He thought it was important to have a good business background. Business was just simply the way the world operated."

But a businessperson can't operate without a solid grasp of numbers, and from the very beginning Jeff was indifferent to mathematics. "The first time I flunked a test was a math test when I was a little kid. From what I remember of the way my father scolded me about it, apparently I wasn't fully accepting of the fact that I had flunked. He raised his voice and said, 'You got an F on this test!' as if he was trying to *convince* me of it. I remember him saying about math, 'You can't do anything in this world without mathematics. You've got to *know* this stuff!' "

We wouldn't be fair to Jeff if we neglected to mention that he *did* have a career goal—of sorts—as a child. "I wanted to be a baseball player. All I thought about was baseball. I would cry when the Kansas City Athletics lost leads in the bottom of the ninth inning—lose seven-run leads to the Yankees! One of my first memories is watching a game back in the late fifties. I asked my Dad, 'If they say he's walked, why is he running to first base?' I had a very literal interpretation of the game back then." He also had a simplistic notion of what it takes to play the game. "I would try out for teams—rather unsuccessfully. I was a terrible baseball player. Here I was saying I wanted to be a baseball player, and yet I was terrible at it. That was pretty difficult to deal with. Even when my interest in baseball began to wane, I would still tell myself I wanted to be a baseball player."

He took one more shot, from a different angle, at working in the national pastime. "In ninth grade we had a career section in one of our classes. Pick a profession and go interview people in it. I wanted to be a baseball journalist. I interviewed a couple of guys who announced for the Athletics. I also interviewed some guy who was the sports editor at the Kansas City paper." But here, too, Jeff's career goal was more stated than felt. "Even after that I don't remember thinking, God, I'm going to be a baseball broadcaster. Little ambition, very little ambition. I was happy just sitting around at night playing my guitar."

Wide-ranging intelligence, sensitivity, respect for authority, and lack of direction: the four warning signs of the Hamlet Syndrome. We want to repeat that not all children exhibiting these tendencies become Hamlets. Their turn of mind simply predisposes them to the syndrome. For a young person to become a Hamlet, his wide-ranging intelligence has to lead to tolerance, curiosity, and skepticism. His sensitivity has to develop into conscience and consideration for others. His respect for authority has to take an unconventional twist and cause him to respect the values of his own heart. And his lack of direction has to—well, remain lack of direction.

9

Mild in the Streets

W ith the possible exception of the terrible twos, no period of a
child's life exasperates parents more than the high school
years—adolescence. Junior can no longer be trusted to honor every
parental command. The renowned child psychologist Jean Piaget, in his
book *The Psychology of the Child,* explains that adolescent rebellion
results from the maturation of a child's reasoning abilities. Adolescence
brings "a liberation from the concrete" leading to "a transformation of
thought that permits the handling of hypotheses and reasoning with
regard to propositions removed from concrete and present observation"—in other words, the child gains the ability to think critically. With
critical thought comes the awareness of other possibilities, and with the
awareness of other possibilities comes the realization that things don't
have to be the way Mom and Dad have set them up.

But why should Hamlet rebel against the way Mom and Dad have

set things up? His life is pretty good, and the larger society expects him
to conform, not defy. Even if he wanted to rebel, his isolation has limited
his sense of what's possible—he hasn't *seen* enough to know how far he
can go. Thus in most cases Hamlet's rebellion is aimed merely at establishing an identity separate from his family's, not at overturning everything society stands for. He just wants a little room for himself. He takes
charge of his appearance, for instance, and sports a haircut and clothing
that offend Mom and Dad. But regard for a moment Hamlet's friends.
They've cut their hair the same way, and their apparel resembles Hamlet's too. In violating parental standards, Hamlet usually conforms to the
standards of his peers. He's not rebelling so much as transferring his
allegiance. Wiser parents tolerate this defiance as a necessary step in
Hamlet's self-development and socialization—all the while giving thanks
the kid isn't engaged in drag racing or drug abuse.

Generally, older Hamlets made for more rebellious teenagers than
younger Hamlets. Much of that has to do with the times in which the
elder Hamlets grew up. Hamlets pushing forty went to high school in the
1960s, when the culture opened up and any kid wishing to remain in
good standing with his peers had to do his part to widen the Generation
Gap. New ways of thinking, behaving, and dressing trickled down from
college, where older brothers and sisters, newly freed from the padded
walls of suburbia, reacted to the horrors of racism, an expanding war,
and the desiccated standards of the 1950s. Even so, older Hamlets
generally shunned the more radical behavior patterns of the time.

Hamlets in their early thirties, having gone to high school in the
early to mid-1970s, routinely experimented with alcohol and marijuana.
They grooved to rock and roll music and let their hair grow long. Rarely,
however, did they get so out of control that their families stopped
thinking of them as nice kids. The youngest Hamlets, those in their
twenties, went to pep rallies, homecomings, and proms during the disillu-
sionment of the Carter years and the grim conformity of the Age of
Reagan. External goads to rebellion had largely disappeared. Conformity
was *in,* and consequently the youngest Hamlets saw only disadvantages
to forsaking the security they were raised in.

Jeff, our hippie, is one of those Hamlets pushing forty. He went to
high school from 1967 to 1970, at the counterculture's zenith. He grew
his hair out, learned how to play guitar, and spent his time thinking
about Vietnam and the environment. But the worst he did in terms of
rebellion was argue with his father during dinner. "What inevitably

happened was that I would pick up on something my father said, or bait him, and we would just go round and round. We'd argue about Vietnam, we'd argue about the environment, we'd argue about civil rights. It was probably a way of hashing out other issues, getting a chance to vent my anger and unhappiness with him."

Nevertheless, there are circumstances under which Hamlet will rebel in earnest. Uncontrollable rebellion, which can begin as early as age twelve, results from a sudden, traumatizing loss of security. Once Hamlet feels the cold wind of vulnerability against his skin, his defiance takes on a desperate, dangerous fury. Usually the security is lost when the family moves from the comfortable surroundings in which Hamlet grew up. Hamlet adapts poorly to his new environment. He may have been an outsider in his old environment, but at least he was settled in that role, feeling to some extent that he'd chosen it for himself. In his new haunt he's *automatically* an outsider. His new classmates long ago established a social order among themselves; their primitive, clique-ridden society makes no accommodation for new arrivals. Bitter toward the parents who transplanted him, strange to his house and his neighborhood, he has nowhere to turn for solace. To ameliorate his alienation and fear, he takes the you-can't-fire-me-I-quit attitude toward his new surroundings. He rebels not only from his parents (because of his age he'd rebel against them anyway) but from his new peers and neighborhood as well. Cowardice and common sense alone restrain his insurrectionary impulse. The previously benign Hamlet becomes, in his uprooted adolescence, a wild, unpredictable child.

Jessica, our perpetual student, serves as a case in point. She moved to an affluent suburb of Madison, Wisconsin, when she was twelve years old. "I think I must not have liked it there, because I started acting up," she says, confessing, "I started getting involved in acts of juvenile delinquency. My friends were misfits and maladjusted people. We'd get into trouble together, and then one or another of us would be sent to the school psychiatrist to be straightened out. My parents were shocked. They couldn't understand where all this bad behavior was coming from. It wasn't until many years later that I made some sense of it myself. I'd been cut off from all my friends and cooped up in this area where I didn't know anyone. And everything was very spread out, I couldn't go anywhere. I was bereft, and I couldn't adjust to it for a very long time."

The plight of Antonio, our artist Hamlet, was even more desperate. He was born in Panama, not far from the Canal Zone. His mother married an American soldier and left for the United States, entrusting Antonio, her second son, to her mother and father. "In most cultures, the first son is the favorite, and the second son fends for himself. That's part of why my mother left me with her parents. But I didn't mind. With my grandparents *I* was an only child, the favored one." Although he grew up relatively poor (and without television), he had all the security and isolation of a middle-class American-born Hamlet. And as with American-born Hamlets, so long as he kept his end of the bargain—good grades and obedience, mostly—his life was idyllic. "My life was a joy," he acknowledges. "I was spoiled. My grandparents were very orderly, but very loving. I knew what I could and couldn't do, knew what time to be home. I could do whatever I wanted as long as my work was done and I was where I was supposed to be.

"One day, before I turned thirteen, this dispatch came in the mail to pack me up and send me to America. Nothing was explained to me. I just woke up one Sunday morning and my grandmother dressed me in my Sunday finery. But instead of going to church we took the train and went to the Panama City airport. I'd never seen an airport in my life. They put me on this plane—still not a word about what was going on—and I started to cry. Something in me knew that I was not coming back." That something in him was correct. His mother, living on an army base near Oakland, had decided she was ready to include him in her family. And so in less than a day Antonio went from sheltered tropical Panama to the bustle of a sibling-filled California home.

He had neither the will nor the ability to assimilate quickly. "Talk about culture shock! The transition from being Latin to being American drove me crazy. It just didn't take. Latins and Americans have different ways of dealing with the world. We eat different food, we move differently, everything is different. I didn't know English that well, and that didn't help. [He grew up speaking Spanish.] My mom thought it absolutely imperative that I assimilate right away, so she told my teachers to admonish me and even spank me if I spoke anything other than English. I felt like everyone was trying to erase me. I went crazy. I got into a fight just about every day. I remember one Saturday it got to me so much that I just walked and walked and walked. My objective was to run away, past everything, but the damn city just kept on going.

"In the span of a year and a half I went to three public schools and two Catholic schools. I started my second Catholic school when I was in eighth grade. It was the habit of the Catholic Church at that time to recruit for their religious orders by going around the Catholic school system and speaking to the graduating males about the advantages of joining a religious life. And I thought, this is a way to get out of this crazy thing I'm in, to get away from Mom and all these other people I don't know who I'm supposed to call brother and sister." So prior to his freshman year of high school Antonio, with his mother's consent, joined a religious order and moved to a monastery in northern California. There he continued his rebellious ways—"I was on penance all the time for doing what I wasn't supposed to be doing," he admits with a mischievous grin—but also (excuse the pun) found the order he'd been craving.

Rebellion against the values and life-styles of elders marks the onset of the Hamlet Syndrome. From here on, Hamlet's separation from the mainstream will deepen and broaden. Yet just as the cry and shape of a newborn baby can't tell us whether it will grow into Einstein or the village idiot, we cannot tell from a teenager's rebellion whether he's going to become a Hamlet or an Iacocca. If in addition to being mildly rebellious he's logical, principled, sensitive, and unambitious, *then* there's a good chance he'll turn out a Hamlet. Otherwise, don't waste your time fretting over his future. You'll find out soon enough whether your high school grad is a Hamlet—he sends out unmistakable signals to that effect by the end of his sophomore year in college—and if he is you'll have more than your share to worry about. But you'll also have more than your share to be proud of, as we'll see later on.

10

The Tale of Arden Forest

As a child, William Shakespeare had a smack of Hamlet in himself. His mother, Mary Arden, inherited land and wealth when her father died. She married John Shakespeare, an ambitious glover on his way to becoming one of the most prominent men in Stratford. They were as middle-class as anyone could be in Elizabethan England. Through the first thirteen years of his life they provided well for their little prodigy, raising him on a quiet street that ended in orchards, groves, and wild country. After learning to read and write, William formally enrolled in grammar school around age seven, taking his lessons from men who held master's degrees from Oxford. In school he learned Latin, starting with *Aesop's Fables* and progressing over the next six years to the poetry of Ovid. His parents took him every Sunday to the local Protestant church, where he heard homilies urging obedience to family, neighbors, and queen. In his spare time young Shakespeare sat in the rose garden behind his house, wandered in the woods, and hunted deer. Despite the turmoil in England—the Northern Rebellion broke out when he was five, and his father, who served briefly as a public official, sometimes had to be escorted to official functions by guards—he experienced little genuine danger. In short, he grew up intelligent, sensitive, and obedient, three of the warning signs of Hamlethood, amid happy and secure surroundings.

But when William Shakespeare was thirteen his family's fortunes reversed, the result mostly of his father's financial recklessness. All sense of security was lost as Shakespeare's family mortgaged more and more property to pay off his father's debts. The chance for a college education slipped beyond reach—too expensive. Yet as Shakespearean scholar A. L. Rowse puts it, "in Elizabethan times people lived their briefer lives more gregariously, more intensely," so rather than lament his misfortune, Shakespeare immediately set out to make a life for himself in Stratford. By age eighteen he'd impregnated Anne Hathaway, a woman eight years his senior—a significant age difference in an era when few people reached fifty—and three months into her pregnancy he married her. By the time he was twenty-one he had three kids to care for. He made a living helping in his father's shop, selling wool, and teaching school. Unlike modern Hamlets, Will Shakespeare was a man of the world while still in his teens.

And thereby hangs the tale, the moral of our story. Once the security of his childhood was taken away, Shakespeare engaged the world, and he didn't stop engaging it until he'd become the most famous author of all time. By contrast, the secure childhood of modern Hamlets holds them, like a magnet, in the easy chair of complacence. So long as they don't have to, they won't resist the force that's pulling them down. That leaves them frightfully unprepared for the inevitable crises of adulthood and does tremendous, perhaps irreparable damage to their coping mechanisms. No wonder they're so afraid of grown-up responsibilities. Any middle-class, suburban parent reading this book should resolve to expose, expose, *expose* his child to the dark side of the human experience. Show him the consequences of anger, jealousy, greed, hypocrisy—and complacence. Show him other customs, other values, other ideas. Take *fewer* responsibilities for his welfare, make him do for himself, and let him live with his decisions, especially the mistaken ones. Let him know there's more to the human equation than getting good grades and staying out of trouble. The child may still become a Hamlet, but he'll have a better idea of what awaits him once he's on his own. "I grew up very secure, but now I feel very insecure, and it's a big contrast," confesses one twenty-seven-year-old Hamlet who is unemployed and starting her second graduate school curriculum. "Maybe if I hadn't grown up so secure I wouldn't feel so insecure now."

III

THE GREAT AWAKENING: HAMLET GOES TO COLLEGE

O God, God,
How weary, stale, flat, and unprofitable
Seem to me all the uses of this world!

Hamlet, ACT I, SCENE ii

C ollege almost always represents the turning point in Hamlet's life, especially for the Hamlet who spent adolescence placating rather than fighting the family, community, and nation he was raised in. The college campus serves as a way station between childhood dependence and adult independence. It allows Hamlet the time and freedom to define his relationship to the world. Free from the fetters of his upbringing, Hamlet can indulge his curiosity and skepticism to the fullest. His horizon expands a thousandfold as he discovers the world beyond his secure, middle-class environment. For the first time in his life he realizes just how much the social law has restricted his behavior and perspective, and as with anyone suddenly plunked into exotic but safe surroundings, Hamlet is eager to explore his possibilities.

His explorations lead to revelations that permanently alter his outlook on the world—and himself. He learns from the social sciences and the liberal arts that many seemingly disconnected phenomena stem from common roots. From the hard sciences he learns that every action causes a reaction—there are consequences to events. And of course he learns a million things about human nature from the people he meets on campus. The world is not nearly so atomized and simplistic a place as his high school education and favorite television shows made it sound. Hamlet may feel betrayed by the icons of his childhood—how come they never *told* me about all this?—as he understands at last the price he and his family paid for security: numbing, stupefying isolation. Appalled by his previous ignorance, he resolves not to fall into the intellectual and spiritual torpor that his parents did.

Because he's in a completely new environment where few if any people know him, it's easy for Hamlet to discard childhood traits and values and become a new person. Within months he moves well beyond the world view he had in high school. The transformation is so rapid that when he leaves campus to visit Mom, Dad, and his friends at home he's stunned by how differently he regards his old milieu. It's one step removed now, a little bit loathsome. He gets angry when his loved ones, who haven't kept up with him every day, either don't recognize how different he feels or express the opinion that he's becoming a stranger. They expect him to remain the child he was, which he greatly resents. He sees that he can no longer depend on family and old friends for satisfying companionship. On his own emotionally, exposed to insecurity and doubt—a refreshing change after all those years of suffocating protection—he senses that the time has come to determine his own direction.

The problem, of course, is *finding* that new direction. Hamlet realizes that the future he envisioned for himself when he was a child isn't right for him, so he abandons it even though he doesn't have any new plans. He's looking for *the* right path, one that has few, if any, negatives. But his crippling thought processes make all his options seem inadequate. Acutely aware of his ignorance, he figures he just hasn't yet discovered the appropriate path for himself; someday he'll come upon that magical, right way, but until then he'd better not make a move. When prospective alternatives *do* present themselves, his skeptical nature inevitably finds them flawed, meaning his search must continue; problem is, it continues and continues and continues. For the more Hamlet knows, the easier it is for him to debunk the new life-styles and philosophies he encounters. He becomes adept at uncovering negative associations and disastrous consequences that discourage him from taking any course of action. He wallows in overthink.

Hamlet would have enough problems if all he had to do was figure out where to turn next. But college, for all its wonderful attributes, also has more than its share of frustrations. Hamlet's courses are a lot tougher than they were in high school; he has to work harder than ever before just to keep up with the class, never mind get an A. Whereas at home he had his own room and plenty of privacy, now he's forced to share a crowded dormitory or apartment with a herd of roommates and neighbors, many of whom like listening to heavy metal at all hours of the night and don't share his ideas about cleanliness, decorum, and interior design. He worries about paying for his education; if his parents are footing the bill, he worries that their financial support compromises his independence. College is also the national mating ground, and like everyone else on campus Hamlet is desperate to find the love of his life. Few people feel their loneliness more profoundly than a college student with nothing to do on a Friday night.

Sooner or later all the changes and pressures and frustrations come together, and something goes awry. Hamlet suffers a crisis of monumental proportions, the first severe test of his character. He screws up a few final exams and winds up on academic probation. He argues incessantly with his parents. He falls out with a lover. He reaches the deadline for declaring a major without having found a course of study that he likes. However the crisis manifests itself, it's the biggest stumble of his life, and it soon mushrooms into an all-encompassing, debilitating trauma. His confidence withers, his internal security disappears, and he questions *everything* except the importance of tolerance, curiosity, and skepticism. He moves away from the middle-class values of his upbringing, but toward almost nothing. To concerned observers, Hamlet the obedient child and good student has suddenly and inexplicably lost his way. He's rejected the practical route in favor of a twisted, brambly trail that leads nowhere. Up he climbs, groping along, losing time to indecision and false steps, oblivious to warnings and signs of danger. What his distressed observers don't understand is that he treads on not necessarily because he wants to, but because in his heart he knows *he has no other way to go*. The Hamlet Syndrome has a complete hold on him now.

At last Hamlet can be distinguished from young people destined for material success. Faced with mounting pressure from family, peers, and society to *do something*, and faced as well with his own self-doubt,

Hamlet can make only one decision about his direction in life: to post-pone making a *real* decision for as long as possible. Success-track colle-gians can be just as doubt-ridden as Hamlet, but they don't let their misgivings blow up into a full-fledged crisis. They push on, determined to fulfill their yearning for the good life. Hamlet bristles at their outward confidence as they seemingly waltz their way to independence, affluence, and adulation. Half from envy, half from principle, he comes to hate them.

We can readily understand why Hamlet would *envy* peers bound for success, but why he hates them on principle requires some explanation. It's no secret that, be they liberal, conservative, or in between, most college students who think about it decide that the system is riddled with contradictions, hypocrisies, and injustices. What can a person do to right those wrongs? Aspiring yuppies tell themselves they can best help others by joining the mainstream and working into a position of power from which they can effect change. But Hamlet has trouble accepting that rationale. To him, the compromises required by the mainstream dilute an individual's commitment to change. Once you're profiting from the system, Hamlet's logic goes, you're not going to do anything to endanger it. Thus the concerned Hamlet (and most Hamlets are concerned with social issues) feels more comfortable, more *pure*, on the outside, and regards those going after the dollar as perpetuators of misery.

Another way Hamlet differs from future executives: He's not inter-ested in systematically digesting great volumes of facts, a talent often essential to success in pre-professional college courses. Hamlet is a conceptual thinker, given to contemplation and generalization rather than memorization and application. (He can also be a dilettante easily bored by long explanations and too many details.) Although we found a surprising number of Hamlets able to master college chemistry and accounting courses, even *they* expressed preference for the broader thinking characteristic of the arts and humanities over the applied intelli-gence typical of science, engineering, and business. In an age where the more specialized one becomes, the more money and status one usually commands, Hamlet clings stubbornly to the generalist ideal. Western civilization, to his way of thinking, would do well to hold up for emula-tion that paragon of Shakespeare's time, the Renaissance man.

The college crisis throws all but the dropout Hamlet off the career track. If Hamlet's in a pre-professional program, he's likely to leave it or cease caring about his grades. If he's a student of the humanities, he may have trouble showing up for class or finishing papers. For the first time in his life he suspects he may be a failure, and as a result he suffers a considerable loss of self-esteem. The negative feelings are exacerbated by the bewilderment or disapproval of family and friends and the go-for-it, dress-for-success bravura of the proto-yuppies around him.

Let's take a look at Hamlet's college crisis through the eyes of three people currently going through it. Later on we'll get a more mature perspective on the crisis from Martin, Brent, and Antonio, who will help us understand just how much Hamlet's college crisis sets the tone for the next fifteen years of his life.

11
The Kids Today

There may be at most a dozen academic programs like that offered by the Department of Rhetoric at the University of California, Berkeley. Shunning the trend toward specialization that extends even to the humanities these days, the Rhetoric Department "looks back to when the humanities were regarded as a whole," says Arthur J. Quinn, chair of the department and author of *Figures of Speech: Sixty Ways to Turn a Phrase.* In the last few decades we've come to associate the term *rhetoric* with empty words, as in "the President's speech last night was just a bunch of rhetoric." But classically, rhetoric has little to do with hooey. It's the formal study of the strategies a communicator uses to inform, entertain, or persuade an audience. As such, it incorporates elements of philosophy, psychology, religion, history, and even dramatic art in its effort to understand the fundamental principles of human communication.

"The department sees everything as audience-related," says Quinn, "so what we try to do from the very beginning is have students realize that what they write should be seen in its consequences toward social groups. On the freshman level students get used to writing for one another, as a kind of realistic audience. We expand that at the sophomore level to where they have to worry about the oral component of discourse—speech and debate. Juniors and seniors take a whole range of discourse and try to look for its common elements, so they might be reading science or politics, law or poetry, and judging it as an effort of one person to influence others."

Each year this integrated approach to the humanities prompts about one hundred of the university's several thousand undergraduates to declare Rhetoric as their major. Most of these majors intend to pursue careers in law or advertising, vocations that require a close acquaintance with persuasive strategies. But the Rhetoric program also provides a haven for young questioners devoid of granite-etched career goals: Hamlets in the making. They choose the Rhetoric major over more traditional—and easily explainable—academic disciplines for three reasons. First, rhetorical technique, as handed down from the Greeks and Romans, demands tolerance, curiosity, skepticism, and the ability to recognize the consequences of actions, qualities intrinsic to Hamlet's way of thinking. Second, because rhetoric includes speech and debate, students must look at issues from a number of perspectives, giving Hamlet excellent training in the black-and-white and shades-of-gray fence-sitting logic he's already predisposed to. Third, the Rhetoric Department's interdisciplinary approach makes it possible for majors to pursue graduate education in a variety of fields, meaning Hamlet can hold on to the possibility of enrolling in a professional program later on.

The doubt and indecision that separate Hamlet from his career-oriented colleagues are achingly familiar to the nascent Hamlets among the Rhetoric majors at the University of California, Berkeley. These troubled students share a pronounced skepticism about virtually any value you care to mention. They feel misunderstood by mainstream America, that vast contingent that often includes their family and friends. They're also uniformly reluctant to engage the world on terms they consider repugnant, yet are still consumed by pressure to conform and go for the dollar.

For Amy the pressure to succeed began in early childhood. "I *had* to be a good student. If I got an A minus my mom would ask me why

I didn't get an A. My dad wasn't into it as much. He just kept telling me to make lots of money when I grow up. He'd tell me architecture was the way, or business, or real estate." Amy worked diligently to please her parents. The family moved to a well-to-do suburb on the San Francisco peninsula, and she attended a fairly competitive public high school. The pressure to be an academic standout increased, driving her to regrettable extremes. "I didn't cheat a lot in high school, but even if I didn't use the cheat sheet I'd have to have it there. If I didn't get an A, how was I going to explain that to my mother? The good thing was the other kids in high school didn't have this problem, so they messed up and I came out ahead most of the time anyway.

"My junior year of high school I came to Berkeley with Model United Nations, and it was wonderful. There were so many individuals, *real* individuals, not all these cookie-cutter types. Berkeley was a way for me to break out. I could meet people who weren't all wearing preppy clothes." And so, after graduating near the top of her high school class, Amy enrolled at Berkeley for precisely the reason many mainstream Americans forbid their children from even applying to that campus: its tolerance for diversity. At her mother's urging she took courses in math, economics, and accounting, intending to major in business administration. But once away from home Amy's crisis began. She discovered she wasn't interested in computing bottom lines. After getting a D in calculus, she wound up on academic probation.

"I was falling apart the second semester of my freshman year. I was on academic probation. My mom was driving both of us crazy telling me what to do. But I also had some very supportive teaching assistants that semester." Among those supportive teachers was the one in charge of Amy's Rhetoric composition course, who turned Amy on to the pleasures of critical thinking. "For the first time in my life somebody asked me what I thought," Amy recalls. "It wasn't what do you think the author is saying, but what do you think *about* what the author is saying. To be effective on your paper you had to know what you thought, or at least sound like you believed it. For one time in my life I actually *thought*, whereas in high school they tell you to regurgitate everything, they promote memorization. After that I thought, well, maybe I'll consider Rhetoric as a major."

But blind to the depths of her daughter's crisis, Amy's mother resisted the proposed departure from the success track. "My mom ignored the idea of Rhetoric. She pretended she didn't hear me when I said

I wanted to major in it." Yet Amy stuck with the program, and after wrestling with the decision for months she became a Rhetoric major in her junior year. Her mother has had a hard time coping with Amy's rejection of definite career goals, "but I think she's starting to accept it," Amy says hopefully. "Now she says, 'I know you're set on Rhetoric, but don't push aside accounting and business completely.'"

Amy's problems are compounded by the fact that she's Chinese-American. She grew up more or less accepting the stereotype of Asian women as dim-witted and docile—a stereotype reinforced, unfortunately, by her mother, who said Amy wasn't intelligent and had to study harder than everyone else to succeed. Amy's dawning sense of ethnic identity led her to spend much of the summer of 1987 in China with a group consisting mostly of white students. From the other side of the Pacific Ocean she gained an unsettling perspective on Americans and their society.

"China. What an experience," she sighs, shaking her head. "Only when I went to China did I realize how frustrating this subtle racism, this subtle ethnocentrism that Americans have, really is. One example was a basketball game. Our student group got into a pickup game with the Yunan professional team, and when the students were doing the scoring they wanted to make it U.S.A. versus China. I tried to say to my friends, no, let's not make this a national thing, let's just say U.C. students versus the Yunan team. Why make this a political thing? Why make this so nationalistic? It just seemed like, 'Yeah, we're Americans, we're gonna kick ass. We're gonna *win*. We're gonna show these Chinese people we can really play basketball.'

"In a sense I should have been able to get along with everybody, the Americans in my student group as well as the Chinese. But I'm too American to really click in with the Chinese, and because I'm Chinese I can't close my eyes to some of the things I saw as inappropriate behavior by my fellow students. It was very frustrating. I felt as if something was wrong with *me*. Whenever I talked to someone other than my roommate or a couple of teaching assistants, other people would make me feel like I was a freak, like, 'Gosh Amy, what's wrong? There's nothing wrong with this. You're too sensitive, you're taking it the wrong way.'"

Upon her return from China, Amy came to the end of the first stage of the college crisis: She recognized the dichotomy between the values she was raised on and her own sense of what's right. Now that she's distanced herself from the success-oriented values of her childhood, she's heading into stage two of the crisis: turning her attention inward and trying to define her own beliefs. "I feel very insecure about a lot of things right now," she says. "My whole philosophy of life seems to be self-centered. In the past year I've alienated myself from friends, as if somehow I've developed into a person that nobody can understand. I feel like only a couple of people have really been able to help me get in touch with my feelings." Impeding her search for a new direction is her tendency—enhanced by the study of rhetoric—to think in shades of gray. "I see infinite reasons for why I should do something and infinite reasons for why I shouldn't. I don't know what's going to make me happy. Sometimes I feel like I don't know anything."

But she does know one thing: Just because the majority believes in certain values, that doesn't automatically mean those values are right. From now on she'll be more skeptical. "There's so much pressure, especially with advertising. So many times everybody, family, friends, billboards, tell you what you want. You want to smell like this, you want to have this car. You have to drink this beer and have this certain life-style and occupation. It's frustrating, because how do you know what you *really* want when you're bombarded by all these things?" But though her heart speaks strongly to her and she understands how the system pressures her into going along with the crowd, the dollar continues to tempt her. "In the future, maybe I'll be more competitive. I don't want to be. I don't want to think of myself that way. It's very uncomfortable, too much *you have to be.* Too many shoulds without reasons why, without consideration of my feelings. It doesn't seem real to me. It feels like it's dictated."

A year older than Amy, Eileen has been in stage two of the college crisis long enough to know that she probably won't be more competitive in the future. But that doesn't mean she's decided to follow her heart. She's at the very nexus of the Hamlet Syndrome, where heart and dollar have equal weight. In struggling consciously with the heart-or-dollar dilemma for the first time, she finds going along with "the herd" intolerable but continues to crave the rewards of the dollar—rewards she knows she can easily attain. Torn so completely in two by the dilemma, she's beginning to fear she may never be able to take meaningful action on her own behalf.

Eileen has been a skeptic from the start. Her mother is an accountant, her father an engineer. Together they earn well over $100,000 annually. Eileen grew up in a plush suburb of San Jose, and was expected to excel scholastically and take up a lucrative profession. There was no questioning her strict parents on this count, nor on any other for that matter. Nonetheless, Eileen did question. Because she had lightning intelligence her mother and father respected her, but when she applied that intelligence to scrutinize her family's conventional, success-oriented values she was punished—sometimes severely.

"When I was in sixth grade I had a teacher-parent-student conference," she recalls. "For some reason in the car on the way home I said to my parents, 'You know, I don't really want to be the best in the class. I like being number two because Ruthie'—my best friend, she and I were always neck and neck for best student—'everybody knows she's the best and nobody really likes her. She has no friends, they think she's really weird. I don't want to be that way.' My father got so angry when he heard me say that that he took me into his den, closed and locked the door, and then beat me until my mother broke into the window, *climbed through the window,* to make him stop. He was picking me up, holding me five feet off the ground, and then throwing me down. What kind of message is that, that you have to be the best?"

Despite her early skepticism, Eileen continued to respect her parents' authority, striving to be number one until high school. In her early teens she rebelled, but it was the mild form of rebellion we described in Part II. She conformed to her peers' expectations rather than her parents'. "Throughout grade school and junior high I always felt people didn't like me. I didn't have very many friends. When I was a freshman in high school I realized I was miserable about a lot of things. A lot of the misery had to do with my family and all the pressure they were putting on me, but I attributed the misery to the fact that I had no friends, and I attributed the fact that I had no friends to the fact that I was getting straight A's. I broke down and cried so hard. After that I decided I was never going to feel like that again. I made a conscious decision that I was going to be a cool person. I wasn't going to be the aristocratic upper crust anymore. So I started refraining from raising my hand in class. I stopped offering to help people, and I stopped talking about school. I stopped talking about the things that interested me the most, because I felt that was a threat to my happiness.

"Acceptance is really important to me. I don't want to feel that behind my back people are saying, 'She's so awful.' It makes me feel so alone. It hurts. Once you take that step outside and declare yourself a rebel, declare yourself different, dress in a black turtleneck and trench coat, people don't feel as great a need to be there with you. I guess that's what it is, I'm afraid that when I'm in really great need, if I separate myself out, no one will be there to help me, buck me up."

Typical for a Hamlet, Eileen applied to only a few colleges. "My mother said apply to fourteen or fifteen schools, so I got applications for Northwestern, Stanford, Berkeley, and Columbia. I never finished applying to Northwestern and halfway completed my application to Stanford." A gifted writer, she had thoughts of entering Columbia's vaunted journalism program, but after being accepted there and visiting the school she deemed it a "hierarchical, snot-nose place." Berkeley, a public university, appealed more to her democratic sensibility.

"Seems to me I fell into the Rhetoric Department purely by accident," she admits. "I took the introductory writing course and liked the people. Then I took another class and did very well, so I figured hell, this place is for me." Rhetoric provided her with a logical basis for rejecting the mainstream values she'd questioned since sixth grade. "The Rhetoric Department implies in its teaching that ideology is just a tool, that human beings are manipulative by nature. From a political standpoint it means you invoke ideology to make the masses work toward a certain goal. You let people *believe* they have control over what's going on. You steer them into wanting what you want for them. In the end, everything is subjective. Even if the Rhetoric Department's perspective is subjective also, I feel like it gives me a better view of the world than the next guy has, than the masses have."

But in Eileen's case there's a flip side to the realization that everything is subjective. She's developed a shades-of-gray perspective that causes her to see any number of conflicting viewpoints as equally legitimate. That prevents her from taking a stand or acting. "I feel so crippled. The more sensitive I've become and the more I try to understand why anybody does anything, the less I've been able to define my own actions. Even when I see a villain I have to try to understand him. I don't want to hurt anybody.

"Besides, if I were to act on half of what I see and believe, I'd go nuts. I've *got* to accept it. I keep all those things in mind because to

ignore them would make me as bad as the mainstream, but I'm not about
to hop on a horse and fight every windmill I can find. I have to hope that
someday I'll be able to fight it in my own way. But injustice happens all
around me and I don't feel empowered in the slightest to help make the
world a better place."

Eileen hopes to write serious fiction someday, but her perception
of what it takes to be an author—nonconformity, adherence to the values
of the heart—causes her anxiety. She hesitates to go the unconventional
route even though she understands she *must* do so to fulfill her dream.
Although "the life I'd want for myself would be a house in the mountains
with a typewriter and a table, and enough money so I could eat yummy
food, Brie cheese and French bread, every once in a while," she knows
that "it's socially unacceptable to want to be a writer and base your life
from one typewriter. You have to wear a business suit and go to work
from nine to five and have a boss and people under you and have a lunch
break and a water cooler you socialize around. How do I battle that? How
do I fight against an entire world of people telling me not to do what I
want to do? Will I be considered insane by everyone else, even when I
think I'm on the right track? When I get that house in the mountains
will I be happy? I don't know. Damn it, I don't know!" And mired as
she is between the heart and the dollar, it will likely be years before she
ventures out far enough to answer those questions.

Darren, at twenty-three one year older than Eileen, still doesn't
know what direction he's going to take, but he can no longer afford the
luxury of pondering: He's only weeks away from graduation. Being the
philosophical type, he continues to ponder anyway. He's past the questioning stage that Amy's in, and he's also past that first tangle with the
heart-or-dollar dilemma that preoccupies Eileen. Darren's in the third
and last phase of the college crisis: accepting the fact that his values are
different from the mainstream's and, for lack of appealing alternatives,
deciding to drift wherever his heart leads, even if that turns out to be
nowhere. In trying to understand the larger context of his predicament,
he's come up with the modern Hamlet's version of Shakespeare's "All
the world's a stage" soliloquy. But whereas Shakespeare says there are
seven stages of man, Darren cuts the number of stages to three—a
sparkling example of the extremes to which Hamlet's black-and-white
thinking can lead.

"The first stage is called What Will I Do?" Darren explains. "It deals with all your schooling. It's where you get all the information you need for life. You're exploring what you could be or what you might want to be. The next stage of life is called What Am I Doing? That's the stage I'm reaching now. You've spent—maybe wasted—twenty-odd years to reach this plateau, and now it's time to act but you don't know what to do. Then there's stage three, which I call What Have I Done? You look back, and you've blown it. Life has passed you by. Your best years have gone down the drain thanks to years of indecision, and now it's all over."

Darren characterizes stage two, What Am I Doing?, as a "terrifying time I've been worried about vaguely ever since I was seven or eight. You always think that someday you're going to stop school and do something, but I wonder what it is? One year from now, ten years from now, I'll be doing *something*, but I don't know what it'll be. In this stage you become deeply aware that time is going by. You don't know what to do, and you've only got a limited time to do it in. It's like being on a game show: Bells are going off, the audience is yelling at you to do this or that, and you don't know, you're totally confused.

"The time between stages holds the greatest stress. I was thinking of the ways different people handle it. Between the first two stages they'll either get a secure, safe kind of job, they'll get married, or else they'll postpone the stage by entering graduate school or taking an extended tour of Europe. Me? I think I'm going to Europe."

The Rhetoric Department's interdisciplinary approach compelled him to declare the major. "Rhetoric was what I always wanted to do, but I didn't know the name of it. It's a culmination of all the other things I'm interested in, philosophy, logic, psychology, sociology. There's history and political science, too. Rhetoric pulls all these things together. It's knowing your audience. If you really understand people, you can do anything, sell ice cubes to Eskimos."

Although Darren doesn't want to use rhetoric to sell ice cubes to Eskimos—or anything to anybody, for that matter—he readily applies it to his college education. "Rhetoric taught me there's an implied message in everything, and as far as college is concerned, at first I thought the implied message was to become a socialist, because we had to read Marx and these other books that were pointing in that direction. But starting last semester, everything seemed to be pointed toward nihilism—nothingness. All my professors were lecturing on it in every class. Every time the word is mentioned in class I'll go, look at that, there it is again. We have to read Kafka again, or Schopenhauer or Joseph Conrad, talking about meaninglessness. Why are they doing this to me at this point in my life, when I'm already worried enough about what I'm going to do?"

The worry about his future seems to have overwhelmed Darren. Like many a Hamlet, he's procrastinated past the point of making a graceful transition from college to the workaday world. "I don't know if all this schooling really prepares you for stage two of my theory of life," he says ruefully. "In elementary school we didn't learn about junior high until day one of junior high. Same with high school. As far as college preparation, I think I had about half an hour's worth of it one day. Now here I am in college, and there's a Career Planning and Placement Center, but I've never been there. It just seems so *vague*. A degree in Rhetoric is very valuable, but I don't know how it fits into anything. I don't quite understand my options."

Skeptical, confused, and reluctant to engage the larger world, Darren does nothing. "I didn't apply to graduate school because the whole thing was so *hairy*. I just let time go on. I didn't even research it. I thought about it constantly, but I never actually did anything. I froze. I was thinking of going to school in either philosophy, journalism, or library sciences. Logic is one of my favorite subjects, but I know a grad student in logic, and he's doing things like proving the existence of *one*. That's not going to help him a lot in life. I like journalism because I like to write. My father's an editor, so I feel like I've inherited something. Library science is a cop-out grad thing [tell that to Maxine!], but I like books and libraries, and I know a lot of neat librarians. If I did that I could be out in a year and get a good job with benefits, but I don't know whether that's selling out or not, a cop-out."

Copping out—a good old-fashioned sixties phrase for compromising ideals, for quitting the heart and chasing the dollar. Why, Darren shows signs of becoming a full-fledged hippie Hamlet! "I care about copping out. Now is the time to be idealistic. I'll get cynical later on. I think, what is the whole purpose of living? There's got to be some goal that you're working towards." Darren wants a goal that's true to his heart, but he regards his possibilities in such stark black and white that nothing can measure up to his expectations. "For a while when I was little I wanted to be a lawyer, because I liked to argue about things. But then I realized,

I don't want to be a *lawyer*. I mean, do lawyers really change things, or do they just get disillusioned and give up? If they get disillusioned they still practice but they don't care about it, they do it for money, and they'll sometimes argue things they don't believe in. I couldn't do that.

"It took me two years of college to figure out my three main evils. Those evils are ignorance, apathy, and security: not knowing, not caring, and doing things not based on whether they're right or wrong but whether they're easy. The worst is the combination of all three: intolerant indifference. It just amazes me when people don't care but they're still prejudiced." Darren is at a point where ignorance, apathy, and security—especially security—offer a tempting panacea for his frustrations. He's aware of that, and is determined not to succumb to them. "I don't remember who said it, but someone said most people die at age twenty-five but aren't buried until they're eighty. When you stop learning you die, and all you can talk about is [he mimics an old man here] 'When I grew up movies were a nickel.' Once you settle down, no one pushes you to learn, so you don't. It's so easy to work during the week and garden on the weekends and not read Plutarch."

Despite his uncertain future, Darren refuses to pity himself. "The fact that I was born at this time, this place, a middle-class white male, I can't really put out some kind of sob story." One good thing: His parents aren't pressuring him to get a job or become an instant success. He believes that stems from their own experience; in addition to being an editor, his father is a minister, and his mother, a medical technologist, went back to school so she could learn to work in an emergency room—at a job that pays less.

Still, Darren regrets that the time has come for him to join the work force. "I love school," he says. "If I could get into the university computer and erase all my credits, I would."

The college crisis is Hamlet's initiation into the syndrome. All of the elements converge: the conscious application of critical thought; the expanded world view; the sense of standing apart; the tug of conformity; the fear of engaging the world; and, of course, the indecision. Elsewhere on campus young people are connecting to the mainstream, earning professional degrees, seeking membership in clubs and organizations, interning and volunteering. They're going through rites of passage that bind them to one another and to institutions. But Hamlet's rite of passage leaves him feeling that he's joined a group of *one*. He may engage in just as much beer-soaked revelry as any Fraternity Fred or Sorority Suzie, may have more friends than ever before and have twice the fun he did in high school, but his laughter rings hollow. He's alone now, and he knows it. He has no direction, only the nebulous importunings of his heart. Tossed about in a swirling stream of conflicting emotions, he has one question above all: Will this confusion ever end?

12

The Crisis in Perspective

The good news for Amy, Eileen, Darren, and the hundreds of thousands of Hamlets their age is that the madness of the college crisis
recedes. Not until his mid-thirties will Hamlet again struggle over the
heart-or-dollar dilemma with the intensity that he does in his college
years. The bad news is that the Hamlet Syndrome never goes away
entirely, except perhaps for the first few years after college when Hamlet
finds gainful employment and exults in his complete independence. But
though finding a dead-end job that pays for rent and groceries makes
Hamlet happy for a while, it only delays the resolution of his inner
conflict. Ambivalence and lack of direction will continue to plague him
until he addresses them directly, through positive action—something
he's constitutionally disinclined to do.

The college crisis permanently alters Hamlet's view of the world.
Once he reaches the final stage of the crisis—acceptance of his in-

dividuality—he adopts an outsider's perspective. He gets more analytical, developing his abilities to think associatively and foresee the consequences of actions. With a dispassion he may previously have thought impossible he probes deeply into his own nature and the nature of his fellow humans. At the same time he begins to form a protective shell around the psychological traits that predispose him to the Hamlet Syndrome, the better to defend himself against the whips and scorns of contemptuous mainstreamers. He figures out at last that society is just as responsible for his disaffection as his own recalcitrant spirit, and comes to the sad understanding that life isn't—and can never be—as simple, easy, or happy as he imagined when he arrived on campus. His pleasures become more subtle and idiosyncratic, his disillusion and resignation more pronounced. If he didn't before, he now starts to identify with the underdog, the disadvantaged, the modest and weak. Slowly, haltingly, he gathers his first few nuggets of philosophical wisdom.

We can see how the college crisis sets a pattern for Hamlet's later life by talking to Hamlets who have long since left campus. Older Hamlets, having developed the perspective described in the previous paragraph, can give us wider insight than Amy, Eileen, and Darren, who are still too close to the crisis to understand its scope. Painful as the crisis may have been, the older Hamlets are in many ways grateful that it happened. For in going through the ordeal they discovered their innermost selves—a discovery that more than compensates for the agony of the struggle.

A few lucky Hamlets, such as Maxine, manage to sidestep the crisis in college. She came out of Philadelphia's best public high school ranked third in her class and was promptly "bought" by New York University. In addition to covering her tuition, the university granted her a $2,000 yearly stipend for cultural enlightenment. "I went to operas, I went to shows, I went to concerts, I traveled overseas," she recalls fondly. "I had such a posh time. I can't afford to go to plays or the opera now." She spent her junior year in Paris, where she went through a period of depression. But she turned the low mood into something positive. "I knew if I was that depressed and could still be okay then I could do anything. I could always survive and let moods like that pass." She double-majored in French and history and graduated summa cum laude, picking up a Phi Beta Kappa key for good measure. But though she escaped the crisis in college, Maxine wasn't spared. "I delayed the panic that usually comes with graduation from college. I was in New York, so I figured I'd do something like go into publishing when I got out. But I went to Russian school for the summer, and then I delayed further by traveling around California." A few years after she graduated the crisis caught up with her—as we'll see in Part IV.

Brent, our dropout Hamlet, suffered a prolonged crisis of academic indirection. In high school he snapped off a perfect score on his Scholastic Aptitude Test, won a National Merit Scholarship, and gained acceptance to all the big-name colleges he applied to. The crisis started his second year on campus, when he couldn't figure out what he wanted to study. "I had the sophomore slump with capital letters. At first I was interested in science and political policy type things, but come the first set of midterms I wiped out in my science courses." He realized he didn't have the discipline to succeed in the sciences, so he concentrated on economics. "I studied economics gung ho for two years, until I totally burned out on it. Economics is not particularly fun to study. It involves a lot of math, which I had trouble with. I bombed out on applied math courses." Then he bombed out with his girlfriend. "That was a major traumatic and disillusioning and embittering experience. It was a big mess, devastating to my view of life."

Trying to put the pieces back together, the following summer he read Robert Pirsig's *Zen and the Art of Motorcycle Maintenance.* The tome impressed him so much he added philosophy as a second major. He also began to indulge his interest in music, studying music appreciation and history. Right up to the last few weeks of his undergraduate career Brent didn't know what field he was going to graduate in. "I had to take honors exams in each of my subjects, and the philosophy honors exams were really difficult. I didn't have the time to handle them. So I ended up at the last moment, April or May of my senior year, switching to just economics."

The confusion over his academic direction left Brent with "no firm idea what I was going to do after college," and set a pattern for his postcollegiate career. With the same frequency with which he changed majors and interests in college, he's changed directions in adulthood. He took a job as an economic analyst for a year, then quit; hung out in the mountains and Alaska for a time, then plunged back into the mainstream; went to law school and took a job in a high-powered law firm, then quit. It's not that Brent failed at any of these endeavors—he enjoyed the kind of success that turns most people green with envy. It's his inability to choose between the heart and the dollar that keeps him lurching from one to the other, just as he shifted from science to economics to philosophy in college.

Martin serves as a good example of what happens when a Hamlet is diverted from the path his heart demands he follow. He finished seventh in his high school class of 236 and was readily accepted into the honors program of the only school he applied to, the University of Connecticut. College frightened him. "I had no conception of what it was like. I didn't know what I was getting into. Being away from home for the first time was one thing. My parents had done everything for me, so I was scared to death. Then I was also scared the social structure in college would be like high school, seniors hating freshmen and pounding them into dust." But Martin was very pleasantly surprised. "It wasn't like that at all! I enjoyed being away from home, and all the guys were great." He went from studious loner to the life of the party.

But that wasn't the only change Martin experienced; it was merely the only *happy* change. His very first semester on campus he discovered that his lifelong dream would never come true. Because dinosaurs fascinated him, from earliest childhood he'd assumed he was going to be a paleontologist. "But four things turned me away from paleontology," he says, ticking them off on his fingers: "calculus, chemistry, computer science, and physics. I was required to take three semesters of calculus and two semesters of chemistry, so the first semester of my freshman year I took honors calculus and honors chemistry.

"Well, after the first semester I *knew*. I mean, I learned nothing, *nothing*, in either calculus or chemistry. I floundered from day one. Calculus, to this day I have no conception what they're trying to show me. The area under this curve is what this formula means. What the hell is that? Who cares? Chemistry was interesting, but I couldn't even balance simple equations. The head of the honors program taught the class, and it was his personal feeling that anyone in the honors system shouldn't get below a C. So I think I actually failed the course, but he gave me a C.

"Midway through my second semester, I was still in the honors program, again taking honors chemistry, and this class was even worse than the first one. I had to go in practically every week to talk to the professor, and finally he said, 'You know, this just isn't your subject.' I agreed. He asked what my major was, and I said paleontology. He shook his head and said, 'You're not going to be a paleontologist.' "

Martin, so well known for his ability to draw photolike pictures that his friends dubbed him "the human Xerox machine," went home and tried to tell his parents, who were paying for his education, that he wanted to switch his major to art. "They almost had a heart attack," he remembers. "I've never seen them so upset. I could see how it would be a blow to them, because I'd brainwashed them for the last ten or twenty years into thinking I was going to be a paleontologist. But when I told them about art, they panicked. They told me, 'No no no, you're not good enough, you don't have enough talent, you have a bad imagination, it's a brutal field, too much competition, there's no money in it.' They said, 'Stick it out another year,' and having been told all my life what I was going to do, I went along with them. I ended up taking all four years in paleontology, but my heart wasn't in it."

Martin can still be the life of a party. He's a trivia buff, a connoisseur of fine beers, and possessed of a dry, self-effacing Yankee wit that instantly endears him to others. But even though he's been on his own for almost a decade, he hasn't done a thing commercially with his artistic ability. He continues to draw—an uncannily lifelike portrait of Jackson Browne hangs from his apartment wall—but he's never gotten over the discouragement of his college crisis, when his efforts to strike out in his own direction were snuffed. He has yet to make a second attempt at forging a path of his own, proving that you can't "straighten out" a Hamlet by forcing him to follow the dollar instead of the heart.

As a final example we turn to Antonio, our artist Hamlet. You may recall that he sought refuge in a Catholic religious order at the age of thirteen. He remained with the order for ten years. "After you take your first vows you have a choice: to teach or live a life of reclusion. I decided I wanted to teach, and those who decide to teach have to go to college." So at the age of twenty-one Antonio was sent off to a Roman Catholic college—and the world opened up to him. To get to campus he had to drive a car. His superiors permitted him to eat at restaurants. Most important, for the first time in almost a decade he came into regular contact with people from the secular world—and many of those people were female.

"My first trouble with the vow of chastity came when I was approaching twenty-two," he says. "I was in my sophomore year, and I decided that I had some skill at music and was going to pursue it academically. But my school didn't have a music program, so the order sent me to the nearest Catholic school that did, which was all-female. My superiors required me to wear a robe, so there I was, the only male in a female school, finally reaching puberty—and wearing a dress."

His path forked; the symptoms of his crisis became acute. "I was learning more and more that I had skill as a musician, and could very well *be* a musician. But the parameters of being a musician in the modern world don't fit religious life. There are rehearsals, there are performances, there are after-performance receptions, and none of that fits into being at the religious community for office and dinner. So a conflict arose between my professional aspirations and my religious life. I knew I had to make a choice.

"I can tell when it's time for a change. I can't get myself to form cogent thoughts for any period of time. The day I decided to leave the order, it felt like forever. I started making arrangements in my head. Then I called a lady I knew who had gotten permission to come to our chapel and sit with us at mass, told her what I was doing, and asked if she could put me up until I could get my life organized. After that I went to my superior, the director, and told him what I wanted to do. I wanted to leave that day, but there are a lot of formalities to leaving, and normally it takes several months to separate yourself from the order. But I didn't wait for him to tell me what I needed to do. I dictated the terms of my leaving, and it was accomplished in three days.

"When I took my vows I meant them, and I really lived them. But when I left, I left. I wanted to be somebody else. I was going to be the butterfly coming out of the chrysalis." But without the religious community to take care of his every need Antonio immediately ran into problems. "In the order you don't have to worry about food or clothes or rent or anything, you just do whatever they want you to do and everything's taken care of for you. So for a twenty-three-year-old I was fundamentally unprepared to live in the modern world. The first system I dealt with was getting a job. I thought you go to a person, say you want to work there, and they hire you and pay you money, and then you can do things. I didn't even know how to go shopping. Where do you go to find food?"

Antonio quickly caught on to the nuts and bolts of everyday life. One of the first things he did was go back to school. True to his word, he acted like a butterfly, flitting from discipline to discipline, learning enough about the academic bureaucracy to forestall dismissal. "I wanted to know a little bit about everything. I studied in anthropology for a while, and I don't mean for just one or two courses. I was in the history department. I was in Romance languages. Finally I ran out of time because I was heading toward two hundred credits. I would lie and say I'm declaring this major now, but the music department got up in arms and decided it was time for me to graduate." He was twenty-six years old.

Although his college crisis culminated in a sweeping change of life-styles, Antonio soon forgot its central lesson: Follow the yearnings of your heart. A few years after he finished college he abandoned music in an effort to gain the dollar. The chase for material success left him in the same traumatic position he was in when he had to choose between monastic life and art. On the one hand he had security; on the other he had his essence. He put off making a choice between the two, until one day he realized anew that his first loyalty was to his heart. Because he'd forgotten his past, he had to relive the upheaval of his college years.

13

Facing the Real World

J ohn Lennon said it best:

> When they've tortured and scared you for twenty-odd years,
> Then they expect you to pick a career
> When you can't really function you're so full of fear.

Just as Hamlet arrives at the final stage of his college crisis and accepts himself as different, it's time for him to graduate. The transition from student to worker is hard for every student, but as we saw earlier with Darren, Hamlet has a particularly rough time of it. He's devoted most of his energy to figuring out who he is, putting career considerations on the back burner while he consolidates his new identity. Now suddenly it's time for him to stop thinking about himself, put away his books, and *perform.* We understate the case when we say that Hamlet isn't ready; in most instances he's downright afraid of leaving the ivory tower. As Darren put it, "If I could get into the university computer and erase all my credits, I would."

Ask Hamlet about his future and he's likely to well up with resentment. His childhood is irretrievably gone, and with it a good chunk of the things he believed in. Adulthood doesn't look very appealing; every text he reads provides further proof that humankind is thoughtless, duplicitous, ruthless, and evil, and he wants no part of that. Yet his parents and friends are starting to ask him what he's going to do when he gets out of school. They don't seem to share his misgivings about the way the system operates. Hey gang, don't you see that even if you win the rat race you're still just a rat? he asks, barely able to conceal his contempt for people indifferent to the values of the heart. By the time he graduates from college he may be convinced that, except for intellectuals, artists, and his fellow Hamlets, nobody understands him.

Having come from a middle-class background, Hamlet never *had* to work before. He may have taken a job to pick up some extra pocket change, or his parents may have made him work out of principle, to teach him the "value" of a dollar. Under those circumstances he found it easy to take a flunkie job, working the counter at a fast-food restaurant or doing the filing in a small office. But now work is for real; he has to pay his own way. He has to figure out how much cash he needs and what he'll do to get it. Accustomed as he is to living well, one would think Hamlet would want to maintain a high standard of living, but in most cases all he wants is just enough to survive. Consequently, he's willing to take any odd job that comes his way.

We found seven reasons why Hamlets are so willing to accept underemployment; doubtless there are more. For some Hamlets all the reasons apply, while for others only one or two pertain. The first and foremost reason, which we'll look at more closely in Part Four, is that menial labor protects Hamlet's purity of heart and, theoretically at least, keeps the dollar within reach. The second reason is that immediate independence is extremely important to Hamlet's self-esteem. Having abandoned the success track and struggled for years with the heart-or-dollar dilemma, he carries a burden of self-doubt that feels even heavier when his bills are paid by someone else. Any job that allows him financial independence lifts his confidence dramatically. The third reason for

Hamlet's willingness to accept underemployment is that he realizes he doesn't need all the trappings of a middle-class life. The college town or city he lives in has plenty of low-cost housing. He may not need a car, depending on how close he is to shopping and how much he likes to travel. As for furniture, he needs only a table, a chair, a bed, his stereo, and a shelf for his books. His dishes don't have to match; he can cover the cracks in his apartment walls with posters. A simple and unpretentious life, he discovers, has a wholesome, connected quality seldom found in the superficialities of middle-class existence.

The other four reasons for accepting underemployment are less flattering to Hamlet. For one, he may lack the confidence to apply for good jobs. "No, I'm not qualified, I'll never get that one," he thinks as he pores over the Help Wanted section. He'll never know if he doesn't try—but he refuses to try. Second, he's not practical enough to look for a job in which he can utilize his special strengths and interests. He equates any accommodation to the workaday world with selling out his heart. The third unflattering reason is the panic factor. If he doesn't get some kind of a job right away, he fears he may not get anything at all. He'll go broke and face a humiliating choice between eviction and begging his disappointed folks for a handout. Lastly, Hamlet's just plain naive. Short on work experience, he doesn't necessarily know what constitutes a good salary or benefits package; nor does he know whether his employer is taking advantage of him or not. So long as he has enough to pay the rent and buy Brie cheese and French bread every now and then, he may figure he's got a decent job.

James Briggs, director of the University of California, Berkeley's Career Planning and Placement Center and author of *The Berkeley Guide to Employment for New College Graduates,* expresses a measure of admiration for Hamlets like Darren, who deal with the approach of graduation by doing nothing. "They just do what they want, study what they want, and enjoy it without this need to measure every decision in terms of how it's going to look on their resume," he says. "To have the career factor dominate every aspect of your life, your decisions about courses and major and extracurricular activities, *can* get a little obsessive."

Darren is one of many Hamlets who think of places like the Career Planning and Placement Center as flesh markets where people go to sell out. Personnel reps coldly evaluate nervous, overdressed job applicants on the basis of appearance, ambition, and grade point average. The heart has no place in the process. Such was once the case, Briggs concedes, but in the last ten years the purpose of offices like his has expanded from job recruiting to life planning. Starting from the premise that no one can make a wise career choice without researching the options first, career centers today offer students reams of information on various careers. Counselors help the young job hunter distinguish between the things he'd *like* in a job and the things he *needs* in a job. And through internships and cooperative education programs, career planning centers provide interested students with direct experience in fields they may want to work in after college.

Employment counselors dismiss fears that an individual's first career choice will limit him for life—a major anxiety for Hamlet, who likes to keep his options open. They cite the fact that the average American worker changes careers—not jobs, but *careers*—at least four times. (Of course, some students don't find that reassuring at all. "You mean I have to go through this three more times?" they've been heard to cry at workshops and seminars.) The counselors also discount the fear that a job must become, as Darren believes, the sum of a worker's existence. For principled job-seekers Berkeley's Planning and Placement Center even conducts an ethical-issues program that considers the implications of working for companies that pollute the environment or trade with South Africa.

Unfortunately, Hamlet has yet to get the message that places like the Career Planning and Placement Center have a newly enlightened outlook compatible with his own. Briggs estimates that each year the center formally registers between 8,000 and 9,000 students and informally serves a couple thousand more. But there are over 30,000 students on the Berkeley campus. A number of those students not using the Career Planning and Placement office are, like Darren, graduating seniors caught up in the Hamlet Syndrome. To reach those people, in 1987 Briggs and his fellow counselors sponsored Berkeley's first-ever career information day. The program was called—quite coincidentally—What to Be or Not to Be.

"The largest percentage of students who attended career information day were seniors, and an overwhelming percentage of those students did not know what they wanted to do," reports Jackie Sproul, a career counselor for eleven years, the last seven at Berkeley. Over 1,000 students attended the event, of which 411 responded to the Career Planning and Placement Center's questionnaire. Seventy-two percent said they had *some* idea what they wanted to do, but weren't sure. Another 14 percent were completely undecided. Only 14 percent knew exactly what they wanted to do.

Granted, students who know exactly what they want to do don't need to attend a career information day. But the fact that 86 percent of those who *did* attend the first What to Be or Not to Be day had at best only a fuzzy notion of what they would do after college ought to refute those who think our campuses are churning out careerists by the millions. Those who accept—and hail—the popular opinion that today's students are motivated by competition and materialism must explain why so many of the nation's brightest young people—for the Berkeley campus is among those schools having the highest admissions standards in the country—have so little direction.

The career counselors we spoke to agreed that students today are under unprecedented pressure to find a "good" job, good defined as prestigious and remunerative. Amy earlier pinpointed the external sources of that pressure: parents and society. "Dealing with parental expectations is a big one," acknowledges Jackie Sproul. "Some of the students I see are really pressured with 'Once you graduate you have to get a job because we've been paying all this money for your education, and when you get that diploma, that's it.' "

Then there's social pressure, the need to have a job one step higher than everyone else's. Jim Sullivan, who counsels liberal arts majors at Berkeley's Planning and Placement Center, notes, "There are students whose view of the work world is doctor, lawyer, engineer. For some reason they feel they need to get a position that has some kind of status or pays a certain amount of money. There are some liberal arts students who say money is real important to them, they want to get an M.B.A. How much thought they've put into what an M.B.A. does, what that life is like, I don't know." Adds James Briggs, "This is probably the first generation that's not going to do as well as their parents. And yet the expectation, particularly for middle-class and upper-middle-class kids, is, 'Well, when I graduate and get my first job I'm going to maintain exactly the same kind of life-style it's taken my parents twenty-five or thirty years to attain.' "

The pressure to be a conventional success hasn't always been this bad, says Briggs, but it's exerted a powerful influence on students for the last fifteen years. "In the late 1960s you didn't breathe that you were even thinking of a career because there were so many important issues.

How quickly that changed! In eighteen to twenty-four months, at the end of the Vietnam War and the end of the draft, bingo!—we had a very career-oriented student population, and that hasn't changed. You don't hear quite as much as you used to about wanting to help society, or contributing in some positive way to the lives of other people."

Since the oldest Hamlets are around forty, very few of them graduated from college back in the sixties when, as Briggs remembers, career aspirations were unfashionable. They graduated starting in the early 1970s, as the Vietnam War and student activism wound down and campus life quieted. These older Hamlets confirm Briggs's observation that the pressure to get a good job has existed for at least the last fifteen years. Further, they maintain that the pressure to make it was just as difficult for them to handle as it is for Hamlets graduating from college today.

Martin graduated in 1979. He panicked when he realized he'd have to find employment. "It was time for me to start making decisions which I hadn't paid any attention to my first three years of college. My parents were starting to get on my case, asking me what I was going to do—they weren't telling me anymore. I knew, despite the fact that I was going to graduate, that I knew nothing. Paleontology gave me a background in geology, but I didn't want to try to fool some geology company into thinking I would be some great benefit to their firm, even though this was the time of the energy crisis and I would have been hired in seconds. I had no idea what I was going to do.

"Grad school was out. For one thing, I didn't think anyone would want me, and secondly, the GREs [Graduate Record Exams] came around and I didn't even know what they were. My advisor never told me about them. I was worried at first that I missed them, but then I said to myself, what do I care, I'd just be buffeted with more calculus and chemistry in grad school anyway." His father got him a summer job as a janitor. Once that ended, Martin postponed the search for permanent employment by traveling across the country with a friend.

Antonio, having prolonged his college education as long as he could, finally graduated with a degree in music in 1974. His reaction to graduation illustrates the depth of Hamlet's anxiety over the end of his school days. "My graduation consisted of finishing a Bach harpsichord concerto at the graduation recital," he recalls. "Not staying for the ceremony, not even staying for my bow, I walked out. I didn't collect my diploma for four years; it was mailed to me because they got tired of holding on to it. I took a bus and went up into the hills, up to a park, and I sat in a stream in my suit and I cried. Just cried. I'd just graduated from a university with a degree in music. Who was going to hire me? How was I going to feed myself? All I felt was despair."

James Briggs sees employment prospects improving for the Hamlet type. "The old attitude among employers was, 'Give me a college graduate, I don't care what the major is, and I'll do their training.' But higher education exploded in the fifties and sixties, and with many more people getting degrees, the employer's attitude changed to 'No, I'm not interested in any old college graduate, I'm interested in someone who's trained to do such-and-such.' Couple that with an economy that was not terribly expansionary, and you can see how the supply-demand situation changed. Students, particularly those in non–career-specific majors, were faced for the first time with really having to be clear about what they wanted to do.

"Now the cycle is beginning to come back around. The nature of the economy is changing. It's demanding more generalists. You go to an employer and ask what he's looking for to fill the vacancies he has, and he gives you a list of all the abilities and personal qualities a liberally educated person is going to have. Some employers who only three or four years ago came in saying, 'I want this specifically trained major,' are now open to identifying high-potential people out of any major."

High potential—that's Hamlet. Low action—that's Hamlet too. Even in a job market that values people with his abilities, he has neither the confidence nor the desire to hire on at a promising, entry-level position. He equates work with regimentation and responsibility. Remember what Maxine said? Work is a prison, day care for adults. She can handle a certain amount of responsibility well, but only at a slow pace. Employers can clean up their baby and dress it in the finest clothes—flex-time schedules, profit sharing, quality circles, job sharing arrangements—but the newly graduated Hamlet is still going to think it the absolutely ugliest child he's ever seen and refuse to kiss up to it.

14

Danes of Rage

O ne of the biggest changes on campus since the sixties and early
seventies is the lack of commitment to social causes. Except for
South African apartheid, no issue since Vietnam has inspired America's
college students to demonstrate, sit in, teach in, die in, and make the
nation take note of them. This in contrast to twenty years ago, when
administrators on many campuses had to call in the national guard to
suppress all the protests. Although many of the participants in the
campus revolts of the 1960s were conformists lacking genuine commitment to the ideals of the time, there were also plenty of principled
students courageous enough to protest despite hazards ranging from
academic suspension to beatings, tear gas, jail terms, and bullets. That
type of student doesn't seem to exist anymore.

Regardless of the mood of the times or urgency of the cause, Hamlet
rarely turns out for demonstrations or sit-ins. He's not ignorant of poli-

tics; he may know more about the cause of a demonstration than most of the people taking part. It's just that he prefers to keep an arm's length from the dirty work that signifies real commitment. Hamlet is a thinker, not a doer. He's happy to ponder the revolution but reluctant to help bring it forth. In the good old days of the early seventies a few Hamlets here and there did participate in protests, but their plunge into the realm of political dissent almost always ended in disillusion. Working for social change confirmed their darkest suspicions about the system: that it's entrenched, implacable, and unshakably committed to the dollar. Even worse, they learned that the outs fighting for change are often just as bad as the ins presently in power: dogmatic, combative, manipulative, and willing to employ any means to accomplish their ends. Thus chastened, Hamlets rarely engage in large-scale political action again.

Jeff, our hippie Hamlet, went to the University of Kansas in Lawrence seeking a community of like-minded people, and he found it. "Lawrence is a relatively small town, about sixty thousand people. Over twenty thousand of those people are students, so there was a sense of community there. Then there was also the community of the movement, a sense of us having similar ideas about the direction in which things should move and the way issues should be resolved. That was pretty heady.

"The spring before I started college was the Kent State thing [four students were shot to death by national guardsmen during an antiwar protest on May 4, 1970], and they'd closed down the University of Kansas early. There were plenty of ready-made villains, even local ones. It was fun to be part of that scene. I blocked a few highways, broke windows at the ROTC building, went to die-ins during the Kansas Relays [an internationally renowned track-and-field meet]. My dad was very concerned that I'd get caught up in the radical wave—you know, drugs, rock and roll, sex, political activism. I remember one Sunday I was heading down to Volcker Fountain, which is right in front of Kansas City's large art gallery. That's where the hippies were. My dad said, 'I don't know if you should go down there, there are all sorts of trouble-makers and something might happen.' It was obvious he disapproved of that type of life-style. But I was a pretty good kid. We just didn't happen to share the same ideas about how the world should be."

And just how did Jeff think the world should be? He took courses in the social sciences and humanities, trying to get a larger perspective on humankind and the state of planet Earth. Profoundly troubled by the way things were going, he developed some fairly radical views. "My first major in college was political science. I took all the political theory courses I could sit in on. Anarchism really appealed to me. I was so deeply offended that the system seemed to be built on this construct whose philosophical underpinnings were teetering. I had a great time writing papers. I got a generally positive reaction from my professors, but it wasn't until I took history as a second major that I found a kindred spirit, a professor in the history department. We had fun sitting around his office speculating about ways things might be slowly shifted, changed."

Change things did—only *not* in the direction Jeff had hoped or worked for. The community in which he felt so comfortable abruptly disappeared. "By the time I left Lawrence it was changing dramatically. I'm sure the same thing was happening all over the place, but particularly so there, where the norm is rather traditional and conservative. You could smell it from a mile away. I didn't feel a part of the place anymore. I don't know how much a part of it I ever was, but it did seem like home for a while. That community no longer existed, and looking back on it—depending on what mood you catch me in, I can be rather cynical about it—that community may *never* have existed."

Since his college days Jeff has steered clear of politics. So cynical about the system has he become that he refuses to vote. But beneath every cynic there lies an idealist who's been hurt once too often. Although he may not act on his beliefs anymore, in his heart Jeff remains profoundly concerned about the state of the world. When asked whether he'd consider taking to the streets again, his pleasant voice fills with irritation. "We all ought to be out in the streets *now*," he says. "This country is making war economically and otherwise *right now*, and has been for as long as we've been an empire. What this country does to other countries and other cultures is awful, and it does it in such an insidious way: economic tyranny, arming the world to its teeth. The exploitation, just the way we take advantage of two-dollar-a-week labor to pay for the niceties of middle-class living . . ." He throws up his hands, unable to finish the thought.

Hamlets among today's student population are just as politically aware as older Hamlets, but the tenor of the time completely discourages them from participating in protests. In Ronald Reagan's America, political activism strikes young Hamlet as quaint and futile. Amy, newly returned from China, says, "Sometimes I wish I could be like Gloria

Steinem, a leading figure. But right now I don't have the means or support to do what people in the sixties did. It wasn't easy for them, it's just that things were rolling in their direction."

When an issue strikes close enough to home, however, a few of today's college Hamlets consider agitating. Amy sees an alarming increase in anti-Asian prejudice as Japan, Taiwan, Korea, Hong Kong, and Singapore continue to improve their position in the global market against the United States, and so "I've gotten involved in the Asian Student Union. They lead discussions that are really important for me. Even if I don't go out and change the world, at least I end up knowing that I'm not the only person who feels this way. Right now I don't feel capable of crusading, but sometimes I'd like to do that eventually. By discussing these things I can help myself, and maybe then I can help other people."

Notice that Amy's activism takes the form of discussion. Hamlet can talk for hours about social conditions that upset him, but even when Hamlet himself is the potential victim of injustice—as is the case with Amy—he's loath to go beyond the talking stage. He looks back on the effort that went into making the sixties such a tumultuous time and realizes that if all *that* failed to straighten out the system, nothing short of a revolution will significantly change things now—and that's not going to happen anytime soon, at least not the way Hamlet would want it to. So why make a fuss? Hamlet keeps his rage at the system to himself, sharing his frustrations occasionally with trusted friends, and when people with causes accost him on his way to class he smiles politely and ignores them.

15

Hamlet Makes a Decision—Sort Of

W e live in a society riddled with contradictions. We go to church on Sunday morning and pray to a deity that commands us to love one another as we love ourselves, and then a few hours later we let out whoops of satisfaction when the other team's quarterback leaves the game with an injury. And that's one of the more innocuous examples of our cultural schizophrenia. We long for peace as we daily augment our nuclear arsenal, as if one more warhead will make a difference. We condemn South African apartheid and forget that the Boers modeled their homelands policy after our own system of Indian reservations. We criticize our political candidates for avoiding the issues, then vote for the one with the most appealing personality. The list goes on and on.

And it's not just the big issues where we think and act inconsistently. Contradiction has become so commonplace, and as adults we've adapted to it so well, that we don't even notice it anymore. But it's there, especially in the dichotomy between work life and home life. When we go to work we adopt a "professional" attitude. That means we act with a ruthlessness and self-preservation we'd be ashamed of under most other circumstances. Then, after we've spent the day baring our teeth to other human beings, we cuddle up to our loved ones—or try to, anyway. Sometimes we take the job home with us, another way of saying the line between our professional and personal lives gets fuzzy. When that happens we blame ourselves for "stressing out," as if we should be able to snap in and out of such contradictory roles without any strain whatsoever.

This is old news for most of us. But sheltered Hamlet knows nothing of our cultural schizophrenia until he reaches college, and then it hits him with the force of a heavyweight's punch. He recognizes right away that it's a form of mass insanity, different from pathological insanity in only one respect: It's so common it's considered normal. How do people cope with all these contradictions? he wonders. They do it by not thinking, not caring, and doing what's expedient—Darren's three evils. In order to survive, people have to give up their principles. That's why they say idealism's nice but impractical: It gets in the way of the usual coping mechanisms. Hamlet, still young and unsullied, sees a different way of coping, one that allows him to retain some semblance of sanity: He can hold on to his principles. He won't get along as well as he might, but he'll have his integrity and peace of mind, which ultimately counts for more than a suitcase full of $100 bills.

By the time he's ready to graduate from college, then, Hamlet has rejected all the popular rationalizations for heartless behavior: that we have to look out for number one; that we help others most when we help ourselves; that the system is imbued with a wisdom, foresight, and capacity for self-correction that no individual can match; that humans are by nature depraved, and we're foolish to fight our instincts. No matter how hard he tries he can't bring himself to act *professionally*, which he defines as a consistently selfish, hostile, *ad hoc* manner. At the same time, he can't imagine living without principle, conscience, and consideration for others—the concerns of the heart. Therefore, in spite of his desire for the dollar and his fear of standing apart from the mainstream, he feels he has no choice but to follow the dictates of his heart.

This is the closest Hamlet ever comes to resolving his heart-or-dollar conflict. Never again will he be so sure of his direction.

The decision to follow the dictates of the heart and forget about the dollar is a fairly easy one in that it requires no real *action*. To make money, to obtain power, to fit in, you have to *do* things. To retreat to the fringe of society you need do nothing at all. And so even though Hamlet is making a decision, it's not the sort of decision that requires a tremendous output of energy. Make no mistake, the commitment to his heart *will* cost Hamlet, but the expenditure will come in defending his passivity and nonconformity, not in actively pursuing some worldly goal. And that cost is lower than the one he'd incur if he were to join mainstream society and take active steps toward success. In that instance he would have to justify his behavior to *himself*, an impossibility given his way of thinking—as dropout Hamlets discover. The heart-or-dollar dilemma is thus something of a no-win situation: Whichever way Hamlet goes he's sure to face criticism. Since, like most people, he's his own worst critic, he takes the path of least resistance and follows his heart.

Here begins the most crippling pattern in Hamlet's life. Henceforth, whenever he's faced with a difficult choice, his first and strongest impulse will be to do nothing—or as little as possible. If he doesn't do anything, he thinks, he doesn't do anything *wrong*. Besides, if he does nothing for long enough there's always the chance that the forces pressing him to act will go away. Thus Hamlet's life becomes a series of *faits accomplis*. He falls into things rather than aggressively determining his fate. Eileen, as we saw earlier, just fell into the Rhetoric major by accident. Martin, as we'll learn in Part Four, fell into the first job that came his way. As the years pass it gets harder and harder for Hamlet to make a positive, action-oriented decision—and that handicaps him terribly when the heart-or-dollar dilemma gains a renewed intensity in his middle to late thirties.

IV

CONTROLLED FLOUNDERING: HAMLET IN THE REAL WORLD

Thou wouldst not think how ill all's
here about my heart . . .

Hamlet, ACT V, SCENE ii

"Life just kept getting better and better. I was awestruck by how wonderful it was. I'd always had good years—until I got out of college." So Maxine describes the turn in fortune suffered by most Hamlets after they leave the university. Once the diploma is awarded and Hamlet returns his rented cap and gown, he can no longer put off the question "What next?" In college he decided what *not* to do. Now he has to make a different kind of decision, one that requires *positive* action. Hamlet has to stop thinking and start doing. The question, though, is what?

He has three choices. The first is to continue doing what he enjoys: going to school. This option especially tempts Hamlets with an intellectual bent. Spending three, six, even ten years obtaining an advanced degree that may have little market value strikes Hamlet as honorable and principled, the sort of sacrifice for knowledge and culture that made the monks of the Middle Ages the unsung heroes of Western civilization. *Someone* has to compile a concordance for the writings of the Druids or resurrect French poems of the seventh century; it might as well be Hamlet. If he gets lucky someone will recognize the importance of his scholarship and offer him a job as a professor, meaning he may *never* have to leave school. Tenure completes the cycle of security that began with Hamlet's birth into a stable, middle-class home; it's a happy ending to the Hamlet Syndrome, ensuring good pay, good benefits, job security, and a minimum of entanglements with the workaday world.

Hamlet's second choice is to delay for as long as possible the decision about what to do. The most popular delaying tactic is travel. The extended postcollegiate journey to wherever is an old European tradition, but though it's still observed on the Continent and in Australia it hasn't gained widespread acceptance in the United States. Nevertheless, many Hamlets, like Darren in the previous part, find the lure of an open-ended trip irresistible. Travel is exciting, much more stimulating than graduate school or work. Despite occasional bouts of loneliness and homesickness, the traveling Hamlet savors each sweet swallow from the cup of adventure. The fun ends when his money runs out and he has to move fast to stay alive. He's back at square one, figuring out what to do next, only now he doesn't have the money that cushioned him before he went on his trip. As a result he often chooses a hasty, unwise course that condemns him to a prolonged stay in society's lower echelons.

Female Hamlets have another delaying tactic to fall back on: raising children. (We'd love to report that male Hamlets also exercise this option, but even the most open-minded of them generally shun the role of primary parent. Part of the reason is biological, of course, but most of the reason is social. Men are still expected to do their part for the family by earning money, not by sitting at home with the kids.) Female Hamlets find the child-rearing option tempting because having babies remains a "legitimate" women's occupation. "If I can't find a job I can always have a baby," the typical thinking goes. Female Hamlets with strong feminist leanings sometimes worry that abandoning the workplace in favor of rocking the cradle represents a retreat from responsibility, a betrayal of themselves and their sex. They often return part-time to the workplace once their youngest child can be trusted to day care.

Hamlet's third choice—and the one he usually winds up making— is to enter the work force. Work gives Hamlet economic independence, which for the first time in his life makes him entirely self-powered.

Beholden to no one but his boss, Hamlet exults in his newfound freedom. Why, he even gets weekends off, whereas in college he often had to spend his Saturdays and Sundays studying! Pretty soon, however, he stops finding pleasure in his work. Among other things, it's boring. In college each semester brought new courses, new instructors, new classmates, and Hamlet reveled in the fresh stimulation. But work, especially the dead-end post Hamlet almost always takes after leaving college, consists of the same tasks with the same co-workers day after day, month after month. Hamlet starts to feel that he's stagnating, that his brain is in danger of rotting away. He gets restless, develops a bad attitude, and either moves on to something else or sinks into the sort of funk that makes the whole world seem gray. Dropout Hamlets who hold more remunerative, prestigious positions tire of the pressure and politics of the office. They count their savings, and if they have enough to live comfortably for the foreseeable future they up and quit. Hamlet, small-time or big, finds no fulfillment in the life of a working stiff.

Hamlet's choices are circumscribed by his past. For example, if he majored in the liberal arts and neglected to plan for a career, he has no specific occupation to pursue after graduating from college. That leaves him feeling he has no place in the vocational world and increases the likelihood that he'll go to graduate school or travel for an extended period. If he decides to work, he usually accepts the first job offer he gets—even if it's nothing more than minding the cash register for a small business.

Whichever choice Hamlet makes—and sometimes, as we'll soon see with Maxine, he makes all three—he's often regarded with suspicion. *What's he doing that for? Why can't he make up his mind? He's going nowhere. He's a loser.* Hamlet may not hear the whispers, but he picks up on the doubt—and, at times, contempt—in the faces of his friends and family. He's not a loser, he knows that. The real losers are the hordes who play society's game without taking a moment for self-reflection. But how does Hamlet explain his redefinition of the word *loser* to mainstream people? How does he explain to people frightened or incapable of critical thought that being your own person, thinking for yourself, *questioning*, is more important than struggling toward a $200,000-a-year job in a Madison Avenue advertising firm? Most of the time he doesn't. He lacks the language or patience or faith in his listeners to make them understand. And so the suspicion that he's a loser grows unchecked, and Hamlet soon finds the number of people he can *really* talk to shrinking.

Maxine, as you may recall from Part Three, managed to avoid the crisis that usually strikes Hamlets in college. Her life since college, however, epitomizes Hamlet's ordeal in the adult world. A Phi Beta Kappa graduate of New York University, she figured on getting a job in the publishing business, but she delayed her entry into the work force first by spending the summer studying Russian at an academy in New England, and then, that fall, by traveling around California. When she finally returned to New York the only "publishing" job she could find was with a tiny company that made posters. "It was basically a clerical job," she remembers. "I was promoted to head of the administrative department because everyone else had left. The company was awful. They paid shit, and they treated me like shit. It was a good experience in that I learned right away that employers don't care about you." She quit after seven months. Eking an existence out of a part-time job and a small inheritance, she wrote a mystery novel, participated in the antinuclear movement—and fell apart.

"Everything went bad at the same time, around May of 1985. I lost my job. The person I was living with moved in with her boyfriend—who was my best friend. The novel didn't sell. Communists got involved in our antinuclear group and created a horrible situation that broke us up. I was totally destroyed." The crisis she'd avoided since college finally caught up with her. Lonely and depressed, she returned to her mother's house in Philadelphia to regroup. Over the course of several months she made a new start for herself, working part-time in a hospital, volunteering at a community coffeehouse, and applying to graduate school. She mulled over her options. "I knew I couldn't keep on having these part-time jobs and trying to write. It wasn't enough to live on," she says. Yet she stayed true to the Hamlet within her. "I thought, if I'm going to spend eight hours a day at a job, I want it to be something I believe in. The only institution I believe in at this point is the public library, so I thought for a long-range thing that would be okay." In the autumn of 1986 she enrolled part-time in a graduate librarianship program. She expects to graduate in 1989 and take a low-key, probably low-paying position in collection development. "I realized I'm not interested in living on top of things, in a fast-moving place like New York, and having a high-powered job. I couldn't handle having too many people depend on me." So half a dozen years after finishing her undergraduate degree, having sampled all of Hamlet's postcollegiate options, Maxine at last has a direction—and still it's not the direction mainstream America looks favorably upon. "The conventional notion of success is money," she acknowledges, a conviction echoed by virtually every Hamlet we talked to, "and I see myself getting rich only through dumb luck: if I write a book that for some reason appeals to people, or if I marry into money. Those are the only two possibilities. I can't imagine any job I would be in where I would make a lot of money."

Forced to choose between the heart and the dollar, Maxine has decided to follow her heart. Most Hamlets make the same choice when they first get out of college. (Dropouts initially go for the dollar.) Like the Buddha, Hamlet's secure and comfortable childhood has provided him with enough knowledge of the good life to realize that material success—money, power, a slick appearance—doesn't bring fulfillment. Happiness lies elsewhere, in the free and easy wandering of the mind and the serenity of a clear conscience. But though Hamlet *understands* he can't buy happiness, deep down he still wants to be well off. He's grown up with money, and each day society tells him that the purpose of life is to accumulate wealth. So even as he follows his heart he feels guilty about not chasing the dollar. That gnawing desire for material success spoils his happiness and frequently makes him regard himself the way everyone else does: as a washout. Keep that in mind as we explore in more detail Hamlet's three adult options. Although he manages to live by the dictates of his heart, Hamlet's tone is anything but prideful. He tends more toward the apologetic, the ashamed—and the defensive. Only when he's completely comfortable will he admit that in being true to his noblest self he's accomplishing something rare, beautiful, and, perhaps, just as difficult as making a million dollars.

16
The Grad School Grind

Throughout this book we've extolled the merits of critical thought. As with any good thing, however, too much critical thought leads to problems, one of them being the Hamlet Syndrome. For their own good, Hamlets should resist the temptation to overindulge their skepticism and analytical skills. But many find the pleasures of critical thought so intoxicating that even after four years of college they thirst for more. No place offers them a safer, more structured environment for intellectual chugging than graduate school, especially a program in the humanities or social sciences. Graduate school also attracts Hamlets who don't have any idea what they want to do, but need a temporary haven. Doctoral programs last upward of four years, and many allow dilatory students to hang around for a decade or more. The security of his childhood long gone, Hamlet can cocoon himself anew in the self-contained world of his graduate department. Grad students work as teaching assistants or researchers, usually earning just enough to support themselves without having to leave campus. When they need companionship they need only saunter down the department hallway, where they're bound to find people with the same interests and background as themselves. They may even *live* on campus. The ivory tower, indeed.

Yet as we mentioned, graduate school has its perils, including the tendency to encourage Hamlet's need for rational answers to *everything*, even personal, emotional matters. When confronted with a threatening question—for example, "When are you going to finish that dissertation and start earning a living, old boy?"—Hamlet submits an intellectual explanation: "Well, the topic I'm working on is incredibly complex and it'll take a ton of time to write up correctly." He can't admit that part of the reason he's taking forever to write his dissertation is personal: He's afraid to leave school or he's just not up to the writing. The irrational is unacceptable. Only after he's gotten his Ph.D. and a job can he reveal how scared he was of leaving graduate school—if, indeed, he can reveal it even then.

Other pitfalls dot the trail to a graduate credential. Hamlet may feel guilt or shame for hiding out and studying esoterica that society considers worthless. (And just for entertaining such irrational feelings he gets even more guilty and ashamed.) He shares the general impression that graduate school is easier than life in the working world, and consequently his voice takes on a defensive tone whenever working stiffs ask him how school is going. He may sense that his wage-earner friends condescend to him, and that behind his back they make fun of him. How can he explain to such a patronizing audience that sheltered as it may seem, the daily life of a graduate student is anything but idyllic? For indeed, academia is a business just like any other.

As one Hamlet puts it, "In graduate school you see the reality of how a field works, and you may decide you don't want to live that way." Academia has a hierarchical structure: full professors at the top, non-tenured professors lower down, year-to-year teaching staff down further still, and graduate students at the bottom. Hamlet resents his relegation to the lowest caste, especially when he discovers that he has more on the ball than some of the full professors who teach his seminars. But if he is to flourish in his graduate program he has to please the old goats, so he says what the professors want to hear and he writes sycophantic papers. That violates the ideal of unfettered intellectual inquiry he brought with him from his undergraduate days.

Many graduate programs also require Hamlet to help teach the department's introductory courses. Although Hamlet believes in the importance of teaching and goes to it eagerly, he's soon worn down by grade hassles and unthinking students. Was I ever this bad? he wonders after trying to explain a key concept for the tenth time to an uncomprehending undergrad. The number of students who don't care for his subject matter disappoints him—he may even take the lack of interest as a personal insult. He grades a seemingly endless stream of tests and papers that bore him into a stupor while eating away at his study time. And what is he paid for all this labor? The same as any other teacher in this society: peanuts.

But the worst part of grad school is the series of exams that stand like ten-foot walls between Hamlet and his desired degree. They're the performance evaluations of the academic realm. M.A. exams, language exams, oral defenses, all require months or years of intensive preparation. Should Hamlet stumble over any one of them he may wind up disqualified from his program—fired—out on the street sans degree, sans employment, sans everything.

If with each semester Hamlet's disillusion with graduate school grows, he may leave, recriminating himself all the while for wasting several years of his life. This is especially true of Hamlets in the humanities and social sciences. A doctoral degree in those fields generally has little economic value except within academia, so if Hamlet doesn't want to fight for a tenure-track position he has little incentive to complete his Ph.D. Nonetheless, many Hamlets persist in the paper chase despite what they know about academia's dark side. They have something to prove to themselves, their friends and family, or their department; or, after prolonged consideration of their other options, they realize that graduate school remains the best place for them. And so they slog on, in some cases completing their formal education *thirty years* after entering kindergarten. By the time they graduate they're often too old to get a good job, so unless they find work as teachers they end up—as has one Ph.D. in philosophy who declined to talk to us—tending bar or toiling at some other menial occupation.

Jessica, our epitome of the perpetual student, spent ten years in graduate school. She despised her undergraduate major, communications arts. "I would get C's because I'd take these courses on interpersonal communication or nonverbal communication, and it was all such garbage. We'd talk about feedback loops and stuff and I'd have to do hokey research projects, which I'd always sort of blow off. One teacher asked me into his office one day and said, 'You never look at me in class. What's going on?' And I thought to myself, the reason I never look at you is because I have no respect for you and what you're doing, but I have to have this class for my major."

It doesn't sound like Jessica was much of a candidate for graduate school, does it? Well, never underestimate a Hamlet's desire for sanctuary. "After college I knew I wasn't ready for a job and I thought, how do I get out of this? I know—I'll go to graduate school! I applied because it seemed the least offensive alternative open to me." She chose a field she knew hardly anything about: Chinese literature. "Why did I want to study Chinese? I just wanted to." She shrugs. "There was a book called the *Tao-te-Ching,* and in one of my undergrad courses someone mentioned this book had been translated into English over a hundred times, all different translations. And I thought, how is it possible that one book can be translated so many different ways? I've got to find out what's going on here. Then another professor mentioned that a whole collection of volumes in the Taoist canon had never been translated, and I thought, what a treasure trove for scholars! Later I found out why it had never been translated: It was so deadly boring that no one would ever want to look at it.

"I never thought about whether I would be marketable or not. I had no thoughts at all about career or long-term goals. My only goals were year-to-year—what courses am I going to take this semester? I needed several years just to learn the languages—ancient Chinese, modern Chinese and Japanese—and then learn the culture. After that my dissertation took forever. Part of it was that I enjoyed it so much I didn't want it to end. I knew that when it ended I would have to get a job, and I wasn't ready for that."

Every now and then Jessica, aware that she was using grad school as a haven, questioned the value of staying in the program. "A lot of times I had this fantasy, why not a normal life? Why not the house in the suburbs, the kids, and everything all laid out the way it's supposed to be: the VCR, nice clothes, trips here and there, a car that doesn't need to be fixed every two months? But at the same time I longed for that life, I didn't think it would really be me. I'd get bored. That's my greatest fear, being bored. I'd rather have poverty than boredom." So she followed her heart and stayed in graduate school long enough to earn a Ph.D. "My mom keeps saying, 'You could have been a doctor or two and a half lawyers by now!' But I feel like I've done what I've wanted to do. There hasn't been much reward for it, but I've had a lot of freedom. That's why I've hung on the way I have."

For Jessica, the shelter provided by graduate school justified her remaining there a decade. Other Hamlets, disillusioned by academia, leave. Jeff traveled to Europe after finishing college, but when his money ran out he had to return to the United States and decide what to do. "I thought to myself, God, the choices are not great here. I can go to work, or I can go back to school." Opting for the latter, he scrambled to get into the history program at his alma mater, the University of Kansas. "There was almost no forethought. Suddenly I was back at this thing that I had left a year earlier, and in no way was I prepared for it." Disillusion set in quickly. "My main interest was American intellectual history. There was a really influential instructor, and I became one of his students. But I got tired of reading a thousand pages a week. And I got tired of the idea that it didn't really matter in any significant way. This professor I was studying under had written just a few years earlier that history is a dead movement, at least the way standard historians handle it. I thought he was absolutely right." So nine months after hustling to get into graduate school, he dropped out and went to work full-time at the campus bookstore.

Hamlet has an easier time staying in graduate school if he knows his program will lead to a decent job, and thus Hamlets in the sciences are more likely to finish their advanced degrees than Hamlets in the humanities and social sciences. The thing is, fewer Hamlets enroll in science programs, perhaps because the volume of detail daunts their more conceptually oriented minds. Hamlets in the sciences, in addition to all the problems outlined earlier, face the prospect of working on projects of dubious moral value—for instance, experimenting on live animals. One Hamlet who dropped out of a Ph.D. program in biology but still works in a lab says, "I've avoided seeking jobs that might be harmful or unethical. I choose not to do animal research. It's too hard to figure out what's justified and what isn't, so I don't do it at all." Also, the hierarchy in graduate science programs is more pronounced than in the humanities. Professors lord over their labs, taking full credit for anything produced even when grad students have done all the work. And as specialized as humanities Hamlets like Jessica may be, candidates for the Ph.D. in the sciences burrow into even more obscure holes. "Just intensely studying one little process in plant cells, there came a point where I understood as much about it as anyone in the world," says the Hamlet who won't experiment on animals.

Of course, Hamlet can always go to professional school. Completion of a professional degree virtually guarantees lucrative employment. But for moral, political, or other reasons, Hamlet rejects almost every professional avenue to the dollar—except for one, which we'll now examine a bit more closely.

A Hamlet was shopping with her father one day when they ran into a neighbor. After exchanging the usual niceties, the neighbor admitted he was having problems with a business associate. He didn't want the problems to lead to litigation, but he didn't know how to word a letter to that effect to the troublesome associate. "I'd be more than happy to pay someone to write that letter for me," he said in exasperation, and the Hamlet offered her services. "Jeez, you'd do anything for money, wouldn't you?" chided her father. "You know what that makes you?" "Yes," the Hamlet replied drily, "it makes me a lawyer."

These days the few good words we hear about the legal profession come in jokes. What's the difference between a dead snake in the road and a dead lawyer in the road? There are skid marks in front of the snake. Why didn't the sharks eat the shipwrecked lawyer? Professional courtesy. Lawyers have developed such a bad reputation that one of Shakespeare's throwaway lines from *Henry VI, Part II*—"The first thing we do, let's kill all the lawyers"—gets quoted almost as often as the gems from his more famous plays. Lawyers are scoundrels, rip-off artists, bombasts. They'll exploit any little loophole to help a client—provided the client has the money to pay exorbitant legal fees. Perhaps it's because so many of our politicians start out as lawyers that we innately distrust anyone with *attorney-at-law* attached to his name.

Yet law attracts a disproportionate number of Hamlets. James Briggs, director of the University of California, Berkeley's Career Planning and Placement Center, offers this theory as to why. "When you're a college senior, if you don't know what you want to do, you can always say you're thinking of going to law school. If you say that three or four times to three or four different people, you become very committed to going to law school, because you have to live up to what you told people. So you go to law school, and you have no idea why you're going except it was a good answer and people said, 'Oh, that's very prestigious, very lucrative.' "

But there are other reasons law appeals to Hamlet, one being that it's the quickest and easiest path to a doctoral-level degree. Health professionals such as doctors, dentists, and optometrists require at least four years of advanced training; lawyers need but three. Before they go to graduate school aspiring healers have to flourish in mind-bending courses like organic chemistry; all a Hamlet needs to qualify for law school is his liberal arts degree. Hamlet's analytical mind and silver tongue—or, as some would have it, his ability to BS—better indicate his likelihood of success in the profession than the grades on his transcript.

But the main reason Hamlet wants to become a lawyer is that it offers him a chance to fulfill his two conflicting desires. Law, as James Briggs said, is prestigious and well-paid. With a practice of his own or a partnership in a solid firm, Hamlet can establish himself as a productive member of the community. He can afford a middle-class life-style comparable to the one he grew up in. His hunger for the dollar, conventional success, can be satisfied. Yet at the same time Hamlet can do good. Lawyers don't *have* to be bad guys, and Hamlet, carrying his idealistic convictions into adulthood, can use his law degree to fight for justice. He may even hope to work in public interest law, going to court on behalf of oppressed peoples or endangered species. In such a way Hamlet can preserve the purity of his heart.

This chance to have *both* the dollar and the heart explains why Hamlet opts for law over other short but lucrative graduate programs, such as the master's in business administration—better known by its acronym, the M.B.A. The American Assembly of Collegiate Schools of Business reports that between 1974 and 1987 the number of M.B.A. programs in the United States soared from 389 to 650. Almost one quarter of all master's degrees awarded in the United States each year are in business administration. Yet we found no Hamlets who aspired to an M.B.A. The reason: Business, in their eyes, offers little chance to satisfy the needs of the heart. Sure, it's a quick ticket to an upper-middle-class existence, but the very notion of business often makes Hamlet recoil. He hates competition, aggression, and the amorality of the marketplace. The bottom line is that Hamlet doesn't like the bottom line.

Yet law is a bottom-line profession also, and deep down Hamlet knows that. Before he even applies to law school he knows he'll have to pay back student loans (thus precluding public interest work right after passing the bar), and knows the firm he works for will expect upward of forty billable hours per week from him. He knows too that he won't always be a Perry Mason for the oppressed. He'll be spending the better part of each day wading through acres of legal texts, composing letters and briefs, kowtowing to partners in the firm, and toting up his billable hours in service of clients who may be arrogant and amoral. Not much room there for a heart that wants fulfillment. The law-school–bound Hamlet has to come to grips with the fact that concern for the dollar, at least for the first several years of his career, will override any ethical considerations.

One way to do that is to try *embracing* the bottom line. Sid, now twenty-seven, hails from the Oklahoma Panhandle. He went to Trinity College in San Antonio, Texas, majoring in English. "I was just out of college, thinking I was ready to set the world on fire, but there was nothing to burn in San Antonio," he says ruefully. He took a nine-to-five job as a copywriter for an advertising agency, earning $11,000 a year. The job bored him, so he tried graduate school. When he found that unfulfilling also, he took the Law School Admissions Test—and got an almost perfect score. "I decided on law because there's money in it, basically," he concedes, adding, "I feel like maybe I'm selling out now, but I'm tired of dealing with people that irritate me. I know there'll be people like that in law, but at least I'll get paid enough to put up with them."

Now hold on, Sid. If money alone could make a Hamlet bear the slings and arrows of a high-pressure, dubiously moral occupation, the Hamlet Syndrome wouldn't *exist*. There's a heart that must be satisfied, too. And if you're having trouble with obnoxious people now, just wait until you're surrounded by attorneys. Almost every lawyer is opinionated, highly motivated, and trained to argue to exhaustion. You, as a typical Hamlet, may be capable of arguing to exhaustion also, but only about something interesting, not dry stuff like torts and due process. For most Hamlets, no amount of money could compensate for a life in that environment. And what if the firm asked you to defend a client you knew was guilty of something heinous? "I'd probably do anything they told me to. I'd be a complete mercenary." Oh yeah? Do you really think you could do that, given your Hamlet nature? "Sometimes I think I might be selling out my ideals to go to law school, but then I think, well, I've just got to be aware of what I'm doing and why I'm doing it." So we're back to square one: As long as the money's right, you think you can do it. Maybe, Sid, but maybe not. Judging from the testimony of the next two Hamlets, law's affronts to the heart are not as easily dismissed as you might be hoping.

Noelle, a top student at Rutgers University in New Jersey, was halfway through law school when she abruptly withdrew. She was raised a standard Hamlet: in a sheltered suburban neighborhood, getting top grades, rebelling but mildly. Early on she developed a strong affection for animals. "I used to bring home every stray I found," she admits. When the time came to consider a career, she decided to follow the inclinations of her heart and help animals professionally. "There were a lot of different ways I could have done that, but I decided to try law and fight for animal rights." She did well in law school, but three of law's harsh realities compelled her to abandon the program.

"First, I didn't feel like I fit in the profession. I was extremely idealistic about becoming a lawyer. I thought I could save the world, or at least the animal world. But I found out that I'm really sensitive, and getting into arguments with lawyers and potential lawyers, well, it seemed their values were different. They were more sneaky and aggressive. I guess I could have forced myself to play that role, but it would have required a major change of personality. I would have had to force myself to become something I wasn't.

"Second, I felt that if I worked for any kind of private law firm I wouldn't have any time left over to devote to animals. Some of the private law firms work you to death, and you have no life of your own. I could have gone to work for a nonprofit organization, but I'd taken out loans to go to law school and I didn't know if I would be able to pay them back if I was working for a nonprofit organization.

"Third, as time went on, it seemed that law was a bunch of bullshit. Even the homework, reading the cases, it seemed like all the law is merely someone's opinion. Everything is so arbitrary. It's just what some guy thought, and he could have been a really stupid or prejudiced judge. It's just one person's opinion, not written in stone from God or anything. There's no such thing as a *law;* it all depends on how you interpret it. There's nothing to hold on to; the law changes every day."

Noelle's three reasons for leaving law school show how a Hamlet's personality combines with social conditions to thwart his chance of finding a suitable niche in society. Noelle's first reason comes entirely from within: She's simply too sensitive to partake in ruthless debate and negotiation. Her second reason is partly her problem and partly society's: She can't afford law school on her own, because it's so expensive. Her third reason is purely social, and punctures one of America's most cherished illusions.

No one knows what John Adams was drinking in 1779 when he claimed that the liberated state of Massachusetts would be ruled by "a government of laws, and not of men," but it must have been potent stuff. For law does not exist apart from humankind. Humans invent, apply, and enforce the law, and when particularly knotty problems arise humans have to interpret the law as well. Yet we still cling to the shibboleth that law can transcend human nature. Ronald Reagan made this very argument when he nominated fringe rightist Robert Bork to the Supreme Court in 1987. "His [Bork's] nomination is being opposed by some because he practices judicial restraint," a legal philosophy that calls for judges not to impose their views on the law, Reagan said. But judicial restraint is a myth. Many legal scholars agree with Noelle that law is nothing more than opinion, perhaps a stupid or biased opinion at that. In the words of Oliver Wendell Holmes, one of America's great Supreme Court justices, the law "cannot be dealt with as if it contained only the axioms and corollaries of a book of mathematics."

The knowledge that law isn't clear and automatic, that it changes from judge to judge, discourages Hamlets like Noelle because it means being right isn't enough; you also have to be argumentative and persuasive. "It doesn't matter whether you're a nice person or not. The person who's going to be best at law is the one who can bullshit more. I didn't feel comfortable with that. It seemed like a big charade," maintains Noelle. She wants a legal system of black-and-white guidelines administered by virtuous people, but like the rest of us she gets a system that rewards obnoxious persistence and silver-tongued manipulation. Halfway through law school she learned why lawyers have such an unsavory reputation—and why Hamlets, despite their initial attraction to law, so often back away from it in the end.

Then there's Brent, our dropout Hamlet. After graduating from college with a degree in economics he took a job as an analyst. He did very well but he hated his work, so after a year, having saved up lots of money, he dropped out. He lived in a cabin in the Rocky Mountains, and from there he went up to Alaska, making money working in canneries. "I had trouble hauling around seventy-five-pound bags of wet salt," says the slender Brent, "and I started thinking, these people can do this better than me, but there are things I can do better than them. That's when I decided to go to law school."

Brent echoes James Briggs's point that many Hamlets go to law school because it sounds good. "Like at least half the other people in my class, I went to law school because I thought it fit with my interests and background and would keep me off the street for three years, not because my lifelong ambition was to become a lawyer." He quickly proved a stellar student. He was named to the prestigious law review, an honor generally reserved for the top 10 percent of the class, and wrote articles on environmental legislation. "By my third year I was working day and night, weekends. It was pretty fun, especially law review." In his choice of classes, however, overachieving Brent betrayed his Hamlet roots. "I was more inclined toward the intellectual aspects of law than the applied aspects. I took courses in philosophy and history of law rather than corporate finance. It didn't matter; whatever job you take afterwards has little to do with what you study in law school."

He continued to distinguish himself after law school, obtaining a coveted clerkship with a federal appeals judge. "I had a great time that year. Once a month the cases came in, and I would plan my workload so I could do my job from nine to five and go home." But there was a down side. "In a sense it was a dead-end job, because you do it for a year and then you have to leave. It also left me socially isolated. You can't talk to any of the attorneys in the case, can't make connections, so it was very much an ivory tower position.

"After clerking, I didn't really want to practice law, go to work for a big law firm. I had an underlying image of what that was like, and I knew what *I* was like. I thought of myself more as someone in a plaid shirt than a Brooks Brothers suit." In spite of his misgivings, he took a position with a large firm—and lasted all of one year. "I liked the people, some of the work was interesting, and the offices were nice. But I was desperately unhappy. I felt very pressured in terms of time and I couldn't put work behind me. I'd wake up in the middle of the night thinking about the stuff I was working on. I felt burdened by billing time. And I didn't like some of my clients. The reason was one of principle: They weren't on the right side.

"I thought I would like law because I'm good at solving problems. I thought I would take a problem, solve it, be satisfied, then go take a vacation. But there's an unlimited amount of work at a law firm, so you can't take a vacation. As soon as you get something done, there's this endless string of more things. You can't take the rest of the day off because then you're not billing time. Despite how hard I was working I wasn't billing enough time. The whole thing was driving me batty. I'd stare out the window for half an hour sometimes—and then I couldn't bill that time." When his girlfriend got a job in Europe, Brent abruptly quit his job and went with her. He dropped out a second time, and he hasn't been back to the mainstream since. We'll come back to him later when we look more closely at dropout Hamlets.

In like Sid, out like Brent; the law school grind eats at Hamlet until he has to run away to save his soul. And law school, as we've noted, is the *easiest* professional school for Hamlet to handle. By definition, then, it would seem that professional work demands more grace under pressure than Hamlet can summon. My son the doctor he can never be—at least not my son the *happy* doctor. For Hamlet to be happy, as Sid will probably discover, money simply isn't enough.

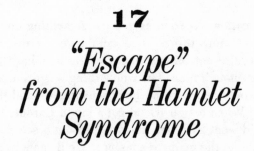

17

"Escape" from the Hamlet Syndrome

Especially when Hamlet first comes out of college, he's plagued by the feeling that he needs more experience. He's read some interesting books, he's met a few people from different places, but he really doesn't know what's going on outside middle-class America. To most of his acquaintances experience means *work,* but to Hamlet that definition is too limited, too prosaic. For him experience means exploring the whole world, not just the outer reaches of the office. So many different things to eat, wear, see, do, and ponder! He feels naive, culturally and intellectually impoverished. Determined to make up for his ignorance, Hamlet just says no to grad school, scoffs at making a living, and walks off to look for enlightenment. In this one respect, at least, Hamlet may be said to have ambition.

Middle-class as he may have grown up, Hamlet refuses to travel Ugly American style. He doesn't roll from campground to campground in a thirty-foot recreational vehicle, doesn't gawk at peasants from an air-conditioned tour bus, doesn't curse at foreigners who don't speak English. Whether backpacking through a wilderness area or Youth Hosteling across Europe, Hamlet immerses himself completely in his new environment. Most of the time he travels alone in an effort to know himself better. Rocky as the road sometimes gets, he learns more about the world and his inner self with every bump he surmounts, and the ride gives him such a thrill that he comes to regard traveling, particularly that first extended adventure on his own, as the high point of his life. For the rest of his days, whenever he feels the need for renewal, he breaks out the maps and starts planning a journey.

Travel broadens Hamlet. He took the first (and biggest) step in overcoming the handicaps of his sheltered upbringing by going to college and turning on intellectually. Now travel expands his horizons even further. He learns that people are very different—and yet, deep down, they are the same. They may live under different economic, political, religious, or cultural circumstances, but they laugh and cry for the same reasons he does. This comes as a revelation to Hamlet, conditioned by TV newscasts and high school social studies classes to believe that anything or anyone outside the American middle class is inferior, irrational, and worthy of suspicion. Meeting foreigners or nonconformist Americans in their own context, he sees that Dan Rather tells him only half the story. These ostensibly inscrutable people have perfectly understandable (although not necessarily acceptable) motives for doing what they do. Sometimes their customs or ideas make so much sense to Hamlet that he adopts them for his own.

Traveling has a second beneficial effect on Hamlet. An intrinsically insecure endeavor, travel becomes even more insecure when done à la Hamlet: cheaply, impulsively, and for an extended period of time. Somewhere along the line Hamlet will find himself without food and water, or without a place to sleep. He'll wander into a dangerous area ignorant of the perils at hand. He'll put his trust in rip-off artists. When he makes that mistake he'll have only himself to fall back on; Mom and Dad and the American flag won't be there to protect him. But frightening as that exposure may be, it's the best antidote known for the overprotection of his youth. For the first time in his life Hamlet knows risk, danger, *insecurity.* He understands that one little mistake—drinking the wrong water, turning the wrong corner—could mean his end, and he at last learns what it is to be fully human: vulnerable, lonely, afraid. To his parents, who usually view travel as a trip to Grandma's or a week at Waikiki, Hamlet's perambulations are inexplicable except as a dodge from adult responsibilities. What they don't understand is that by traveling Hamlet finally learns what it is to *be* an adult. Upon his return he'll be better prepared to take on the world—that is, if the wanderlust wanes sufficiently for him to accept anything as mundane as full-time employment.

How do you keep Hamlet down on the job once he's seen Paris? Although his wanderings expose Hamlet to insecurity and thus prepare him for the tribulations of the workaday world, they also condition him to constant stimulation. As a traveler, whenever Hamlet tires of a locale he can go somewhere else and delight himself anew. That's not possible at a job, especially the kind of job Hamlet usually gets. Penniless after his travels, lacking the credentials or experience for middle-class employment, the newly returned Hamlet takes a menial position. After the excitement of the first few paychecks wears off, he gets bored. This is quite a comedown, he thinks, and he may end up chronically depressed, romanticizing his travels and despairing of ever having such happiness again. He lets everyone know how restless he is, constantly regaling co-workers and acquaintances with stories of his exploits, and that reinforces his depression. Hamlet may need months to adjust to his fixed circumstances—and even then, he may harbor a sense that he's trapped and only half alive.

For some Hamlets, wayfaring becomes more than an escape from the workaday world—it becomes the very purpose of existence. Give Hamlet the money and the time and he's off. He cares not that he's interrupting a career or abandoning his household; he finds far more fulfillment on the road than on the job. And his style of traveling remains unconventional even into his thirties. Go to Flamingo Campground, the southernmost part of Everglades National Park, in the dead of winter. There, in a little tent amidst a fleet of recreational vehicles, you'll find a graying Hamlet watching the crepuscular flight of the ibis to their offshore rookeries. Go to the train station in Belgrade and grab yourself a seat on the overnight local to Athens, Greece. Sitting across from you: a Hamlet in her late thirties, carrying in a battered suitcase everything she needs for a six-week stay. Unburdened of responsibility, excited by fresh surroundings, Hamlet is free of the dilemma between heart and dollar, his state of mind transcendent.

Brent is one of those Hamlets who, if traveling were a career, would have a resume worthy of a corporate president. An avid backpacker and hiker, he's covered trails across the United States, Mexico, and Europe. As we noted in following his path through law school, he twice dropped out to travel: once to the Rocky Mountains and Alaska, once to Europe. "For five years, from law school to clerking to working in a firm, I worked *hard*. Not to make myself out as a hero, but that was a five-year period where I got more and more locked in. And I realized, when I left the law firm, that I hadn't been camping since before I started law school. I really like backpacking and camping. I just like to be off in the woods. I'm happy. I smile. I relax. Just me and dirt and rocks and trees and insects. But between the ages of twenty-five and thirty, the prime time for doing that sort of thing, I had a car, a tent, all the equipment—I was Mister Backpacker—and yet I never got out. I really felt *deprived*. Now I backpack more, go kayaking, try to make up for that lost time."

Maxine's brother and his family live in Brazil, which gives her an excuse (as if one were necessary) to go to Rio de Janeiro for weeks at a time. Her immersion in Brazil's largely native, predominantly Catholic, non–English-speaking culture gave her new insight into the great American ethos. "People in Brazil would walk two miles out of their way for you, just because they knew you were so-and-so's sister. If they were your friend, they'd double over backwards to make things easier for you. That's because they don't have anything else but each other. They're happiest sitting around with other people. I don't think that's true in the United States. Americans are antisocial in a lot of ways. They want their own house with a white picket fence, and they don't want to share what they have. They don't even want to share time. They're like squirrels. They want their own little pile of stuff for a rainy day. I'm torn between the two ways of living. I want my own little place the way I want it, but after a few days of that I want company in the evening."

Unfortunately for Hamlet, travel can't go on forever. Sooner or later the learning has to cease, the respite from the Hamlet Syndrome has to end. Like an escaped prisoner hauled back to jail, Hamlet finds his sentence to the workaday world all the more intolerable after his taste of freedom. One Hamlet couple, having run out of money after camping all over the United States and Canada for a year, vowed to save enough principal to travel permanently on the interest. On their paltry salaries they'll need years to reach that sum—but it's the first worldly ambition they've ever labored to fulfill.

* * *

Some Hamlets try to escape the heart-or-dollar dilemma by leaving home; others try to escape by *creating* one. For the female Hamlet convinced that the only way to win is not to play the game, motherhood seems a golden opportunity to bow from competition gracefully. A baby gives her a perfectly acceptable excuse for delaying—perhaps permanently—the choice between following her heart and toiling for the dollar. But motherhood isn't as clean an escape from the torment of the Hamlet Syndrome as she might think. To understand why, we first need to understand the female Hamlet in the context of society.

Since the beginning of the twentieth century the United States has made great strides in its treatment of women. Today America may even be the least sexist country in the Western world. But that's faint praise when one considers just how sexist our society remains. Sure, a few women are slowly percolating toward the top levels of business and government, but our basic assumptions about male and female roles have gone largely unchanged. Men dominate. They go out into the world, make a living for the family, and perform the duties that require aggression or physical strength. Women submit. They keep the house, take care of the children, and perform the duties that require emotional support. The fact that most women now work hasn't changed our assumption about their role; the vast majority of working women labor at *support* positions, and then are *still* expected to do the bulk of housework, shopping, child care, and emotional buttressing.

The feminist movement of the sixties and seventies sought to change our assumptions and equalize the relationship between American men and women. Contrary to the allegations of the movement's detractors, the new feminists, except for a few extremists, had no intention of demeaning the role of motherhood or housewifery. They simply wanted women to have the same opportunities men did, and wanted men to play a more supportive role domestically. If, with the entire spectrum of choices open to her, a woman still opted to become a housewife and a mother, that was fine. The important thing was that she *have* a choice; no one quibbled with her decision to be a wife and mother so long as she made it of her own free will.

Female Hamlets grew up with the feminist movement. They read Germaine Greer and Betty Friedan and maybe even Simone de Beauvoir. They watched Gloria Steinem and Jane Fonda and Billie Jean King on TV. Smart young women, female Hamlets realized the movement was fighting for *them*, and to one degree or another they came to identify with the feminist cause. But by the time they graduated from college the women's movement had withered under a resurgence of traditional stereotypes. The effort to change our basic assumptions about male and female roles collapsed, and society went on expecting women to shut up and take a backseat to the men in their lives.

What's happened as a result of feminism's flowering and subsequent decline is that the female Hamlet, a firm believer in women's rights, feels an obligation to capitalize on the opportunities her older sisters struggled so hard to open up for her. But that requires great courage of conviction in these reactionary times. How much easier it would be to escape from the rat race and have a baby! Ms. Hamlet thinks. (Only after baby keeps her awake every night for a week does she realize how wrong she was to think that.) At the time she decides to conceive, motherhood strikes the female Hamlet as a socially acceptable delaying tactic.

But motherhood doesn't delay the choice between heart and dollar—motherhood *makes* the choice. A pregnant female Hamlet *has* to go for the dollar, and here's why. She needs money, lots of it, to pay for furniture, strollers, clothing, diapers, toys. She needs doctors and hospitals, health insurance and child care. She needs a blender and a television and an automobile. She has to start caring about the quality of the neighborhood, the size of her dwelling, and the reputation of the local schools; if any of those fall short of her standards she has to spend incredible amounts of money to make an improvement. Previously she got by on next to nothing. Now she may reel from shock as she discovers that her would-be escape from the Hamlet Syndrome has made her part of the mainstream, money-crazy world.

Perhaps because they understand how motherhood can trap them, few female Hamlets, even those in stable, long-term love relationships, elect to have children. But what can we say about those who do? Generally, the stronger and happier a female Hamlet's network of relationships, the less concerned she is about professional success and the more willing she is to play wife and mother. (Female Hamlets with leaner support networks tend to focus more on their work lives.) A strong network of relationships consists of a stable sexual partnership, a number of close friends, and meaningful family ties. A female Hamlet fortunate enough to possess such a network still has feminist leanings, but identifies more with the *people* in her life than with her job. Her heart is therefore likely to tell her that it's all right to become "just a housewife," to extend her network of happy relationships to a new generation.

A Chicago Hamlet who describes herself as a "shaman, home-maker, mom, and eternal scholar," says, "When I got pregnant, I couldn't find it in me to have an abortion, even though having a child conflicted with my educational aspirations. I couldn't give it up for adoption, either." So she dropped out of college and put her personal goals on hold. For her, the feminist battlefront has moved from the workplace to the hearth. She tries to instill in her daughter a healthy mix of male and female attitudes: "Open-mindedness, yet strength of conviction. Self-sufficiency, yet interdependence. To feel deeply, yet retain emotional control. And this above all, to her own self be true."

Despite the worldly hassles of raising a child, many female Hamlets consider it a relief from the pressures of the workaday world. Says one, the mother of a two-year-old: "I hate to say it, but if I don't have to make money, I won't. My husband and I look forward to the day our various debts will be paid off, and then I may do something with my Ph.D. in psychology, but I hope it won't be full-time. I just don't feel any frantic need to get more and more power or money. I'd rather live in my head and with my friends."

Ma Hamlet can make motherhood work to her advantage. By having a baby she's conformed to society's expectation of women, so she might as well make the best of it and add the convictions of her heart to baby's upbringing. She can bring feminism to the home, insisting that her husband participate extensively in child care and teaching her child to assume sexual equality. We've seen how some Hamlets seek to combine heart and dollar by going to law school, and we've noted how their attempt usually ends in failure. We suspect that motherhood harbors more potential for success. Ma Hamlet, after all, is her own boss (although sometimes she suspects the real boss is Hamlet junior). She has no competition. And unlike Hamlet the attorney-at-law, she loves her little client. As long as she keeps guilt and boredom at bay, remains committed to sexual equality, and continues to grow intellectually (and those are *very big* provisos), there's a chance her ersatz delaying tactic can turn into a happy resolution of the Hamlet Syndrome.

18

To Do or Not to Do

Thus conscience does make cowards of us all,
And thus the native hue of resolution
Is sicklied o'er with the pale cast of thought,
And enterprises of great pitch and moment
With this regard their currents turn awry,
And lose the name of action.

Hamlet, ACT III, SCENE i

That's how Shakespeare's Hamlet says, "Once we start to think about the great things we want to do, they stop looking so wonderful, and we lose our will to do them." Modern Hamlets share their namesake's ability to diminish ambition through the power of thought. Hey, that sounds really neat! the modern Hamlet may exclaim when he first hears about some project, but when he thinks about it, maybe gets involved in it a bit, he finds a dozen reasons not to follow through. He's especially skilled at finding reasons not to work at jobs commensurate with his ability. We saw some of that in Noelle's and Brent's reactions to a career in law. Hamlet may desire the dollar, but the more he thinks about it the less compelling that desire becomes.

Hamlet thinks too much about the consequences of making a living, and that puts a damper on his ambition to succeed. But look at it another way: By alerting him to the compromises he would have to make to compete in the American free enterprise system, his proclivity for pondering actually *helps* him. Accepting those compromises would destroy his heart and leave him forever miserable and bitter. Realizing that his integrity means more than a pile of C-notes, he heeds his dissuading thoughts and forsakes conventional, material success. He removes himself to the fringes of society, reasoning in typical black-and-white fashion that if he can't make money the right way—that is, without harming himself, the environment, and others—he'd rather not make money at all. In this respect the rest of us could take a lesson from Hamlet; if we all gave some thought to the consequences of our livelihoods and had the guts to put our principles ahead of our paychecks, the world might be a more livable place.

From Hamlet's perspective, the system routinely and unapologetically harms everyone it touches. It starts by glorifying masochism, known more familiarly by the euphemisms *dedication* and *sacrifice*. Especially during these times of economic decline, employers expect their employees to make up for corporate shortfalls by working harder for less compensation. To Hamlet's astonishment, more often than not his coworkers eagerly oblige. "That's sick!" he thinks. Why should anyone slave away for extra hours or in dangerous conditions if it doesn't interest him or he has better things to do? Let the stockholders do the filing and typing if they're so concerned about the company's performance! Sacrifice yourself for someone who'll appreciate you, not for someone who'll fire you the minute you show signs of burning out from stress.

Hamlet detests the conformity imposed on the average American worker. He's a genuine individualist—uninterested in wearing massproduced clothes, drinking mass-produced beer, and driving massproduced cars—and he balks at wearing a business suit or other uniform, eating the processed slop that passes for lunch in most downtown cafeterias, and reining in his wry sense of humor because he knows the office nitwits won't understand him. Work imposes too much order on his schedule: nine-to-five, nine-to-five, nine-to-five, nine-to-five, nine-to-five. And how is anyone supposed to be happy with just two weeks' vacation? As we discovered in the section on travel, Hamlet's idea of a vacation starts at two *months*. The worst part of the conformity game, however, is the company's demand for loyalty, as if Hamlet should value the business's welfare above his own. A corporation is nothing more than a legal entity, lifeless in itself; how can he care for that above his flesh and blood? That, he thinks, is fascism, and Hamlet's not so afraid for his job that he subordinates his interests to the company's.

Remember, too, that Hamlet comes out of college an idealist. He regards as reprehensible the business world's obsession with profit to the exclusion of all else. Want to get a rise out of him? Tell him about some corporation that knowingly marketed a deadly product because it calculated that after all the lawsuits it would still come out ahead. Although Hamlet doesn't usually subscribe to socialism, he does believe that people should come before profits. For that matter, the environment should come before profits, too. To better live in accordance with his ideals, Hamlet seeks work that does as little damage to the world as possible.

For most people, money is the prime consideration in choosing a job. They measure their self-respect in direct proportion to their salary. But Hamlet measures his self-respect in terms of how true he is to himself. He evaluates a job not just by its earnings potential, but by the level of commitment it demands, by the amount of stress it causes, by its moral implications, and by its environmental consequences. That doesn't leave him much to choose from. He can go into the public service professions, such as library and hospital work. He can join the customer service sector by waiting tables in a restaurant or stocking shelves at a bookstore. He can accept a position on the clerical staff of a nonprofit organization. None of these jobs pay very well or present much opportunity for fulfillment, so he puts off work as long as possible, looking for other options. But sooner or later Hamlet will have to deal with the great bugaboo: getting a job and earning a living.

Although Hamlet has compelling reasons for renouncing the dogfight for the dollar, he's not *so* radically opposed to the capitalist system that he drops out of it entirely—joins the hard-core unemployed or becomes a revolutionary. He's grown up too middle-class to fall *that* far outside the mainstream. He prefers what looks to him like middle ground: a job that allows him to remain financially independent yet keeps him on the fringe of the nation's corrupt economic system. Whereas his buddies in engineering may be designing weapons and his friends in business may be bilking old ladies out of savings, Hamlet can't harm the public as a flunkie. That kind of security—the security of conscience—matters more to him than the security of a hefty investment portfolio. Whenever others judge him by his paltry salary, he can respond that it's better to be poor and true to one's self than to be rich in the service of an inhumane system.

Hamlet doesn't object to work per se. Indeed, he's happy to work hours on end, day after day, at something he enjoys. Even in a conventional work setting he makes an excellent employee, because he's conscientious, thorough, and capable of solving problems quickly and efficiently. But Hamlet does bring a monumentally bad attitude to the job. Except for the paycheck, he sees little reason to forfeit the best forty hours of his week to labor that's not fulfilling. Since he doesn't tie his identity to his job, he resents that work takes up the bulk of his time and energy, leaving none for projects of his own. The people he works with may bother him as well; once he knows the parameters of his responsibilities he detests supervision, and he often wishes his nattering mainstream co-workers would shut up or disappear. And always there's that emphasis on money, money, money that makes him want to throw up. Here he is, convinced there's more to life than a BMW and the bottom line, and everyone around him is carrying on about their latest technological gewgaw and the company's quarterly statement.

Fresh out of college, Hamlet can take a lowly post and not raise consternation among his family and friends. The folks may be tickled that he's finally on his own, no longer a financial burden. They may even mistake his getting a job for boldness, considering that so many of his friends run off to Europe or to grad school. If he's working at a dead-end position, Mom and Dad can reason that Hamlet's young, with plenty of time to fiddle around before he gets serious about a career, and besides, the experience will do him good. Friends treat Hamlet just as they always have. He's still the same old guy, a little weird but fun to converse with. There's no reason to look down on him, because he may be making as much in his dead-end job as his friends are making in their entry-level positions. He's certainly earning more than his friends in graduate school. Those first few years after college Hamlet can flounder without feeling like he's drowning. He's so happy just to be on his own that his modest way of life entirely contents him. *I'm afloat,* he exults, *and ain't life grand. I can go on this way forever.*

Perhaps, in a vacuum, Hamlet could go on that way forever, but by his late twenties the situation changes. Time and expectation begin to intrude on his relationships with other people. He's had several years to find a niche for himself, so why is he still running the office photocopier and fetching coffee for the bosses? Mom and Dad wonder.

They think he's had time enough to establish himself. Their friends have a kid younger than Hamlet whose income is swelling toward six figures, and another couple down the street just announced their child's graduation from medical school. What are Mom and Dad supposed to say when they're asked what Hamlet's doing? Hamlet's friends also wonder at him. Those who started as entry-level auditors and adjusters now hold spots in middle management. They're buying new cars and houses, starting families. To them, Hamlet hasn't changed since college, and his complaints about society and the world in general are getting old. It looks like a split is inevitable; his friends think Hamlet's refusing to grow up, and Hamlet thinks his friends are selling out. Before long, Hamlet feels the only people who understand and accept him are a few close friends and family members.

If Hamlet languishes without direction into his thirties, he comes to resemble the two composite characters we described at the beginning of this book. To look at him you'd swear he was a winner—but he's going absolutely nowhere. Time begins to work some subtle but profound changes in his personality. After so many years away from college the intensity of his convictions dissipates; the choice between the heart and dollar no longer appears as stark as it once did. As a result, he now leads his unconventional life-style as much out of habit as out of principle. The prolonged separation from a learning environment affects him intellectually as well: Although he still reads and keeps up on what's happening, his mind loses some of its sharpness. And several years as a petty functionary condition him to think that he's capable of nothing more, that he's reached his limit and will never attain conventional success. His world takes on a static quality, and Hamlet begins to steel himself for a life of disappointment.

But let's not shed tears for our workaday Hamlet just yet. In many ways his life is better than that of his conventionally successful peers. He's remained true to himself, and has kept his conscience clear. His job may frustrate him, but he doesn't spend sleepless nights fretting over it like his middle management counterparts. Fuzzy as his thinking may have grown, he's still more alert, more turned on, more intimately connected to the wider world than friends who've retraced a path back to America's sheltered way of life. And, ironically, Hamlet may be more secure financially than high-salaried go-getters the same age. Perhaps it's a legacy of his secure upbringing, or perhaps it's the inevitable consequence of his realization that material possessions don't bring happiness, but more often than not Hamlet manages to *save* a portion of his meager salary. He lives below his means and doesn't go into hock buying gim-cracks and nights on the town. He doesn't take out loans to finance cars, vacations, houses. His conventionally successful friends may be living from paycheck to paycheck, but some Hamlets have so much money saved that if they stop working they can survive in the style to which they're accustomed for a year or more—and still have a cushion left over. Indeed, many Hamlets use their extra money in this manner, quitting a job and going unemployed for months before they take another post. Hamlet may deem money the root of all evil, but he's not above using it to buy time and freedom, commodities he genuinely covets. He may also use his savings to take extended vacations, satisfying whims that jealous mainstreamers, limited to two-week respites, have to postpone until retirement.

Still, by his mid-thirties the stigma of his second-class status frus-trates Hamlet. He knows he's better than his job, and he knows that people far less intelligent and talented than he have risen to remunera-tive posts—witness his supervisors. He wants something better than he has. But now it's pretty much too late to start climbing the career ladder. By the time he'd get someplace successful he'd have to retire. Besides, the system is just as screwed up now as it was when he graduated from college—why should he compromise himself after all these years? Torn between his desire for more and his reluctance to get it, knowing his options are slipping away for the last time, Hamlet arrives at the great crisis of his adult life: *to do or not to do.* He has too much sense of self-worth, too much of that old desire for the dollar, to accept going through the rest of his life as an underling. But even though he thinks about it all the time, he can't bring himself to *do* something, to swallow that pride and principle and summon some ambition! In many ways Hamlet's adult crisis resembles the crisis of his college years: Which way does he go? The major difference is that he no longer has the luxury of time; whichever direction he chooses now, that's the one he follows to the end. Nor will doing nothing suffice, as it did in college. This time Hamlet *has* to take action, make a move for himself, if he hopes to avoid a permanent malaise.

Let's say our thirty-five-year-old Hamlet decides to shoot for con-ventional success. The quickest route to the top of the corporate hierar-chy is sales, yet Hamlet can't even call up the courage and aggression to sell ice cubes to a desert dweller. It's simply not in him. Most Hamlets know themselves well enough not to seek employment as salespeople, but at the very beginning of his work life Jeff, our hippie Hamlet, tried to make a go of it. Lacking the boldness to bargain face-to-face (and not wanting to cut his hair), he went to work as a telephone solicitor for a firm that sold aluminum storm windows and awnings. He found the job very entertaining—but in the end he didn't have the touch.

"You had these people in these boiler rooms—that's what we called the phone rooms—who were never going to make it in the mainstream, *ever.* You had one guy who weighed four hundred pounds, one guy with a bum leg. These are people you see on downtown streets and you wonder where they fit in. They don't look like spare-changers or boozer types, but they're just a little bit odd, and they're always downtown, which makes you think they probably sleep in some five-dollar-a-day hotel someplace. Then you have an occasional suburban kid like me pass through. There was one seminary student there, a really shy, introverted guy, nice in a midwestern sort of way. He looked like he should have been on the back forty milking cows. But put him on the phone and he just immersed himself in this different personality. He shoved it down their throats! He'd have more leads at the end of a day than anyone, day after day. He was fascinating to watch. For me it was always difficult to stuff it down their throats. I couldn't quite bring myself to do it.

"I remember one time when I did try. We had these out-of-town lines, and they were the easiest. These farmers out in Olathe or some-place—actually there aren't many farmers in Olathe—just get it in their skulls that they want some aluminum awnings. They probably just want a visitor, they don't see too many people. Of course half of them probably waited for the salesman on their front porch with a shotgun. Anyway, I was having a real frustrating day on this out-of-town line. I should have had four or five leads by then, but I had none at all, so I was determined to get the next call I made. This woman answers the phone, and I say, 'Hi, my name is Jeff Fakename and I'm from Pacemaker Products, wondering if you have aluminum combination storm windows on your house.' 'No, we're quite happy with our wood frames, we have a lovely house here, it's a three-story home about seventy-five years old and aluminum wouldn't be right.' I'm really pitching it, really going after her, but she's hanging tough. I was determined to make this sale, so I said, 'Did you know that in your town it's *illegal* to have wooden storm windows?' And she says, 'What's your name again?' I hung that phone right up. Turns out she was the wife of the editor of the town paper, and in that afternoon's edition there was a front-page article about some scam telephone solicitor telling you it's illegal to have wooden storm windows on your house. She identified the company and everything. Three deals had been made in this town the night before, and the salesmen were canceled, losing something like ten thousand dollars' worth of business in twenty-four hours. It wasn't long after that I left that job."

Jeff's next post: working as a janitor in the dental school cadaver rooms at the University of Missouri, Kansas City. That, understandably, didn't last long. For the next eight years, into his mid-thirties, he worked at a string of clerical jobs, taking several months off "blissfully unemployed" between each assignment. "I save up money rather easily. I don't buy a whole lot, just records, books, and food," he explains. But at age thirty-three Jeff began to wonder whether he wanted to live on the fringe for the rest of his life. He hit Hamlet's mid-life crisis, *to do or not to do.* We'll see how he handled this ultimate battle with the Hamlet Syndrome in the final part of the book.

Rarer still than a Hamlet in sales is the entrepreneurial Hamlet. One would think that Hamlet would *want* to be in business for himself, since then he could be his own boss and run his concern as ethically as he wished. But Hamlet simply has too much trouble putting himself forward to succeed as an independent businessperson. As Antonio, one of the few Hamlets to try entrepreneurship, can attest, unpleasant aspects of self-employment such as securing customers, negotiating payments, and deciding where the capital goes are much too troublesome to address head-on. "After I graduated from college I stopped playing the harpsichord for almost two years. But people approached me about starting a group, so I did. Not only did I start a group, I started three: a trio, a quartet, and a small chamber orchestra. I bought a 1938 Packard hearse to schlep everyone around in. I'd buy violins and have them rebuilt into baroque instruments—five hundred dollars a shot or more. It was a hoot—talk about a bohemian life-style! We played weddings, funerals. If someone even casually mentioned an event I gave them my card. But I didn't have any business acumen. I thought, if you're good enough, people will *give* you lots of money. Dead wrong! When the time came, I didn't know what to charge people. I charged them in terms of what I thought they wanted to pay, instead of what the music was worth in terms of buying tires and gasoline and violins. I lost money, I owed money. I went bankrupt."

So the chastened Antonio went to work as an accounting clerk. The fact that he had absolutely no background in accounting deterred him not a whit; if there's one thing Hamlet knows about service and clerical jobs it's that he's sharp enough to master them in a matter of days, maybe hours. Antonio also exemplifies Hamlet's ability to *make it* in the work world if he wants to. "I taught myself accounting and progressed from one job to another," Antonio recalls, "and I worked my way up to about fifteen thousand dollars a year. But I wasn't all that happy where I was. One Christmas I wasn't doing anything, so some friends invited me to tag along on a ski trip to Utah. Then they said, as long as you're here why not interview for some jobs? I came home from that Christmas vacation with six job offers. I accepted one from the University of Utah—it started at twenty-five thousand seven hundred dollars."

That's enough money for us to consider Antonio a dropout Hamlet as well as an artist, so we'll pick up his story again in a few pages, when we're discussing dropout Hamlets more fully. In the meantime, let's grant that Hamlet doesn't belong in hard-core business and discuss what happens to him when he looks for "safer" employment, which is what he usually does. Lacking the gumption to go into sales or pursue his own enterprise, and lacking as well specific job skills or qualifications, he falls into the first inoffensive position he can find. The pay doesn't matter so long as it's enough to live on. Nor does he care that the position leads nowhere, and that he'll have to switch companies to advance. Hamlet may even find his first job pleasurable, taking pride in doing well and enjoying the new atmosphere, so different from the university he just left behind.

Martin's work history is atypical in that he's held the same dead-end job for a decade—"find a rut and stay in it," he quips—whereas most Hamlets stick with an unchallenging job only a couple of years or so, then move on to another drudge position. But in every other respect his story is characteristic. He sorts and delivers mail for a large nonprofit organization, putting in the standard eight-hour day five days per week. The job pays well enough for him to afford a one-bedroom apartment, all the books and art supplies he needs, and equipment and ingredients for brewing beer at home. He saves a portion of each paycheck, and so despite the appearance of modest means he's financially secure. Talking to Martin about how he found his job, one is tempted to think he was born six hundred years too late—the fixed destinies of the medieval period may have suited him better. "It would be nice to feel like you're assigned some mission at birth and it's drilled into your brain. I'm not suggesting they do this, I'm just saying it would be nice," he chuckles apologetically. He then invokes shades-of-gray logic to explain why he became a mailperson. "They throw out a billion choices, whether you want to be a flight attendant, a garbage collector, whatever. There are just so many choices I couldn't decide. So I took what fell my way, which was the mail. My friend's mother called and asked me, 'Do you want this job?' and I said yes. That's the only reason I'm there. It's not like I said, 'Oh wow, that's the job for me!' "

Overall, Martin doesn't mind doing the mail, but he admits that his job has its share of frustrations. "In the beginning I didn't know what I was doing, so it took me all day to do the mail. But soon I got everything organized, and I was at work eight hours but actually *working* only four hours. The rest of the time I was either reading, writing monster letters, or doing artwork. They all knew it upstairs, but they didn't know what to do with me. Finally they said, 'Would you like to make more money?' I said sure. So they tacked on all this posting, filing, and xeroxing. That was years ago, and I'm still doing it. I've asked them to dump it on somebody else, but they ask me 'What will you do with all that free time?' And I say, 'I can go back to reading, writing, and doing my artwork.' I don't think they're buying that," he concedes with a laugh.

That's one way Hamlet finds satisfaction in his underemployment: He masters his duties so thoroughly that he gets everything finished in a few hours, leaving him the rest of the day to pursue his own projects— reading, writing, socializing—on company time. He suffers not a shred of guilt; he's done his job, hasn't he? But the bosses, already ruffled by Hamlet's bad attitude, resent what they see as freeloading. They either humiliate Hamlet by finding petty tasks for him or they add to his responsibilities. Money enticed Martin into accepting more responsibility, but now he regrets the decision and wants his time back. Most Hamlets have the same priorities. They aren't the least bit interested in their work; they want to keep the job simple so they have more time for things that *really* matter. To them, job security means coming to the same uncomplicated, quickly finished assignment every day—and being left alone by the bosses.

Because he's so obviously overqualified for his job, friends and strangers alike constantly ask Hamlet what he's doing there. "My former girlfriend once asked me, 'Why is an intelligent person like you doing such a mindless job?' " Martin relates. "I didn't really have a good answer to that." The question puzzles him the same way the question

"What are you going to do when you graduate?" confounded him during his senior year in college. "Maybe it's the confidence factor," he speculates, referring to his expertise at foreseeing the negative consequences of actions. "A lot of people don't give a second thought to what they do. Me, I always think of the worst. I always imagine the worst thing that can happen whenever I consider doing anything, and that's usually enough to persuade me not to do it."

After he ponders a minute, he warms up to the question and waxes more philosophical. "Why should I knock my brains out trying to achieve something? A lot of people say self-satisfaction. But *what* self-satisfaction? You're going through hell to achieve some goal which, if and when you achieve it, you probably don't notice or you realize it wasn't worth it. I'm not willing to go through agony to achieve something that I'm not that determined to do. Maybe I *am* just floundering through life. But it's *controlled floundering*—it's what I want to do."

But where does Hamlet find fulfillment, if he doesn't find it in his work? Surely the knowledge that he's true to himself cannot alone sustain him through the dark nights of his soul, when he questions his motives and wonders whether he really is, as society tells him, a loser. Almost every Hamlet we interviewed seriously pursues an artistic or otherwise creative endeavor that gives him the satisfaction of achievement the workplace can't provide. Antonio, of course, is a concert-level harpsichordist. After a full day of work he often goes home to practice his Bach and Scarlatti until midnight. Jeff plays guitar and draws. Martin also draws, and in the last few years he's learned the rudiments of carpentry, constructing cabinets and backyard decks for friends of his. We can go on: Brent plays the banjo; Maxine plays guitar, sings, and writes mystery novels; Jessica also writes, but she prefers the romance genre.

Hamlet has enormous respect for the arts, steeping himself in music, literature, and the visual media. Although he keeps himself informed of the latest artistic developments, he holds a traditionalist's reverence for craft, and his own creations generally reflect the time-honored standards of his chosen medium. Because the society he lives in undervalues art, his creative endeavors must remain an avocation. But in a world so purposeless and painful, art at least fulfills Hamlet's troubled heart and gives meaning to his otherwise somber existence.

Should Hamlet respond to the to-do-or-not-to-do question with half-hearted actions or no action at all, he risks serious damage to his psyche.

Years of taking orders and performing nondescript tasks gnaw away at his self-esteem, leaving him with the conviction that he's incapable of anything better. He's gone so long without serious intellectual challenge that he's lost much of his ability to think through complicated problems. So down Hamlet goes. He's lived half his life, and what has he accomplished? Nothing, really. His brain's a blob, he hasn't many friends, he lacks material comforts, and he's made no lasting impact anywhere. All he has to show for the first four decades of his life are wasted opportunities, a set of ideals grown cold, and a pervasive feeling of bitterness.

Hamlet often directs his bitterness at the outside world, blaming his failure on a benighted social order, but deep down he's really bitter at himself. He knows that he's to blame for his inability to accomplish anything. Somewhere along the line he should have gotten going, taken a more realistic view of the world and dared to find some middle ground between the heart and dollar. But he got too secure in his flunkie job, his barely furnished apartment, his lonely nights and weekends. He let the time slip by—wasted it—and now unpitying time wastes him.

For dropout Hamlets the question isn't whether to do or not to do, it's whether to keep doing or stop. The dropout Hamlet goes through college feeling much the same as any other Hamlet but, bowing to pressure both internal and external, he either advances to professional school (which he completes) or embarks on a genuine career. Once out in the working world he uses his intelligence to get ahead, and in a short time he finds himself working long hours at a demanding job—and making scads of money. By most anybody's standard, including his own, he's a success. But in the midst of satisfying his compulsion for the dollar he takes a closer look at his life. Is this really worth it? He may own the fancy car he always dreamed of, may live in a plush condominium, may in fact possess all the material possessions he ever wanted—but his heart is aching. He's gained the world and lost his soul. Feeling like an impostor, he wonders what he's doing in this elevated realm, among all these polished corporate pooh-bahs. He's under constant pressure to produce, with no life of his own, and he can't remember the last time he truly relaxed. So before his spiritual angina turns into a full-fledged infarction he quits his high-powered life-style—stops *doing*—and indulges his Hamlet nature to the fullest.

Because he's known success, the dropout Hamlet suffers few of the emotional problems common among Hamlets older than thirty. He doesn't feel the need to prove himself that less-accomplished Hamlets do. He's lived the good life long enough to realize it's not for him, so he's easily contented with an unadorned existence. And whereas other Hamlets privately nurse their bitterness at themselves, the dropout Hamlet carries himself with assurance and dignity. He's secure, but secure in the *best* sense of the word: He knows himself thoroughly and accepts himself for what he is.

However, the dropout Hamlet does have problems adjusting to his new place in society. When he held his prestigious position, he took for granted the respect of the community at large, but now that he's abdicated that life for a fringe existence the people who once praised him scorn him. They can't figure out why he's thrown his life away, but from their point of view the reason can't be very sensible. So they patronize him, sometimes spurn him. The dropout Hamlet gets an up-close lesson in class division: Here he is, the very same bright and charming guy he's always been, suddenly treated as a second-class citizen because he's taken a subordinate job. He resents that society judges him by his earning power rather than his essence—even though he's always known that that's how people measure one another in America.

Too sensitive for the middle class and higher, too proud for the working class and lower, the dropout Hamlet feels he's totally without a niche. Should the dislocation become unbearable he's likely to flee the mainstream entirely. He'll take *years* off from work, living off savings or whatever he can raise doing odd jobs, just to escape the class-riddled judgments of other people. Occasionally he'll try the opposite tack—succumbing to a fit of the "I'll show thems" and chasing conventional accomplishment once more—but his second fling with the big time lasts only as long as it takes him to remember why he originally left it.

We've gotten bits and pieces of Brent's story in other chapters. After a crisis-ridden but auspicious matriculation at an Ivy League school, he became an economic analyst. That paid well but left him feeling dissatisfied, so after a year he quit and roved from the Rocky Mountains to Alaska. He went from there to law school, where he excelled, and he subsequently won a clerkship with a federal judge. He dreaded joining a major law firm, but did it anyway. "I was on the fast track. I was *stuck* in the fast lane. But I realized I wasn't happy there. That wasn't how I wanted to live. People at the law firm used to eat out every night because the money didn't matter, whereas I'd like to go home and cook. There were a couple of people there who on weekends would

fly down to Atlantic City to gamble. They needed more hits of excitement
and challenge than they were getting as leading corporate litigators! They
thrived on being in the spotlight, everything being intense and pressured. But I'd come home and lie down on the lawn for half an hour just
to decompress.

"I always felt like I was in disguise when I was a lawyer, like I was
an actor. I didn't feel like it was really me. A friend of mine described
her first day as a lawyer as someone coming in to talk about some
problem and asking her, 'What do you think?' and her almost blurting,
'Sounds like you need to talk to a lawyer!' That's how I always felt—and
I never got over that feeling."

After a year Brent quit the law firm. His girlfriend took a job in
Europe, and he went with her, there to rediscover an old passion: music.
He picked up the banjo his parents had given him as a law school
graduation present and quickly learned to play it well. "In the spring of
1986 we were living in Europe, and I became a street musician. I just
did it. It was fun, a lark." When he returned to the United States, he
couldn't bring himself to rejoin the workaday world. He started playing
with a country and western band instead, and that's what he's been doing
ever since. "I've been totally stalling on going back to work," he admits,
"because I realize I shouldn't do it until my heart is in it. I feel like I
should get involved in some things, but I don't really want to. Like, when
I came back from Europe I talked to the Sierra Club Legal Defense Fund,
and they said fine, come on down, start doing some stuff. But even though
I'm very committed to the environment, I didn't go. I really didn't want
to, so I didn't."

Brent describes the reaction of mainstream people to his decision
to drop out. "After I left the law firm my mother said, 'Well, he'll never
work another day in his life.' She was really cynical about me. My father
keeps coming up with suggestions like 'Why don't you call so-and-so?'
Then I have friends at law firms who say, 'Gee, we need somebody, it
would be great to have you come here.' But I've been on hold for almost
two years. I'm not to the point where connections are severed, but as time
goes on that's becoming a real danger."

Brent has little idea where to go from here. He hasn't found anything sufficiently exciting to make him want to act. "Last spring I seriously investigated going into private practice, but then I found out how
much liability insurance costs. It's still something I think about. I also

thought about teaching law, but I don't have the ambition to get into the academic rat race. The possibility of teaching actually came up at a certain point, but I thought, they're going to want me to come to the campus, deliver a paper, give a little seminar or speech. Then I'm going to have to write a law review article and start hobnobbing with members of the faculty. I don't want to do that!" Like most dropout Hamlets, he's more or less happy with the status quo. "I think that for me part of the Hamlet Syndrome is arrested development. I want to remain a person with a lot of potential, somewhat precocious, and just freeze at that stage. That's impossible, but I think there's a lot of that in my psychology, not wanting to pay the dues of fulfilling all that potential."

Then there's Antonio, who, we discovered just a few pages ago, taught himself accounting so well that he qualified for a well-paying job at the University of Utah in Salt Lake City. "I didn't know anything about Utah," says the harpsichordist Hamlet. "It wasn't so much the job offers that enticed me to go, but the access to all that money, and not being poor anymore. I went there knowing only that I was going to be a wealthy guy. And I was. It was wonderful making all that money—but as I lived there longer it became evident it was not a good thing. Affluence did crazy things to me. There I was in middle-class American society. I bought a condominium, two sports cars, one of which I modified for racing. I got a cat, lots of clothes. And the prestige! I worked as a senior accountant, and I didn't have a degree in accounting! Ah, the prestige of being the only black, an educated black, among all these gringos." But the abundance of dollars couldn't quiet the longings of his heart. "All the time there was this shadow right behind me, this musician who had been following me around all these years. I was constantly cognizant of him, and I kept denying him, but he finally caught up with me.

"Mine was the sort of accounting job where there's a financial crisis every day. I went to work one day and was called into my immediate supervisor's office to answer questions about some accounts that were my responsibility. He wanted to know why they weren't done, and I just said to myself, 'This is it, I don't want to do this anymore. I'm not this thing I'm pretending to be.' So I quit that day.

"I sold one car right off. The second car I drove to California for a vacation, but it broke down, so I sold it to a dealer and took the train back to Utah. I moved back into the city, got an apartment. I didn't want to do accounting, I wasn't really interested in going back to music just yet, so there was a two-year period of not knowing what to do. Finally I decided to pursue a master's degree in music performance.

"I know at age forty I should be rich or something close to rich. You know, the money, the car. I learned an expression: A man should make as much money as he is old. So my income should be forty thousand dollars a year. But poverty doesn't frighten me. Sure, I want a car, but why does it have to be a BMW? I'm told by people and the media, and sometimes myself, that enough is *not* enough. And yet the thing that always wells out of my gut is that this *is* enough. One *can* live well without being ostentatious. Not only well but comfortably, with integrity."

There's a complicating factor in Antonio's switch from the upper class to the lower: his dark skin. Not only does he have to put up with class bias, but as a black man on the lower end of the economic ladder he has to put up with racial bias as well. "It's a little wearisome to work as a secretary now while I'm a graduate student because I find myself spending a lot of energy making my presence a comfortable thing for other people. A forty-year-old male, black classical musician who's a secretary. People have a lot of trouble with that. They expect me to shuffle, to bounce a basketball in one hand and a baseball in the other, all the while baring my teeth and singing jazz. Wish I knew how to do that!" he laughs. "Where can I go to learn those things?"

How about your future, Antonio? Ever tempted to go back to the good life? "I'm still wrestling with the possibility of having a career. It's really seductive to me. But I'd never go back to accounting. I'm a person who has to do something with his hands. I have to create; I am an artist. The mode of expression doesn't matter to me. But a calculator and ledger book and pencil are not workable vehicles for an artist. I would sweep floors first, I really would. I could go back and start another musical group, but they'd have to be special people. They'd have to be people who weren't afraid of poverty, because there's a lot of poverty in what we'd pursue."

He shrugs and sighs. "My life seems to have been bumbling from one mistake to another, but I don't mind that. I don't fault myself. So I haven't got good foresight, okay? At least I look good," he laughs. Unfortunately, Antonio's prospects for completing the master's program in harpsichord performance don't look as good as he does (and he is indeed exceptionally handsome). While preparing for the concert that would give him his degree, he severely strained ligaments in his thumbs and wrists, necessitating surgery. He'll need two years to heal, rehabilitate, and recover his skills. Had he never known conventional success the deferral of his dream at such a late age would probably have devastated him. But in spite of physical pain, the ignominy of his job, and the delayed gratification, Antonio carries himself with the dignity of a winner.

Even if Hamlet was a typical American in every other respect—and some, like Martin, eat just as many Whoppers and watch just as much TV as anyone—he'd be regarded as a deviant simply because he doesn't define himself by the work he does. Asked "Who are you?" most Americans, after giving their name, say what they do for a living. "I'm a banker." "I run the export division at a scrap metal brokerage." Hamlet, after giving his name, usually just shrugs. When pressed he'll describe his vocation in the vaguest terms: "I work for the Boffo Corporation." He leaves it to your imagination as to what he actually *does* for Boffo. He's ashamed, yes, but he's also saying he's more than his job. I'm a whole person, I have a context greater than the functions I perform to earn money, he says. That attitude doesn't usually go over well in mainstream society, and so no matter how wholesome and upstanding he may otherwise be, Hamlet winds up on the outside. His distaste for the dollar makes him an outsider even when it comes to matters of the heart—love—as we'll see in the next section.

19

Get Thee to a Singles Bar

T here's the story, perhaps apocryphal, attributed to the English dramatist George Bernard Shaw. At a gathering of London's upper crust, his eyes fell upon a gorgeous young dame sitting at the table next to his. "My dear," he asked, plunking himself down in a chair alongside her, "if I were to give you one million pounds, would you go to bed with me?" "A million pounds!" sputtered the lissome lass. "Why, for that much, I suppose I *would* go to bed with you." Shaw nodded his approval and leaned toward her. "My dear," he cooed, "if I were to give you *one* pound, would you go to bed with me?" The dame half rose out of her chair in umbrage. "Why, sir, just what do you think I am?" "We've already established that," Shaw replied, "and all we're doing now is negotiating a price."

Sex and money have always gone together; almost every culture traditionally includes some form of dowry with marriage. The purpose of parentally arranged marriages, still common in some parts of the world, is to enhance each family's financial and social status. In the United States we don't have much history of dowries and arranged marriages, but we still measure our romantic couplings in financial terms, starting with who pays for the date and how much the man shells out for an engagement ring. Women look for men with earnings potential. Men look for women whose physical beauty sparks envy—read that *esteem*—in other men's eyes. We like to think we're more sophisticated than that, that we choose one another for nobler reasons, like love. But Hollywood fantasies notwithstanding, we hardly ever find love between a millionaire and a homeless person, a rock star and a Plain Jane, a female executive and a hobo. The formula is simple: Calculate your financial worth and potential. Add the value of your looks. Now go out and find someone whose overall financial and sexual value is about the same. What's that, Hamlet, you say you don't have much financial worth or potential? Then you damn well better look good, because otherwise you may come away from the sexual marketplace empty-handed.

An attractive female Hamlet, if she's so inclined, can rise above the Hamlet Syndrome by mating herself to a wealthy or ambitious man. So long as she loves him and can tolerate the insecurity of financial dependence she'll be all right. But for most other Hamlets the prospects for finding a satisfying love relationship range from marginal to practically none. Their idiosyncratic world view drastically narrows the field of potential lovers. Consider the male Hamlet. He has minimal earnings potential, meaning he can't provide the material security the bulk of American women crave. Even worse, perhaps, he *thinks* differently. He questions the traditional family structure and may not want kids. He doesn't like the free enterprise system. He has offbeat notions about religion and government. He's honest to the point of rudeness. And fun as he may be to listen to sometimes, after a while his constant intellectualizing sounds like the bleating of a newly shorn sheep. Better to find a regular guy who knows how to have a good time.

The female Hamlet unwilling to sell herself to a Sugar Daddy runs into even greater tribulations. She's a more incisive thinker than most men, and few things threaten an American man more than an intelligent mate. Much as she may try, she can't hide her intelligence for long, and rather than contend with an equal (or superior) the typical American male begs off. Perhaps that's just as well. A female Hamlet wants an honest, communicative, sensitive man who treats her as an equal, not a chauvinistic lunk looking for someone to listen while he lectures about sports and his vocation. What does Joe Mainstream, raised on *Playboy* and ads that display young women more than the product, see when he looks at a female Hamlet? A talkative, headstrong bitch who doesn't shave the hair under her arms. The great majority of female Hamlets, understanding that beauty goes deeper than the surface, only rarely wear makeup or dress in the latest styles. They have too much self-respect to doll themselves up and play sex object. That's more independence than the standard American boy can handle, so off he goes with some vacuous, deferential Madonna clone, and never mind *Ms.* Hamlet.

No surprise, then, that Hamlets of both sexes often remain single. Of the six Hamlets we've featured most prominently, four—Martin, Maxine, Jessica, and Antonio—are by themselves. Jeff, in and out of relationships through most of his adulthood, finally got serious enough to move in with a woman after he turned thirty-five. Only Brent has had a long-term love relationship. He and his girlfriend have been together for a decade. By withdrawing to the fringes of society and cultivating largely solitary pursuits—reading, thinking, practicing his art—Hamlet cuts down on his opportunities for meeting potential mates. He even has difficulty finding other Hamlets, because they're also off by themselves reading, thinking, and practicing their art. Ralph Waldo Emerson noted more than a century ago that Hamlet needs love just as much, if not more, than anybody else. Hamlet is certainly as capable of carrying on a love affair as anyone. But he has a devil of a time finding someone willing to tolerate his quirks and accept his affections.

Martin got serious about a woman for the first time when he was twenty-nine. "Since college I'd only seen two women, and each of those lasted just a few weeks. When you go that long without any indication that the female of the species has any interest in you, it gets to you. Of course, I wasn't putting much effort into seeking them. I didn't go looking for them, and women rarely came looking for me. Except Sabrina.

"The way we got together was very high schoolish, actually. One of the secretaries upstairs came down one afternoon all excited. 'Hey,' she said, 'there's someone upstairs who's interested in you, she wants to know if you're unattached.' She wouldn't tell me who it was, but I sort of had an idea because this one woman always smiled at me in a very friendly way. I was *hoping* it was her, anyway. So I told the secretary I was interested and that I wasn't attached. The next day Sabrina came down. We small-talked it for a while, and I didn't know if she was ever going to say anything. So I said the secretary came down yesterday and told me someone was interested in me, and I'm interested, so let's cut the crap."

The relationship lasted four months. Sabrina, it turns out, was rebounding from a four-year relationship. She didn't want to get emotionally involved again. Martin—and how many American males will openly admit this?—wanted more than just a physical relationship. When he saw that Sabrina was trying as hard as she could *not* to like him, he realized "the whole thing was kind of bogus." They split, but not before Sabrina berated Martin for having Hamlet tendencies. "She even thought I ought to see a therapist. I appreciated her concern, but seeing a therapist is something you do when you're desperate, when you realize you're not going to make it on your own and your friends can't help you. I realize I have this lack of ambition, and that I definitely lack confidence. But I don't see that as anything that's going to drive me to suicide."

Remember when Maxine talked about how torn she was between the American and Brazilian life-style? How she liked the privacy and individualism of the American way, but also enjoyed the camaraderie of life in Brazil? That same dichotomy exists in her feeling about relationships. She treasures her independence, yet at the same time she's desperate for companionship. Her love life is a microcosm of the Hamlet Syndrome: On the one hand she's true to herself and maintains her own life-style, but on the other she desires community, wants to fit in. "I think loneliness is the single biggest factor in my life," she says with great emotion, adding as an aside, "That's one nice thing about going to work: I'm with people." Yet in almost the next breath she expresses pride in her self-reliance. "I feel very independent. I can take care of most things by myself." Oh, for that middle ground! "I don't feel I should have to take care of everything by myself. It would be so nice to have a mate.

"Richard was my first steady boyfriend. I saw him once a week, but it was for two days, from Friday night to Sunday afternoon. It was great, because when you're in a couple, you really don't need much else in the way of society. At least, that's what I thought. After a while I *did* need other society. I missed him and looked forward to seeing him, but I didn't want to see him every day, didn't feel compelled to talk to him on the phone every day. I didn't want him breathing down my neck or restricting my life. I was surprised at myself; I didn't think that's the way I would feel, but I did." Maxine and Richard lasted almost a year before they drifted apart.

We can use Brent's successful long-term relationship to make a couple of generalizations about Hamlets in love. First, Brent and Anne met in college; Hamlet's love relationship often begins early, before he's removed himself to the fringe of society. In his early twenties Hamlet hasn't yet turned into a "loser," and his thoughtful, gentle mien attracts other sensitive persons to him. Especially in college, where Hamlet meets hundreds of new people each semester, the chances for finding that one special person are good. But as the years pass, the male Hamlet loses his earning potential and the female Hamlet loses her looks, making them less desirable to others. At the same time, they're meeting fewer people, owing to their solitary habits and the more static social milieu of the workplace. Hamlet's chance of meeting a partner thus dwindles with age until, by the time he approaches his fortieth birthday, he starts losing hope of ever finding a significant other.

The second generalization we can make from Brent's relationship is that it's nontraditional: Even after a decade, he and Anne aren't married. Hamlet subjects marriage to the same scrutiny he applies to every popularly accepted institution, and like the rest, marriage falls short. The very vows irk him. He sees marriage as nothing more than a medieval property ritual in which the husband exchanges half his possessions for the right to do what he pleases with his wife's body, an arrangement that strikes him as repulsive. Hamlet bases his relationships on trust and affection, not on a silly piece of paper that means nothing in an era of the easy divorce. But then again, maybe living together is just another way Hamlet avoids dealing with the world of commitment. "Anne and I have been together for ten years and we're not married. Isn't that a problem?" Brent asks, laughing defensively. "A lot of people consider that weird. Is that a commitment, or is it a lack of commitment?" As with most Hamlets, he can see one circumstance under which he and his mate would marry: "If we ever had children, which, at our age [early thirties] is an arriving issue."

A few Hamlets try to jump-start themselves out of the syndrome by hitching up with an ambitious but sympathetic partner. One male Hamlet married a go-getter wife in hopes that she'd spur him to greater achievements. So far his strategy hasn't worked, but he hasn't been married very long. One female Hamlet has lived with her significant other, a computer engineer, nearly sixteen years. They take turns working: She gets to garden while he works at his well-paid position, then after a few years he takes time off while she picks up a clerical job. Together they can afford a small house and a few luxuries; for her a neat resolution of the clash between heart and dollar. Her success suggests that with an understanding non-Hamlet partner, Hamlet stands an excellent chance of discovering an acceptable compromise between material wealth and spiritual integrity.

In the end, however, likes attract, and Hamlet usually takes another Hamlet for a lover. The problem of living with another Hamlet is that each partner reinforces the other's self-destructive tendencies. Should one catch a sudden case of ambition, the other can be counted on to exorcise it. Their mutual disgust—and sometimes rage—at the world could, if not tempered by humor and play, lead to premature cynicism. But the benefits of pairing with another Hamlet far outweigh the drawbacks. With a partner in the same predicament, Hamlet can go home knowing that at least within his own walls he'll be understood. He won't have to be defensive about who he is and what he believes. He'll get the emotional support he needs to brave tomorrow's foray into the mainstream world. Love between Hamlets insulates both from the humiliations of the workaday world, and largely inures them to the emotional distress common among Hamlets in their late thirties.

20

Warning: The Hamlet Syndrome May Be Hazardous to Your Health

W e've painted a grim portrait of the Hamlet in his mid to late thirties: He's lonely, misunderstood, disillusioned, and frequently humiliated. It seems he can't win. If he does nothing he wastes away, but taking action requires that he alter his personality to the point of self-annihilation. The sense that he doesn't stand much chance of emerging happily from his to-do-or-not-to-do crisis sometimes provokes Hamlet to behavioral and philosophical extremes. The behavioral extremes may include drug and alcohol abuse; the philosophical extreme is called *nihilism,* the conviction that life is totally meaningless. In both cases Hamlet resorts to self-destructive behavior that worsens his situation and makes it harder for him to conquer the debilitating aspects of the Hamlet Syndrome. Even if he resists the impulse to go off the behavioral or philosophical deep end, chronic stress over his plight may seriously undermine his health and endanger his well-being.

The fact that Hamlets so rarely fall victim to drug and alcohol abuse testifies to their courageous character. Reluctant as they are to take positive action, they're not afraid to face their predicament straight-on. It may well be that substance abuse is actually more common among rich and successful yuppie types than among Hamlets. Jeff, for instance, has never been drunk in his life. When hosting a party, he politely declines to partake of the spirits he freely pours for others. Antonio quaffed his share of wine during his tenure in a religious order, and he's never quite been able to tolerate the stuff since.

Both Maxine and Martin enjoy drinking, but neither has yet come close to crossing the line into addiction. Maxine enjoys drinking beer at social occasions. "In Brazil they're happiest sitting around with other people drinking beer. I feel that way sometimes, too." Martin takes beer drinking more seriously. A connoisseur of fine brews, he not only makes his own beer but regularly samples the offerings of foreign ale-makers and domestic microbrewers. For a while he drank two or three bottles a day, but has cut down to perhaps that many per week. "When you start brewing your own beer, and you can only get two cases per batch, you want to conserve, because this is art you've created. So I cut down, and now I go days without a beer." Still, Martin loves the sudsy stuff enough to have lined the walls of his apartment with shelves full of exotic bottles. "I have five hundred ten imports, another sixty or seventy domestics which are all from microbreweries," he says proudly. The one clearly alcoholic Hamlet we found refused to talk to us, perhaps because discussing his condition would destroy the escape it presently provides.

As for illicit drugs, Hamlet's "problem" is usually the same as comedian George Carlin's: He can't get any. Although Hamlets in their thirties may have used marijuana frequently in high school and college, they've long since parted company with their suppliers. These days even city-dwelling Hamlets don't know where to go to score the good stuff. Nor does Hamlet want any of the harder narcotics; the current drug of choice, cocaine, is too addictive for his taste. We found one Hamlet who'd gone so far as to use heroin regularly, but that was when she was in her teens and early twenties. She stopped sticking a needle in her arm well before the to-do-or-not-to-do crisis of her late thirties. Despite living without a partner and working at a poorly paid clerical job, she hasn't touched anything harder than herbal tea for more than fifteen years.

Although Hamlet may resist the temptation to bury his sorrows in substance abuse, his despair may lead to a philosophical hopelessness that destroys him just as surely. He may come to think that nothing has any value whatsoever, that there is no meaning to existence, that *destruc*tion offers as much possibility for the good life as *con*struction. Such hopelessness, *nihilism*, is the darkest response to existential questions like "What is the purpose of life?" Theoretically it frees Hamlet to act in any manner he pleases, even to the point of criminality—after all, nothing matters, right? In practice, however, Hamlet acts no more on his nihilistic impulses than he does on his more wholesome urges. He merely adopts nihilism as his primary perspective on life, looking upon existence in the most negative, cynical way imaginable. The nihilistic Hamlet feels such bitterness toward the world that even getting what he wants wouldn't make him happy.

Most Hamlets in their thirties look upon the world with a measure of despair and bitterness. Says Martin with utter finality, "People are scum." His recommendation: that the human population be reduced by some 80 percent. More bitter still is one thirty-four-year-old Hamlet from the suburbs east of San Francisco. A talented poet and writer, he's written a polemic *in favor* of nuclear war, seeing in the bloom of a thousand mushroom clouds the only solution for the pain that humans inflict upon each other and their environment. "And then, the great flame past," he writes of the ensuing nuclear winter, "we need fear no more the resumption of the terrible cycle of eating and dying. Instead . . . we ourselves will be grains in that protective sphere of cloud, an eternal, guardian ring of ghosts, preventing reinfection of the planet's surface by forever blocking the penetration of solar energy, until the sun ends and there is no further danger." Well, that's one way of coming to grips with nuclear war and the human condition.

Granted, few Hamlets are so disillusioned with the nature of existence that they'd root for atomic holocaust. But many, like Martin, believe that all people, themselves included, operate from only the basest motivations and thus doom humankind and the planet to increasing levels of misery. Existential despair strengthens their belief that except to satisfy one's own petty desires there is no *reason* to act. "I feel despair about the human race sometimes, even though I'm an optimist," attests Maxine, who hasn't yet lived thirty years. "Sometimes it stops me from acting. I think there's no point. I mean, why bother? Eat, drink, and be merry because there's nothing you can do about these other things."

Even if the stress of the syndrome doesn't drive Hamlet to substance abuse or existential despair, it can still have a deleterious effect on his health. As Hamlet's frustrations mount and his possibilities fade, his susceptibility to stress-related illness rises. He may develop mysterious, chronic ailments that curtail for months or even years his ability to function effectively. Of course, other physiological factors may contribute significantly to Hamlet's sickness, but it's interesting to note how often Hamlets come down with serious maladies just as they're weighing to-do-or-not-to-do type decisions. Brent, for instance, developed "a neurological thing" toward the end of his legal clerkship, when he was trying to figure out whether to seek employment with a high-powered law firm. "It pretty much wiped me out for a month. I couldn't go to work for three weeks," he recalls. "It was right at the time I was going to do some job hunting. When I got back to work there was a backlog of things to do, and by the time I got caught up it was summer, so I never got on track in terms of looking for a job." Fortunately, Brent's illness disappeared of its own accord and has not returned. Its sole long-term effect: a heightened sense of mortality, i.e., do what you want to today, because you can't take tomorrow for granted.

According to a number of medical studies, stress saps the body of B vitamins, and may also interfere with the body's ability to absorb more B's. As a longtime vegetarian (a dietary preference he shares with many Hamlets), Jeff already ran the risk of a B_{12} deficiency, since B_{12} comes entirely from animal products. When, in his mid-thirties, he began to agonize over his dead-end existence, his body gave way. He weakened, felt jittery and nervous. "When you wake up in the morning and your gums are aching and you walk to work and your ankles feel like they're about to break, well, that's bizarre stuff when you're thirty-four," he says. After living with the condition for two years, going to doctor after doctor, he finally received a proper diagnosis: lack of vitamin B_{12}. An ardent milk drinker, Jeff believed he was getting all the B_{12} he needed. But the stress of deciding whether to do or not to do may have contributed to an already-existing deficiency and brought on his illness. His doctor gave him regular injections of B_{12} and restructured Jeff's diet, and today Jeff feels much better. Nevertheless, the experience left him scarred psychologically. "Right after I found out about the B_{12} thing, life just went to hell for me. I read *Laurel's Kitchen* [a popular vegetarian cookbook and nutritional guide]. There's this part that describes the symptoms and consequences of B_{12} deficiency, and one sentence says there's this descent into madness, and eventually death. I read that and freaked out! I had my first anxiety attack—I'd never had anything like that before. It took a long time to recover from that feeling of panic."

In time Jeff overcame the physical and psychological effects of his B_{12} deficiency and got to make his to-do-or-not-to-do decision. But he lost two years of his life to that illness, two years he could have spent striving for something better. Perhaps he wasn't ready to take those first few steps out of the Hamlet Syndrome, and his body, responding to the misgivings of his heart, rebelled. If so, we'd have some fairly convincing evidence of the power of mind over body.

Indeed, when you stop to think about it, that's much of what the Hamlet Syndrome's about: the power of mind over body. Let's explore Hamlet's formidable thoughts more closely to see just why they compel him, at times bodily, to flout the prevailing wisdom and remain the "oddball" person that he is.

V

SOLILOQUIES: HAMLET SPEAKS HIS MIND

There are more things in heaven and earth, Horatio,
Than are dreamt of in your philosophy.

Hamlet, ACT I, SCENE V

.

C all it the if-you-can't-say-anything-nice-don't-say-anything complex: The social law dictates that we not engage in heated discussion of controversial issues unless we're among trusted friends. This is one unwritten law that Hamlet obeys. Although he may be somewhat proud of his status as an outsider, he has no special desire to advertise his differences with the mainstream. He's afraid of confrontation, unwilling to argue or fight. For all he loves to talk, then, he hushes up when it comes to controversial topics. He doesn't want to put himself in a position where he's perceived as a militant outsider, for then he *really* opens himself up to ridicule—especially if, in his mid to late thirties, he makes a decisive move for the dollar and looks like he's contradicting everything he said in the past.

Hamlet may also feel that, except with his fellow Hamlets and a smattering of others, meaningful dialogue is impossible. Few people share his frame of reference. Mainstream Americans see the social law not as a force of tyranny, but as a source of comfort and guidance—that is, when they see it at all, for usually they're no more aware of the social law than they are of blinking their eyes. They see critical thought not as an empowering process, but as intellectual subterfuge intended to make them feel guilty about their beliefs. They agree we should be tolerant—but only up to a point. Curiosity, they recite like school kids, killed the cat—as if that's proof it's harmful to humans, too. And as for all this garbage about principle, conscience, and caring for others, when's the last time anyone got his due for being a Good Samaritan? Hamlet and his mainstream acquaintances exist on different planes of consciousness that intersect only occasionally. Under those circumstances anything more heartfelt than an exchange of pleasantries would seem to be out of the question.

Nevertheless, Hamlet's human. He's always on the lookout for someone to talk to. Although on the surface there's nothing new and exciting in his life, inside his head he's fairly bursting with novel thoughts and ideas that he's desperate to share. The problem is finding kindred souls with whom he can establish rapport. Because of his solitary habits, guarded nature, and lack of telltale physical characteristics, Hamlet has trouble connecting with others of his ilk. Like a prospector looking for the one precious nugget in a riverbed of gravel, he patiently ascertains every new acquaintance's frame of reference. His only tools: an open ear and a handful of broad questions.

So skillful does Hamlet become at this panning for human gold that he can discern within seconds whether someone new has the potential to become a close friend. If the conversation turns to investment strategies, real estate, and tax shelters, Hamlet waits for the right moment to utter a polite "Nice to meet you" and move on—if you can't say anything nice, don't say anything. But should the conversation take a more intriguing direction, for instance to the arts, Hamlet sticks around a few minutes longer. He tries to elicit his new acquaintance's opinions on certain cultural touchstones without violating that taboo about engaging in heated discussion with strangers. If in response to his queries he's told that Prince is the greatest musician of all time, or that Stephen King ranks right up there with Shakespeare, or that foreign films are too confusing and should be more like Charles Bronson flicks, away he goes, off to find someone who shines a bit brighter.

Say, however, that Hamlet does see luster in his newfound acquaintance. His next step is to administer the are-you-like-me test. Maxine
caught on to the test by, of all things, observing Marxists. Shortly after
leaving college she joined a grass-roots antinuclear organization, but
communists, with their own separate agenda, invaded the group and
sundered it. Maxine noticed the communists playing a social game that
she later realized Hamlets play as well. "Commies have this little code,"
she explains. "It's hard to say exactly what it is—whether it's the way
they dress, their body language, certain catchwords and phrases, their
sense of humor, or a combination of all these factors—but just through
casual conversation they know who's a commie and who isn't. We're the
same way. We test people, and we can tell who's like us and who isn't.
I tested Mike, this new friend of mine. I told him I had intended to go
to Canada for a vacation, but the rail workers ruined my plans by going
out on strike. I laughed and said, 'Boy, they have their nerve.' And Mike
said, 'Well, they have a right to go on strike,' which is exactly the way
I felt. I just wanted to see if he felt the same way I did."

We made a little fun of popular taste with our references to Prince,
Stephen King, and Charles Bronson, but we don't mean to imply that
Hamlet is a cultural snob. Indeed, he may appreciate some popular
entertainers very much. When it comes to aesthetics (and also religion,
philosophy, and politics), he can draw pleasure and wisdom from on high
or down low. Martin, for instance, reads with equal ardor texts on
pre-Revolutionary America and Tolkien's *Lord of the Rings.* The difference between Hamlet and mainstream people—and what causes Hamlet
to shy away from folks who think Prince is the greatest—is that mainstreamers generally draw their pleasure and wisdom from down low *only*.
Their cultural insight extends only as far as the latest hyperpublicized
one-shot phenomenon. It's breadth and depth of interest, the willingness
to go past what's popular and accessible, that Hamlet looks for when he
quizzes a new acquaintance. A mind that accepts mass-produced schlock
as the paragon of culture (or, for that matter, that accepts any mainstream
belief as the final word on a subject) is to Hamlet no mind at all.

Nor is Hamlet looking for any particular ideological stance when
he searches for close friends—quite the opposite, in fact. He finds
ideological systems, with their inviolable assumptions and unyielding
precepts, much too black and white. When it comes to the heavy issues—
religion, philosophy, politics—he dwells in the shades of gray. To him

no belief system has all the answers. There are too many in-between situations that established *isms,* because of their absolutist nature, can never address realistically. Ideologies also limit the range of intellectual inquiry—perhaps *the* cardinal sin according to Hamlet's own beliefs. Hamlet insists on the right to examine the full range of an intellectual realm, free from the fetters of orthodoxy, and thus regards communists, religious fundamentalists, and other absolutists with a combination of amusement and contempt.

We're making Hamlet sound like the Hebrew father Abraham, searching fruitlessly through Sodom for a handful of good men. He doesn't like the culturally unsophisticated. He has little patience for fanatics. Whom does he like, then? He likes people with an abiding respect for ideas. They don't have to agree with him on the heavy issues, they don't have to think as obsessively as he does. But they do have to be tolerant of viewpoints other than their own—and capable of discussing those viewpoints in a nonconfrontational manner. They have to be curious. And they have to be sufficiently skeptical to admit that there may be more to heaven and earth than they previously imagined. Should Hamlet discover this openness in any new acquaintance, he's liable to gamble and reveal some of his more heartfelt opinions—and, if his intuition is correct, his new friend will respond in kind and a genuine dialogue will ensue.

Those heartfelt opinions, so seldom shared with the wider world, are the subject of this part of the book. Since Hamlet thinks about himself the most (different as he is, he's not *that* different), we'll start with his musings on himself and his heart-or-dollar conflict. From there we'll move outward: to his regard for other humans; to America and politics; to the state of the world; and finally, to God and the cosmos. In the associative minds of many Hamlets these headings intermingle, so be prepared for an occasional leap of logic or reference to something we've already discussed. Remember too that no two Hamlets are alike; what our six featured Hamlets say on the following pages may not necessarily reflect the opinions of the Hamlet in your life. Hamlets' perspectives range from the stubbornly concrete to the wispily ethereal, their interests from the everyday to the eternal. The sole common denominator: a stubborn insistence on thinking—a lot—for themselves. The best way to find out what *your* Hamlet thinks is to ask him, point-blank. He may display some initial reticence, but so long as you show him you're willing to listen, truly *listen,* without judging him or raising clichéd counterarguments that he's heard a thousand times before, he may agree to make a case for himself. Indeed, before long he may talk you into a stupor—for despite his belief that few people share his frame of reference, Hamlet wants as much as anything to be understood and accepted.

21

To Thine Own Self Be True

The unexamined life is not worth living, Socrates asserted more than two thousand years ago. Even in his time that was old wisdom, for upon the temple walls of the Oracle at Delphi, which predates Socrates by two centuries, were reportedly inscribed the words KNOW THYSELF. Thus the modern Hamlet, in ruminating over his predicament, follows one of the oldest maxims of Western civilization. And make no mistake about it: Hamlet thinks about himself a lot. The *ignorant Hamlet* is a contradiction in terms—especially when it comes to being aware of who he is.

Hamlet's self-image is shaped in part by his perception of others, a problem because most people act and think differently than he does. He comes to see himself as a minority of one: the sole drifter in a world of the firmly rooted, the sole puzzler in a society of the very certain. All people know how to make themselves useful; he alone seems worthless and inept. Nor does any Hamlets Anonymous exist to provide identity and support. Except through chance meetings and the sort of feeling-out process we've discussed, Hamlet remains isolated from his fellow Hamlets. After all, how *do* Hamlets find each other? *Attitude* is the common trait, not anything so discernible as ethnicity, gender, accent, or attire. And so for all Hamlet knows he really *is* alone, incompetent, and deserving of failure.

As with everyone else, Hamlet gains more perspective on himself as he ages. He may go through adolescence unaware of his inner nature, but as he discovers the power of critical thought—a time that usually coincides with his college crisis—he begins to figure out who he really is. Once he learns that he's motivated by values at variance with those of society, he becomes obsessed with himself and his place in the world. Am I screwed up, or is the world? he wonders. In time he concludes that while something may indeed be wrong with him, there's something wrong with the world as well, and for the time being he's better off going in his own direction even if he's not quite sure where it leads. At the same time, he comes to understand that most other people *don't* examine their lives. They're afraid to, or they never learn to think critically. They never ponder the consequences of their actions, something Hamlet finds appalling. During this stage—the early twenties—Hamlet is most proud of his own way of thinking, and most resentful toward the thoughtless majority around him.

As Hamlet matures he sees that life has more shades of gray than he first realized. Take himself, for instance. He sees that for all the high-minded reasons he originally had for following his path, he went that way as much out of fear, resentment, and need as principle. He felt safer in his lowly niche than in the riskier, more challenging realm of the dollar, and obtained more solace from defying the mainstream than joining it. Now he understands that his motive for going his own way was more or less the same as the motive impelling everyone else toward the mainstream: the need for security. So who is he to point fingers at the mindless majority? Nor has his desire for the dollar disappeared; in many respects the only difference between him and a corporate executive is that Hamlet doesn't want to *work* to attain his riches. He'd rather someone just handed him a million dollars, meaning he's not any better than the executive, only lazier. When Hamlet recognizes the extent to which base motives play a part in his decisions (and nondecisions), he forgives somewhat the shortcomings of his compatriots, and he's overcome with an abiding humility that may last the rest of his life.

This humility, although it dissipates Hamlet's resentment of mainstream society, nevertheless has a deleterious side effect. It permanently dispels his illusion that he's better than everyone else. Formerly, the sense that he was more aware, more caring, and more successful at integrating his beliefs into his everyday life served as a major source of self-esteem. Now that he knows he's just an ordinary guy, he has to obtain his sense of self-worth from someplace else. But where? He's made no impact on the world, has achieved nothing concrete to take pride in. Hamlet's new humility may bring on the to-do-or-not-to-do crisis, for all of a sudden he feels a desperate need for external validation. In the resulting scramble for self-esteem he'll either rise to a higher level of wisdom and acceptance, fall into the existential despair chronicled in Chapter 20, or wind up in some shade of gray in between—the last possibility being the most common. Many a Hamlet, one moment reconciled to himself and the world, echoes in the next these words of Shakespeare's Hamlet: "The time is out of joint—O cursed spite,/that ever I was born to set it right!" (Act I, Scene v).

Few *people*—never mind just Hamlets—are as humble as Martin. But then, as he's already told us, much of that comes from the lack of self-confidence he carries from childhood. He didn't have to go through the humbling revelation that he's as base as everyone else, because he's known that from the start. Thus, when Martin pronounces, with utter finality, that "people are scum," he assumes you understand that he's including himself. "Everybody's got it," he says, shrugging, when you ask whether he too is scum. "It takes *effort* to do the right thing. It's so much easier just to not care. I call my lack of action in trying to change the things I don't like scumminess. I complain about things, but I don't see any point in writing letters or whatnot to make things better. I admit it, I'm a complete hypocrite, up and down the line." But before you ask Martin why he singles himself out for such harsh condemnation, he adds with a bemused chuckle that "I assume most other people are hypocrites up and down the line also."

Although he's approaching his mid-thirties, Martin feels none of the symptoms of the to-do-or-not-to-do crisis. He hasn't yet begun to fight, and the fact is he may never. "I have no great yearning for success," he asserts. "I don't even need a definition of the word. Other people may find they have to seek this thing, achieve that thing. But to me that's just keeping up with the Joneses. It's something other people put on you. I derive my satisfaction in life from things other than my job. Money is necessary merely to pay the rent and feed yourself and clothe yourself, and to support your hobbies. Nor do I need to be in charge of anything. I don't like being in charge. I'm a great follower, but I don't have any desire to lead because I *know* I'm unworthy to do so."

He ponders the leadership question a moment longer. "I don't know, maybe I could lead. I go a lot farther than a lot of people once I set my mind on doing something. It's just that I so rarely do so. Like this deck thing. [He's learned to design and build outdoor decks.] I had no idea how to build decks. I just volunteered to do it for somebody, bought a book or two, and taught myself how to do it. I always get hooked on these little hobbies, like tree identification. I walk by all these ridiculous-looking trees and I have no idea what a single one is, so curiosity gets the better of me and I start looking into it. Maybe if I put that kind of energy into leading I could do it."

But then, maybe not. Martin doesn't feel he can ever say with surety how he'll react to a situation. "I don't know if *anyone* really knows themselves," he muses. "I delude myself, and I'm sure a lot of other people are deluding themselves, too. We all have our little lies. You can know yourself to a point, think you have a fairly good idea of what you'd do in a situation, but if you asked me what I would do if some guy started raping a woman right here, I'd have to say I don't know. I haven't the slightest idea. I've never been in such a situation. I might be frozen and do nothing, or I might run over and try to kill the guy. I don't know. People who run into burning buildings to save people, they're not any hero type. They're probably mailmen, just like me. They don't know *why* they do it, they just do it. It's sort of an inner feeling, an urge, that you can't really analyze or predict. So I just don't see how anyone can really know themselves. Not totally. Try and convince me that they can."

Brent, also approaching his mid-thirties, probes his psyche for the motives behind the Hamlet Syndrome. "Maybe I'm spoiled. I've had a lot of privileges and things made easy for me." Those privileges and comforts created too many shades of gray—too many *choices.* "There were choices I had that a lot of people didn't. After high school I could have stayed working in warehouses and doing odd jobs and gotten good enough at it that by now I'd be running a store. A lot of people I know just got plunked into something and stayed there. Sometimes I'm envious of that, but then other times I realize it would probably become onerous to me."

Perhaps early success contributed to the Hamlet Syndrome. Muses Brent, "I think the key question is, do I have impossible standards? Because I was such a hotshot as a kid and had such inflated views of my potential, it created a set of expectations that ultimately were impossible to meet. I'd pick apart each job: This one is dead-end, this one is too demanding, this one doesn't pay enough. Even when I realized I was expecting too much from myself and my job, I couldn't reconcile myself to what I was doing. Once I had an opportunity to leave, like enough money or something else to do, I was gone."

Because he has conventional achievements he can point to, Brent's discovery of unflattering motives hasn't ruined his self-esteem. But then, there are signs that as he learns why he's a Hamlet, he creates new delusions, meaning he's not yet ready to face himself straight-on. "To me it's still an open question as to whether my dropping out has been part of a syndrome or whether it's just been a series of discrete incidents," he says. An open question? He's dropped out not once, but twice, and last we heard he's still playing banjo for his country and western band and shirking regular employment. He's in the prime of his life, but it's been two years since he quit practicing law. "Maybe now I will find something and like it, and life will be beautiful from now on," he says, a faint smile belying the Pollyanna sentiment. "I could just decide I want to settle down, have a job, do something. Not save the world, but just have a job and live a normal life." Of all the Hamlets presented in this book, he's certainly the most capable of setting himself up in a mainstream existence. The question remains, however, whether his heart will permit him to do so.

Let's turn to Jeff, who, being a highly philosophical fellow, is a true connoisseur of shades-of-gray thinking. He renounced all black-and-white perspectives in college when his reading and thinking convinced him that there are no absolutes. The absence of absolutes compels us toward what he calls *radical acceptance,* acceptance of the world on its own terms. "The world can't be any other way than it is, no matter how much we, or *I,* may want to change it," he declares, a curiously absolute statement considering Jeff's shades-of-gray outlook. Jeff says further that human beings, as part of the world, are also immutable, meaning that we must accept ourselves warts and all. No amount of prayer or good deeds will purge us of our fundamental nature, which includes a dark side rife with stupidity, hatred, envy, lust, aggression, and greed. But though Jeff's radical acceptance allows him to forgive people their transgressions, it also causes him to feel powerless—and provides a perfect rationalization for his lack of action. If the world is unalterably the way it is, how can we change anything? If stupidity and evil are intrinsic to human nature, how can we challenge or punish anyone? In Jeff's opinion, the answer to both questions is that we can't.

"It seems to me that, philosophically anyway, we have no grounds on which to challenge anyone's set of beliefs, no matter how crazed they may seem," he maintains. "No two minds are alike—we don't have any idea of what mind really *is* in the first place. For all I know, some minds *might* be in touch with certain powers that my mind isn't. So I have no problem accepting the claims of people who bend spoons or see poltergeists or say the devil made them do things. Of course, that leaves me in the very awkward position of accepting some very gross and hideous things. I don't know what to do with people who rape or murder, for instance. I honestly don't. Philosophically I'm at your mercy on that score."

Tolerant of evil as he may be, however, Jeff does have a personal honor code he tries hard to adhere to. "You try to live according to your beliefs as best you can, even if you come up short a lot. To me, being fair is important. So is being kind. That's one of the things I picked up from my father: being courteous, polite. Those things work, they somehow make life bearable. It's also important to be honest. You know, all that standard stuff."

In the last seven years—since he turned thirty—Jeff has gained a gentler perspective on himself, a brand of humility that lacks the edge of Martin's. Jeff proves that even the most solemn Hamlet can eventually see his predicament from a lighter, more humorous angle. "There are times now when I don't take myself seriously," he admits. "It's fun to take these intellectual positions and make arguments for this, that, and the other thing. It satisfies something, although I'm not sure what it is. It's not that I don't believe in what I say—I do. I want to make that absolutely clear: I'm not saying I have any less faith or belief in my ideas. I still take them seriously, I still believe. But at the same time, to some extent and in some way, it doesn't matter a whole lot. It used to bother me that it didn't matter, but now it doesn't. I can stand back and say, you believe this, but so what? There's a part of me that steps outside it all, and there's even a part of me that enjoys the buffoonery of it."

It's vital to remember Jeff's point that no matter how much distance Hamlet may get on himself, no matter how much fun he pokes at his peccadillos, he still *believes.* He doesn't stop being a Hamlet once he fully understands himself (or, deferring to Martin, understands himself as much as he can); nor does he begin taking decisive steps out of the Hamlet Syndrome. His heart is still with Socrates, who along with the imprecation to live an examined life said, while strolling through a marketplace one day, "How many things I have no need of!" Hamlet knows himself well enough to realize that so long as he has his heart, the only marketplace he truly needs is the one that offers him ideas.

22

Humans—Can't Live with 'Em, Can't Live Without 'Em

Of the nine most frequently used words in the English language, only two are nouns: *it* and *you*. (The other words, as determined by lexicographer G. H. McKnight, are *and, be, have, of, the, to,* and *will*.) Upon examining the list, we're naturally tempted to ask, "Hey, what happened to *I*?" which, after all, is what we assume people think and talk about the most. But follow your thoughts and conversations for a few hours and you'll be surprised at how often your subjects are *it*s and *you*s, especially *you*s. We constantly fantasize about impressing, arguing with, explaining ourselves to, or falling in love with others. In our heads we replay old dialogues or imagine new ones, always making the clever comeback, the compelling case, the convincing plea. Then in *real* conversation we love nothing more than to gossip about others, not just the individual we're with but third parties as well. Our fixation, it turns out, may well be on *you* more than *I*.

Hamlet, as we established in the previous section, thinks about himself a lot. But those thoughts of *I* usually form against a backdrop of *you*. Martin, for instance, thinks not just he, but *all* people are scum, and Jeff's need for radical acceptance stems from the belief that *all* people are unchangeable. Hamlet's personality, like everyone else's, is highly contextual, meaning that to know him it's important to know what he thinks of the people around him. What we find is that Hamlet doesn't think much of other people at all, except for his friends, whom he holds to a higher standard.

Speaking very broadly, Hamlet sees the human race as unchanged from the days of the cave dwellers: xenophobic, paganistic, bellicose, and oriented toward the gratification of short-term desires. Just because we've progressed technologically doesn't mean we've advanced spiritually or intellectually. Cliques of researchers make scientific breakthroughs, a handful of entrepreneurs turn those breakthroughs into marketable products, and the rest of us—meaning 99 percent of the population—go along for the ride, no smarter or wiser than the average Cro-Magnon. Most people have no idea how a television works, or an automobile, or what happens to waste water once we flush the toilet. Maybe one in a thousand truly understands Einstein's theory of relativity. And though we congratulate ourselves for being so civilized, at home crime runs rampant and overseas more than half the world teeters on the brink of starvation and chaos. The reason our own society doesn't disintegrate is that our material needs are thoroughly satiated. Jar the American middle class out of its complacency and all the primitive instincts will instantly resurface—if, in fact, they were ever submerged. Suburbanization, religious orthodoxy, the bloated defense budget, and unbridled capitalism strike Hamlet as nothing more than updated versions of Stone Age tribalism, superstition, violence, and greed.

Maxine, for one, expresses grave doubt about humanity's collective intelligence. "The human race is smart up to a point. I think the tragic flaw is that the human race is extremely shortsighted. *It's a neat idea, let's do it.* They're like real clever children, and they don't think of implications or possibilities. Take these spreadsheet programs for personal computers. The neat thing about spreadsheet programs is that you can ask them *what if* questions. But the what-if questions are things like, what if we raise sales in the northeast region by ten percent, how does that affect our overall picture? That's their level of foresight and imagination—pretty dismal. I mean, why can't you ask, what if we sell all these things and because of increased output in our factory we increase toxic waste production by this much?

"There are so many possibilities! There isn't just black or white, there are so many shades of gray, so many colors in between. It's not like everything is yes or no, this or that. I don't know whether it's because there are two sexes or what, but human beings are used to thinking of things in this-or-that, us-or-them terms. I think it takes a person of great intelligence and imagination to think there's also a third way of doing things, a fourth way, to the *nth* thing."

As Maxine's comments illustrate, Hamlet thinks most people judge too hastily, without considering alternatives or consequences. He finds especially irksome the inclination to draw conclusions from the way things look. To him it's essence that counts, not appearance, but mainstream perception penetrates no deeper than skin and clothes. If you look good, you *are* good, goes the common assumption, and by the same token if you don't look good, you must be less than worthy. Antonio is a very handsome, stylish man, so much so that he's even done modeling work. But in one crucial respect he doesn't fulfill the conventional definition of looking good: He's black in a race-conscious, predominantly white society. Having spent the first dozen years of his life in a more tolerant country, American racism shocked him. "In Panama you weren't judged by what race you were. We had colors from this [he points to his black shirt] all the way to this [he holds up a piece of typing paper], and all of them are Panamanian. Here the first thing an American sees when he meets someone else, because it's meant so much since the inception of this society, is color.

"Once in a bank I saw this old, old black woman, a street person. It was in the days when Reagan was beginning to defund the institutions and the disturbed people were being emptied out into the streets. Once a week or so they'd be rounded up and sedated, and the next day they'd be out on the street again. I was standing in line waiting to have a check cashed, and this lady had taken white shoe polish and put it haphazardly on her arms and face. And she was yelling at the top of her lungs, 'What you mean you ain't gonna give me no money, can't you see I'm as white as you?' Even she understood that it all boiled down to race."

Repugnant as racial stereotyping may be to Antonio, he's realist enough to deal with it head-on. "I make a deliberate effort to fit in wherever I go, and I do that for several reasons. My primary motivation is that I'm aware of the advantages and disadvantages my race and gender put me in—particularly the disadvantages. Whenever a crime in the neighborhood has been committed by a black man the police are liable to stop *me*. My fellow blacks don't know how to deal with me either. There's a certain demeanor I see in blacks when they meet me and start to talk to me. Puerile, I think, but understandable. What I try to do is alleviate that by eliminating fear in myself and my comrades, so we can see each other as persons first, instead of races."

To Antonio, we're not white or black, we're not rich or poor, we're children—or at least we *should* be. "Ever watch children? Even when they're fighting they're having fun. They don't take life seriously. They're bound together by their frivolity, and that's what I try to bring to people. There are serious things in life, there's poverty and death and maiming and mayhem, but the thing that eases it all is the ability to touch someone gently with laughter or compassion or empathy. You turn on the heater for them when the room is real cold, you see to their well-being. The first thing I want to learn is what kind of child you are. We can learn about all of that racial stuff later."

Gender is another social context in which Hamlet must define himself. As we've noted several times, Hamlets of both sexes overwhelmingly reject the narrow boundaries of conventional male and female roles. Jessica confessed earlier that during her decade-long stay in graduate school she often felt the temptation to lead a "normal" life, with a husband, children, and a reliable automobile parked in the driveway of a suburban house. But she resisted that temptation, in part because she'd die from boredom. Another reason for resisting, we learn now, is that she despises traditional sex roles. Her mother, of all people, urged her not to play the mainstream game. "My mom always encouraged my sister and me not to get married. She seemed to see it as some sort of slavery. It would tie you down before you had time to see the world, enjoy yourself." Jessica's mouth curls into an ironic smile. "I think she wishes I were married now, though. She's mentioned grandchildren several times. I told her I'd get her some pictures of kids. Then she can show them to other grandparents, pass them around."

Like most Hamlets, Jessica expresses regret that the women's movement lost the momentum of the seventies. By virtue of being a Hamlet she's already on the fringe of society, and now that feminism's out of vogue she feels almost completely outside. She talks about her last foray into fashion—the realm of the skin-deep. "I have a friend who's very much into fashion, and before I went to the interview for my professorship she said she was going to check out my clothes for me, because she knew I couldn't manage on my own. I'd wear something wildly inappropriate to the interview and blow the whole thing. So she came over and I tried on various outfits for her. She'd say yes, no. Then she didn't trust me to go shopping by myself. She sent away for fashion catalogs from that area, just to see what women were wearing down there, and when I went clothes shopping she came with me and told the clerks, 'She needs a shirt to go with this,' and she approved everything before I could make a purchase. When that was finished, she told me not to buy any more clothes until I got down there. See what the other women were wearing, blend in with their styles. And I thought, this is bizarre!"

Despite their weaknesses—passion for fashion serving as a prime example—Hamlet believes that by some happy accident of heredity or environment his friends have evolved into better than average humans. They're more tolerant, intelligent, principled, and gentle—and they understand *him*, which is no mean feat. As a result Hamlet holds them to a higher standard—the same one he applies to himself. We go back to Jessica. "I'm shocked when my friends don't live up to my moral standards. I can't imagine how the person could do that. Even though I see myself not living up to my own moral standards all the time, it really takes me aback when a friend does something wrong. Whether I confront them depends on the nature of the offense. I tended not to before, but I'm getting more confrontational now, because I'm afraid that if I don't say anything it'll be construed as approval. So I don't hesitate to let them know I don't approve, and I tell them I'll slap their hands if they do it again."

23

Any Way You Look at It You Lose

Hamlet is ambivalent about the human race. On the one hand, experience has taught him that his species is dreadfully and irredeemably flawed. On the other, he can't overcome the conditioning of his relatively strifeless childhood, which taught him that humankind is capable of perfection. When it comes to politics, the conditioning wins out. Deep down Hamlet still expects the best from people. Although he may be too ashamed to admit it, he really believes that individuals can be honorable, honest, and fair. If he didn't believe it, he wouldn't be so disappointed in mainstream behavior—and he wouldn't have to console himself with notions of radical acceptance and the ubiquity of scum.

Nowhere does this dual attitude toward the human race show more clearly than in Hamlet's political creed. He's a dreamer, longing for a utopia in which everyone follows the negative version of the Golden Rule: Do *not* do unto others as you would *not* have them do unto you.

In Hamlet's ideal world every person regulates his own behavior, placing the long-term well-being of the community first. Disagreements are resolved in an amicable, rational manner. But when Hamlet wakes up and reflects on human nature as it really is, his hopeful vision yields to an attitude so cynical it mirrors that of Jonathan Swift, author of the highly misanthropic *Gulliver's Travels*. "I cannot but conclude the bulk of your natives to be the most pernicious race of little odious vermin that nature ever suffered to crawl upon the surface of the earth," the King of Brobdingnag tells Gulliver after the latter describes life in eighteenth-century England. To Hamlet, the King of Brobdingnag's scathing pronouncement rings true to this day. Humans really *are* pernicious.

Thus we have it that Hamlet possesses an almost religious faith in democracy—a faith also attributable in part to the patriotic conditioning of his childhood—yet feels such disgust over the mainstream's preferences that he may not even vote. Hamlet defines democracy as the freedom to choose from a wide range of political options. He sees politics in terms of a broad spectrum, with a nearly infinite variety of shades between totalitarianism on the extreme right and anarchy on the extreme left. But the Democrats and Republicans occupy narrow, adjacent bands somewhere to the right of center, and like so many Americans, Hamlet regards them as Tweedledum and Tweedledee, presenting no real choice at all. If we have so little choice at election time, he wonders, how can we pride ourselves on being so democratic?

Out of apathy or disillusion, many Hamlets never think about political matters. They consistently chuck the front page of their newspaper and change the channel whenever the news comes on. Those who do have an interest generally hold views that fall on the left side of the spectrum, ranging from mild liberalism to outright anarchism. Since he's such a democrat, communism appeals to Hamlet only in that it places the welfare of the community ahead of individual greed. He has no taste for the despotism that usually accompanies a state-administered economic system. Stick Hamlet in a social democracy—something along the lines of the Scandinavian countries—and he'd probably be happiest. He'd embrace the American system more readily if we either added a few parties or had more genuine differences between the existing two.

The developments of the last decade have increased Hamlet's apprehension over the state of American democracy. He found the popularity of Ronald Reagan an especially disturbing trend. Ronald Reagan is Hamlet's antithesis: Whereas Hamlet thinks but hardly ever acts, Reagan acts but hardly ever thinks. He's intolerant, uncurious, credulous, and wedded to the superficialities of Hollywood glamor. His revanchist policies resurrected the values of the 1950s—values Hamlet long ago rejected—and made the eighties a particularly difficult decade for Hamlet to endure. We can safely say that Hamlets casting ballots in 1980 and 1984 voted against Reagan by a percentage exceeding that of blacks, who voted against Reagan by more than five to one.

Hamlet's grievances against the Great Communicator are legion, starting with the very manner in which Reagan thinks—or doesn't think. Against the increasingly complex and urgent problems of the nation Reagan could pit but a feeble intellect, one stupefied by years of *Charlie's Angels* reruns and Rambo movies. No surprise, then, that he justified his policies with melodramatic, distorted tales of welfare mothers in Cadillacs, trees that pollute the air, and conciliatory mullahs. He saw no contradiction in promising to get government off our backs and then favoring all sorts of intrusions on individual rights. He saw no contradiction in committing himself to a reduction in government spending and then tripling the national deficit. He saw no contradiction in vowing to make America strong again and then presiding over our decline into the greatest debtor nation on earth. Were these but minor inconsistencies, Hamlet could chalk them up to the practicalities of politics. But hypocrisy was so endemic to Reagan's administration that Hamlet concluded the Gipper was either a pathological liar, incredibly dense, or a combination of the two. Whichever, in Hamlet's opinion the old man certainly didn't belong in the White House.

Normally we associate anti-intellectualism with practicality, down-to-earth wisdom. But Reagan's anti-intellectualism stemmed from mediocrity and ignorance, not common sense. He operated in as much a dream world as any Hamlet or ivory tower intellectual—indeed, probably more so. He never saw past the insulated, overly secure perspectives of privileged white society. His doctrine had only one tenet: Honor the dollar. In his dismantling of regulatory agencies, his trickle-down tax cuts, and his opposition to environmental legislation, Reagan did obeisance to the dollar by putting the individual's right to make fast bucks ahead of the community's right to ensure its long-term safety. To Hamlet, the standard-bearer of the heart, such a materialistic creed was revolting. He flatly rejected the supposition that money and the marketplace could make everything right. Nor did he see anything other than Pyrrhic wisdom in sacrificing the future for a few years of material prosperity.

In his eyes, Ronald Reagan operated as a Robin Hood in reverse, turning greed into virtue by stealing from the poor and giving to the rich.

What really makes Hamlet fear for the future of American democracy is that so many people *believed* in the Gipper. They never stopped to analyze his simplistic logic, never challenged his misstatements of fact. That Americans failed to repudiate Reagan, even after the Iran-contra hearings revealed he'd forfeited control of foreign affairs to a band of law-breaking, right-wing zealots, convinced many Hamlets that the country is slipping toward dictatorship—with the mainstream's unwitting approval. So long as we're safe and have television to keep us amused, the conventional "wisdom" goes, we don't care that our leaders lie to us and place themselves above the law. Hamlet, already frustrated by the lack of choice in our political system, shudders at the prospect of a power-hungry cabal smooth-talking us out of our basic freedoms. It *can* happen here; all we need do is keep our heads in the sand a few years longer.

"Reagan and his administration were so outrageous it's hard to believe they were taken seriously," says Brent, so incensed by Reagan that he took a rare step for a Hamlet and volunteered to work in Walter Mondale's 1984 presidential campaign. "He lied so much on TV and got away with it. I can't understand it." Out come the contrary views toward the body politic, the simultaneous beliefs that people *should* govern themselves, but *can't.* "I believe in democracy, but if people are so stupid and know so little about the world that they take Reagan at face value, what can you do? It bothers me that American politics have sunk to that level. But other times I say let them have him. They're screwing up totally, but that's democracy and so be it."

Brent doesn't view his work for the Mondale campaign as very effective, except perhaps to soothe his conscience. "It assuaged certain feelings I have, a self-righteous streak," he says, able to laugh about it now. "It reminded me of the white liberal who donates money to the NAACP and then gets held up by a black teenager. 'After all I've done for you people!' he says. People who engage in social causes often develop their own sense of self-righteousness. That's a lot of the motivation. My feeling is it's okay to get involved if you want to do it and feel good about it, but you have to remember you're doing it for yourself, not to get credit from God or other people."

As much as he believes in democracy, Brent sees problems with the system. "A lot of the way I think involves process. That's my legal background, I guess. I see people as the products of institutions and institutions as the products of people. The problem is figuring out where to intervene in that loop. I can point to lots of social problems that I would say are problems of process, like distribution of income. The homeless and people with mental problems should have adequate facilities to take care of them. But where do you break the cycle that allows for homelessness? If it goes on under a president elected by a majority, with the approval of a Congress that's opposed to him, what are you going to do? I think a parliamentary democracy would be better than what we have—the structure of the presidency in this era, with the role of the media and stuff, doesn't work very well—but what difference it would ultimately make is another question."

Jeff's ruminations on the American system take him much further from the political mainstream than Brent. "Democracy was never meant for this country," he declares. "Maybe it could work in some other place, but it was never meant for a group of people as diverse as Americans— and I say diverse with reservations and qualifications. America's just too unwieldy a place. People have different ideas of what it stands for, what's right and wrong, what's good and evil. So compromise, which is what the system is based on, is simply unworkable. I mean, we each have certain issues that we feel *cannot* be compromised." Thoroughly disgusted by the system, Jeff has withdrawn almost entirely from political participation. He hasn't voted since 1972, when to his amazement the nation reelected the corrupt Richard Nixon by a landslide.

Jeff sees America as an oligarchy, not a democracy. A superwealthy few control society by keeping the middle class content. So long as the middle class stays docile everything's fine, no matter how much the lower classes suffer. "Clearly the system isn't fair. Those born into the middle class can take advantage of the system. That's the way it was intended to be. The system works to the extent that it rewards those who are supposed to be rewarded. If someone gets through who wasn't really meant to, like a token black or woman, the system just uses that person to its advantage. It points to him or her as an example for others with the same background. 'Of course the system works, because look, even someone like *him* was able to succeed.' That means anyone like him who hasn't succeeded can only blame himself, not the system." In Jeff's eyes, we're wage slaves of the corporate oligarchy. "If I had to choose between being a slave on a southern plantation and being a worker in an auto plant, I'd choose the auto plant. But that's not to say drilling rivets into a car frame isn't a form of enslavement. There are degrees of oppression. They've gotten more slick—they've somehow convinced us that working for a living isn't a form of enslavement, that you've achieved freedom because hey, we're allowing you to buy consumer goods, we're giving you an automobile, we're letting you watch television. They've gotten more clever, more insidious about it, but the effect is substantially the same as when there was bona fide slavery."

Jeff is a firm believer in anarchy, which he sees as the truest form of democracy. Everyone takes responsibility for his or her own actions and respects the rights of others. "The issue is authority more than anything else," he says. "I never really, and still don't, understand the grounds for anyone or any group claiming authority over others." Asked what shape his ideal society would take, Jeff hedges at first, but then, after acknowledging that such a world could never exist, ventures a description. "It would consist of a lot of small communities of like-minded people. Each community would have its own beliefs and value systems. The overriding rule is that no one community could change any other community's way of living."

Clearly, Hamlet's political views are way out of step with main-stream America's, to a point where his less-enlightened neighbors might think him a radical. That Hamlet, the ultimate democrat, could be seen as a radical is a sad indication of how seriously the level of political discourse in this country has declined—and how limited our notion of democracy has become. Not too long ago politicians spoke for hours at a time about issues of the day, and people listened to them. But that kind of attention went out with television, the McCarthy hearings, and the mass exodus to the know-nothing land of the suburbs. Now if we vote we consider ourselves activists. A nation gets the government it deserves; so long as we care not about matters of state, we'll get leaders who care not about us. The shame of it all is that the people who do care—and thus deserve better—will suffer along with the negligent majority.

24

One Touch of Nature Makes the Whole World Kin

An associative thinker par excellence, Hamlet recognizes that individual actions affect the state of the world. He notes, for instance, that every time we drive a car we add to the amount of carbon dioxide in the atmosphere. The increase in atmospheric carbon dioxide leads to the Greenhouse Effect, the global warming trend that by the year 2100 could cause the oceans to rise upward of five feet and inundate many of the world's coastal cities. Who'll be responsible for the drowning of Miami? Those of us who drive to work instead of taking the bus. Our most routine actions have planetwide implications, and Hamlet feels very strongly that he ought to make the world a little better rather than a little worse.

Of course, feeling very strongly about a matter is one thing; *acting* is another. Hamlet finds just as many reasons for not acting to save the world as he does for not acting to attain success. He may think the situation hopeless. He may be stymied by the huge scale on which any real change would have to occur. Or he may simply have no interest in becoming a martyr or crusader. But despite thinking the world's too big to change, Hamlet still feels a need to act in accordance with his beliefs. So he takes periodic stabs at fusing his actions and philosophy. As Brent noted in the last chapter, even if Hamlet's idealistic actions lack effectiveness, they at least assuage his self-righteous streak.

When he thinks of it and finds it convenient, Hamlet plays the role of conscientious planetary citizen. Knowing that the American obsession for consumer goods does incalculable harm to the environment and perpetuates worldwide injustice (although Americans make up only 6 percent of the world's population, they use up nearly 30 percent of all available resources), Hamlet buys fewer products. This isn't a major sacrifice; he doesn't earn enough to purchase a whole lot anyway. When the globally conscious Hamlet *does* make a purchase, he tries to put his money where his heart is. He boycotts fruit and vegetables from totalitarian Chile, buying his produce from nuclear-free New Zealand instead. He avoids goods wrapped in nonbiodegradable packages or preserved with a host of multisyllabic chemicals; he's the sort whose birthday cards come from those little companies that use 100 percent recycled paper. Wary of big-time capitalism, he shops at locally owned stores instead of national chains, even if it costs a little more. Where possible he recycles his metals, glass, and paper, and dumps his rotten vegetables on a compost heap.

For a number of Hamlets, Jeff, Maxine, Jessica, and Brent among them, doing good for the world also includes experimenting with vegetarianism. The reasons for adopting a vegetarian diet range from health to religion to politics. Jeff became a vegetarian in 1979 and remained one until 1986. "I saw no reason to kill animals. It made no sense to me that people had pets and then would sit down and have cow or bird for dinner. Those animals were too much like me, they seemed to be made of the same stuff I'm made of," he remarks. "Even now I don't eat chicken, or cow products other than milk." He smiles. "I do eat eggs, though. Hey, exploiting them's okay. I just don't believe in killing them."

Maxine and Jessica aren't as strongly committed to vegetarianism as Jeff. They illustrate the dilettantish nature of Hamlet's commitment to changing the world. Maxine doesn't know why she ever became a vegetarian, and now that she's back to eating meat she has no idea why she switched. "Someday I might figure it out. I guess it's just a matter of taste," she says. Jessica's more principled, but she's also less disciplined. "I was a vegetarian for a number of years, then went off it, then went back to it, and back and forth again. I always felt like I was backsliding when I became a nonvegetarian. A chicken's life is important. It has a right to be part of the cosmos, even if it is monumentally stupid."

An aside: Jessica also tries to act in accordance with her beliefs by putting her money where her thoughts are. She sends contributions to Greenpeace and Amnesty International because "animals and nonviolent political prisoners are the most defenseless groups on earth. There are other groups in a bad way, but those two are nearest my heart." Maxine doesn't earn enough to make donations, but when possible she contributes her time to various social organizations. In general, however, Hamlet tends *not* to support charitable causes. Like Maxine, he may not have the money to spare. He may also doubt the effectiveness of cause-oriented organizations, citing, among other things, the fact that many plow a substantial amount of their contributions into administration and fund-raising.

The global issue Hamlet feels most strongly about is environmentalism. He can give a number of reasons why it's imperative we preserve the environment in all its diversity, the primary one being that we depend on the earth for sustenance. When we destroy the environment, we destroy ourselves. Then, too, despite the claims of developers and polluters, the value of the ecosystem can't be weighed in dollars. The processes of life are priceless—not subject to the narrow definitions of cost-benefit analyses. And as the ultimate equal rights advocate, Hamlet rejects the biblical premise that humankind has dominion over all things. He believes that wild creatures have a right to fulfill their destiny free of humankind's interference—just as he has a right to live *his* life apart from the human herd.

In three respects Hamlet's thought processes dovetail seamlessly with environmental consciousness. First, there's his inclination to think associatively. The most basic assumption of ecological science is that all things are connected, and Hamlet can readily intuit the connection between seemingly unassociated phenomena, understanding how each affects the other. Second, Hamlet is naturally inclined to think about the long-term consequences of actions. Environmental forces work over geologic time—centuries, even millennia—and as we noted in the example of automobile use leading to the Greenhouse Effect, Hamlet can project the consequences of actions hundreds of years down the line. Third, Hamlet believes that the good of the community should take precedence over the good of the individual. No person or group of people has the right to pollute the air, water, and earth shared by everyone—especially if the purpose behind the pollution is profit. Environmental problems cross national borders and affect every class of people. If we are to solve those problems (and they *must* be solved, the alternative being disaster) we must solve them together, as one global community, and we must collectively rebuff the destructive practices of individuals, corporations, and nations.

"I'm really troubled by people not thinking about all the ramifications of their actions," says one Hamlet who understands just how much his own actions contribute to the world's environmental problems. "I'm someone who, when I buy a cup of tea to go, I think, this tea is in a Styrofoam cup that will pollute the environment, so by buying it I'm contributing to something that is diametrically opposed to what I believe in. Maybe the tea itself is coming from a country where there's an oppressive government, and all the money is going into the hands of one man and all the peasants are suffering. So what I do now is bring my own glass mug and my own tea, so all I need is hot water. It's working on a small scale, I know, but I feel it's important."

We know how Martin feels about environmental issues—he's the one who thinks the world would be best served by the elimination of 80 percent of the human population. Jeff, who told us earlier that everyone has issues they absolutely cannot compromise on, says that environmentalism is one issue *he* can never compromise on. And then we've heard Brent speak in rapturous tones about backpacking: "I just like to be off in the woods. I'm happy. I smile. I relax. Just me and dirt and rocks and trees and insects." He's so passionate about the environment that he almost went to work for the legal arm of a major environmental organization. But, reflecting Hamlet's abhorrence of ideologies, Brent backed off when he noticed the dogmatic fervor of his prospective colleagues. "For people really involved in the environmental movement, it's a religion," he says with disappointment. "It fits almost every definition—there's even a god, Mother Earth."

It's virtually impossible for a large-scale enterprise to retain a semblance of democracy and humor while achieving its goals in a disciplined, uncompromising manner—yet that's what Hamlet wants. He's always disappointed when he finds that a favorite organization is run by a clique of insiders, or treats itself and its cause as if nothing else mattered, or compromises its procedures and goals to win mainstream credibility. He concludes it's the nature of the beast—as organizations grow it's inevitable that they turn into bureaucratic, hierarchical, compromising monsters. And so, resigned to the fact that no group can change the world and preserve its soul, Hamlet works individually, saving the world one Styrofoam cup at a time. Although that may not be as effective as joining a group that seeks to outlaw the production of Styrofoam, given Hamlet's nature it's the most effective contribution he can make.

25

When Hamlet Gazes Heavenward

As with most Americans, Hamlet makes his first acquaintance with God during childhood. From the daily recital of "one nation, under God" and Sunday school dogma he gets the message that this God fellow ranks right up there with Mom, Dad, and the President of the United States. Higher, in fact, because God has the kind of power his parents and President only dream about. God can see Hamlet *everywhere;* he knows every single bad thing Hamlet does, says, or thinks, and he can mete out punishment in the form of sickness, skinned knees, and guilt. If Hamlet doesn't want God to get him, he has to obey his parents and minister, the grown-ups who serve as God's intermediaries. And obey them he does, even if they can't give him a straight answer to such simple questions as "How come I can't see God?" and "If God loves good and hates evil, why does he allow the class bully to beat me up?"

In early adulthood, when Hamlet becomes a critical thinker, he reflects on his early indoctrination and takes a renewed interest in God and religion. This time, however, he seeks answers from a skeptic's perspective. He learns, among other things, that there are many more religions than he was exposed to as a child—and he may think that some of them make more sense than the one he was raised in. He also discovers the intensely political nature of organized religions; they're hierarchical, territorial, and, as with Roman Catholicism in the Middle Ages and Judaism in Israel today, occasionally buttressed with the power of state. Especially among Western religions, the hunger for influence has often led to corruption, intolerance, violence, and death. Hamlet cannot help but conclude that God is a human power play as much as a supernatural, all-powerful entity. And as for those childhood questions, even in adulthood he can't find satisfactory answers to why God is invisible or tolerates bullies.

The shortcomings of organized religion make it extremely difficult for Hamlet to belong to a mainstream denomination, but he doesn't always abandon religion completely. Let's set up a spectrum of spiritual sentiments, from strict dogma at one end to unbelief at the other. At the far right we'll put fundamentalism. Occupying the right side are mainstream sects such as the Presbyterians, Episcopalians, and conservative Jews. In the middle we have most mystical religions and liberal Western theologies such as Unitarianism and various New Age concepts. On the left we find agnosticism, and at the extreme left we come to atheism, the absence of religious belief. Hamlets form roughly equal clusters at three points on the spectrum: the believers, who fall in with the mystical and liberal Western faiths; the atheists, who perch themselves all the way out on the leftward edge; and the agnostics, who sit in between and wonder whether God exists or not.

The believing Hamlet prays by his own rules. He may at first follow someone else's spiritual teachings, but over time he blends his own ideas with those teachings and develops a unique perspective. By and large he's more interested in contemplation and linking up to a universal consciousness than he is in rituals. In typical Hamlet fashion he sees spiritual connections everywhere. God is not merely a discrete, anthropological being but a unifying cosmic essence. All living things are part of a whole, connected to himself, not a myriad of isolated, exploitable objects. So sure is he that all spiritual paths come together that he often incorporates a wealth of outré ideas into his system—anything from numerology to New Age channeling. Before long his theology may sound like a hodgepodge of every quasi-mystical notion ever propounded. No matter how weird Hamlet's doctrine, though, you can always be sure of one thing: He's given it *plenty* of thought.

Antonio is a believer, but he denies it's simply because he spent a decade in a monastery. "Let's see you make a flower, if you're so damn powerful," he challenges, maintaining that everything he sees in daily life proves the existence of a God. "Spirituality takes a lot of work to deny, so what is the point of denying it? It's like trying to deny your color or gender." Although he says he's still a "papist," in the sixteen years since he left the monastery he's developed a personal religion that most mainstream Catholics would call blasphemy. He knows that, too. "I'm still very religious, but it's a religious life that goes way beyond Catholicism," he explains. "People say the Church is the body of Christ and the body of Christ is the people. That's bullshit. The relationship between a person and God is strictly personal. We come here alone, we leave here alone, and we have to account for ourselves before God on an individual basis. I look at *my* relationship with God and I'm *embarrassed* to be a Catholic, because I've gone much further in my relationship with God than Catholicism could have brought me. Catholicism provided some parameters for me, it gave me a lot of time for meditation, and it taught me something about the human condition. But I was working within it to overcome its limitations."

Judging from his testimony, Antonio has overcome those limitations in a big way. "I am not ashamed to say I've had an out-of-body experience more than once during my meditations," he attests, and in light of those extraordinary experiences he's come to convictions more Eastern than Western. "I believe in something that's generally known by the term reincarnation, although I don't know if that's what I'd call it." Why does he believe in reincarnation? "My ancestors come from western Africa and subcontinental India. How would I know about France and eighteenth-century French culture? By know I mean feel—know how it *feels* to wear the clothes, smell the air. When it came to French music, I already *knew* it. My teachers didn't have to tell me about it. I even knew enough to correct *them* sometimes. I know all the things that made for eighteenth-century French music the same way I know all the cultural pressures that make for rock and roll today. Where did that come from? The only way I can account for it is that sometimes, in middle sleep or near-sleep, I see myself there. We know there were Moors in the French court, some of whom were ministers to the Louises. Maybe I was one of them."

Atheistic Hamlets would scoff at Antonio's testimony. They don't need God to explain flowers or *déjà vu* or the universe—science suffices. To their way of thinking, God is nothing more than the ultimate rationalization. Perpetrators of the most inexcusably evil deed can justify their action by saying it's God's will. God also comes in handy when a demagogue needs that something extra to control the populace. Convince people that disobedience will lead to eternal damnation and they'll do whatever you ask, a neat way of augmenting personal and political power. Hamlet doesn't need the threat of God's wrath to lead a moral life. The ultimate secular humanist, he does the right thing out of inner conviction.

What about the big reason for believing in God, that a supernatural force gives meaning to mortal life? This is one instance where Hamlet doesn't see a connection. Even if God existed, Hamlet thinks it presumptuous to believe God has a special destiny for each and every one of us, let alone believe that he cares for humankind one whit. Here we are, tiny creatures on a little ball orbiting an average sun in a galaxy that's one in a billion, and we're insisting that God made us in his image, has a purpose in mind for each of us, and cares about our every thought and deed! Now *that's* vanity. The atheist Hamlet has come to accept his insignificance—why not? society reminds him of it daily—and has long since gotten over his need for any grand and holy purpose.

But knowing how unpopular atheism is in the United States, most Hamlets soft-pedal their lack of belief. Their life-style and political orientation render them outcast enough; they feel no urge to bring even more censure on themselves by declaring, as Karl Marx did, that religion is the opiate of the masses. Mention God to Martin, though, and you get an outburst of vituperation. No silent dissenter he; he's proud to be an atheist, and figures it's the believers who ought to apologize for how they think. As with most Hamlets, he was brought up in a mainstream religion. "I went to church every Sunday, Sunday school too. Protestant Congregational church. It was more a social thing than anything else. I guess church has always been a social thing, that and a way to support priests and ministers. My folks believe in God in a very low-key way. What they most wanted to see was the three of us kids confirmed, and so we were.

"I was an agnostic for a long time. I only decided I was an atheist two or three years ago. I thought, ah, the hell with it, there's no way. I suppose you could believe in some God-type creature who set the ball rolling long ago, maybe assigned various characteristics and laws to the universe, and then just threw it out there and let Chance take care of the rest. But there's certainly no God paying attention now. Knowing that this is just one tiny speck in the universe, to imagine we're the center of God's plan shows an ego problem on our part. It's ridiculous. Ridiculous!

"I frown on people who dead-set believe that there's a God. These people, because of that strong faith, they're the ones who go out there and don't give a damn about all these things that I worry about. They just figure they've got God behind them, so they don't care. More people have been killed in the name of God than for any other reason." He shrugs. "I don't know if the world would be a better place without religion. Man seems to need something to put his faith in. If there were no religion, we'd worship some scientific fact, or some person. But it would be nice to have something in common that everyone could support, because every day you read about religious wars. It's just religion. I mean, who cares? Why fight over it?"

Why fight over it, indeed? That's the feeling of the Hamlets in between, the agnostics. In typical Hamlet fashion, they can't decide whether a supreme being exists or not. They reject conventional constructs of God, but they can't readily dismiss the possibility that on some level, way past our ability to perceive it, a force or power analogous to God exists. There does seem to be an order to this universe: Atoms are minute solar systems and solar systems are minute galaxies. Did some conscious force design that? Where do matter and energy and the physical forces that govern their behavior come from? The agnostic Hamlet throws up his hands. There's no way of knowing—our minds are just too puny to comprehend anything that could operate on that scale. And if there's no way of knowing, there's no use in thinking about it—and *certainly* no reason for fighting over it.

Yet fight over it people do—and not just in the literal sense. If there's one religious practice that all Hamlets can agree on it's proselytizing, the battle for souls: They *hate* it. Hamlet respects the right of others to worship in their own way, even when they fall under the spell of holy-rolling rip-off-artist preachers, and he expects the same consideration in return. So when others ask him if he's thought about God lately and then try to convert him, he may get so angry he lashes out with uncharacteristic hostility. Yes, he's thought about God plenty, thank you, probably more than the person challenging him! He has a First Amendment right to worship (or not worship) as he pleases, and he doesn't like people telling him what to believe any more than he likes them telling him how to vote.

Hamlet is especially bothered by the missionary zeal of Christian evangelicals, and finds the increasingly political agenda of America's fundamentalist Protestants alarming. Given their way, some of the more militant fundamentalists in this country would turn America into a Protestant theocracy. By definition, Hamlet could never function in such an environment: Fundamentalism requires both unquestioning faith and intolerance of diversity, anathema to the skeptical, curious Hamlet. If the political influence of the religious Right continues to grow, Hamlet will increasingly run the risks associated with adherence to heretical beliefs.

So, scratch a Hamlet and you may well find a self-critical, somewhat misanthropic environmentalist who has strange ideas about God and thinks American democracy is becoming more myth than reality. Not the sort of fellow you'd find attending a Shriners' convention or a motocross race. Hamlet protects himself by not saying anything if he can't say anything nice. Already subject to disrepute because he's underemployed, he fears that people would reject him completely if they knew how he *really* felt. By keeping the talk small he preserves his place on the fringe of society. But the lack of meaningful interaction may distance him even further from the mainstream. As his isolation grows his intellect may atrophy from the lack of fresh input, leaving him confused, frustrated, and bitter. For intellectual as well as emotional and financial reasons, then, it's vital that by his late thirties he make an attempt to connect with the mainstream world.

VI

COPING WITH THE HAMLET SYNDROME

And so, without more circumstance at all,
I hold it fit that we shake hands and part,
You, as your business and desire shall point you,
For every man hath business and desire,
Such as it is, and for my own poor part,
I will go pray.

Hamlet, ACT I, SCENE V

"I used to think I could live on the fringe forever, but something in me snapped. I just woke up one morning and this life wasn't what I wanted anymore," says Jeff. Since his graduation from college in the mid-seventies he'd worked at a series of clerical jobs, saving enough money to take a few months off every now and then but otherwise going nowhere financially or professionally. His hair hung down his back in a ponytail, as it had since the Age of Flower Power. His interests more or less remained the same. But as he came closer to his thirty-third birthday, Jeff started to think differently. He began to want more from life—including rewards that could be obtained only by pursuing the dollar. His to-do-or-not-to-do crisis had arrived.

Although Jeff may have just woken up one morning and realized that his fringe existence was no longer satisfactory, it took him years to actually go out and try for something better. It's not that he didn't know what he wanted. The dollar called, as it had from the beginning of his life. He wanted a spouse, a meaningful career, and, down the line, a house and children. But he hadn't had much practice at asserting himself and taking aggressive steps to fulfill his needs. As a result he acted slowly, tentatively, and only after great expenditure of intellectual and emotional energy.

Over time things fell into place. After years of wooing a woman he was attracted to at first sight, Jeff finally won her over, and they started living together in 1987. He cut his hair; it still falls over his collar, but it's short enough that he's no longer instantaneously recognized as a hippie. The capstone of his emergence from the Hamlet Syndrome was his decision to become an architect.

"Architecture was something that intrigued me from early on," he says. "It didn't only have to do with reading *The Fountainhead* by Ayn Rand in high school. Even when I was twelve years old I drew these designs for a house. In college I had a friend who was in architecture school. His first project was taking a bus outside of town and *making* his own shelter for the weekend. I remember thinking at the time, God, that sounds great. But it wasn't a primary interest of mine, so I didn't think about it seriously."

Most people come to architecture via construction work or engineering or art. Ah, Hamlet!—Jeff's interest in architecture springs from intellectual curiosity. "Architecture cropped up again in the last few years when I read Tom Wolfe's book, *From Bauhaus to Our House*. I'm embarrassed to say that it may have been something of an inspiration, because I thought his argument was ridiculous. It got me fired up, and I started thinking about architecture. I met someone in an architecture program and we talked a lot, and then I read more books, like Lewis Mumford's *Sticks and Stones*. Mumford says a building is no better than the society that creates it, and that surely seems to be true. So over time I started thinking about architecture more and started formulating my own ideas about it."

What clinched Jeff's decision to go to architecture school was his realization that architecture offered an opportunity to combine heart and dollar. Buildings, he learned from reading Mumford and others, have a profound effect on the attitudes of the people inside them. An ornate, naturally lit chamber has a much different impact on a person's mood than a steel-and-concrete, rectangular room with fluorescent lighting. Modern American architecture, with its emphasis on remoteness (setting a building off from its environment, constructing interiors with lots of little rooms and unopenable windows) contributes to *cultural alienation,* the feeling that we're cut off from one another and our surroundings. Jeff, in the best Hamlet tradition, believes strongly in association. Therefore he's aligned himself with the movement toward *vernacular* architecture, a style that takes its inspiration from the intimate, more connected structures typical of native cultures. "Maybe vernacular architecture can provide an antidote to what we have now," he says hopefully. By designing comfortable buildings, Jeff will not only make money, he'll literally give shape to the principles of his heart.

But to become an architect one needs more than an intellectual commitment—one also needs practical skills. Jeff had none of these skills, so he persuaded his office supervisor to let him job-share and work half-time. With the extra time off, he took drawing classes. For the first time in ages he got caught up in competition. Disconcerting as that was, he adopted a philosophical view of the situation and forged ahead. "I took to drawing right away, and fell in love with it. But ego does get in the way a lot: You look around and think, he's better than I am, I'm not as good as he is, so I'm a bad drawer. After enough time in class, and after coming to the realization that there'll always be somebody better than me, I stopped worrying about that sort of thing."

It took Jeff two years to put together a portfolio and application. Part of the reason he needed so long was the illness he suffered as a result of his vitamin B_{12} deficiency. But Jeff also worked slowly. Persistent positive action still ran counter to his nature. Instead of spending his days off drawing up his portfolio, he watched soap operas and afternoon talk shows like the *Phil Donohue* and *Oprah Winfrey* shows. Finally, backed up against his application deadline, he worked fiendishly and submitted his application on time. Even when hurried, his work showed evidence of top-notch talent, so within three months he gained acceptance to a graduate school in architecture. Jeff was on his way to resolving the to-do-or-not-to-do crisis and escaping the fringe existence of the typical Hamlet.

26

Once a Hamlet, Always a Hamlet

How lovely it would be to conclude this book with the encouraging news that, like Jeff, all Hamlets hit upon a creative resolution of their heart-or-dollar dilemma and summon the initiative to attain it. How lovely—and how grossly misleading. For only some Hamlets formulate a vision that allows them both mainstream success and peace of mind, and of those, many never take the necessary steps to turn that vision into reality. Even when they do take the necessary steps, they're still prone to Hamlet Syndrome-like symptoms. For instance, they suffer prolonged bouts of second-guessing—after-the-fact indecision.

Take Jeff. Midway into his second semester at architecture school he took a leave of absence to reassess his situation. Although he was doing well academically, he found the nuts-and-bolts emphasis of his program far less intriguing and enjoyable than the theories that attracted him to architecture in the first place. The workload, the deadlines, the competitive atmosphere, and the constant criticism (both good and bad) from instructors had him riding an emotional roller-coaster. Jeff is currently taking a course in architectural design. His reaction to the course will determine whether he continues to pursue a career in architecture or not. He has no alternate plans; if he quits architecture school, he'll have to go back to the dead-end clerical work he's been doing for years.

Regardless of the physical and emotional sacrifices, plenty of Hamlets persist in their climb out of the syndrome, and in a few years they make their way into a professional position. Are they then happy? Does the heart-or-dollar dilemma truly get resolved? Usually not. Although Hamlet may have steeled himself for the rigors of a graduate program in a professional vocation, he's often unprepared for the commitment and responsibility of the job itself. Working overtime, making countless decisions that affect other people's lives, feeling constant pressure to produce, he's overwhelmed. He sees himself becoming a work machine, a slave to his position, with no time for the dilatory pleasures he so enjoyed when he was underemployed. When Hamlet inevitably discovers that the profession he's embraced comes fraught with cynical expediencies, he may suffer a fresh onslaught of disillusion. At that point he may drop out and go back to the simpler life he led before.

But don't despair; some Hamlets *do* happily resolve the syndrome. Jessica, our perpetual student, serves as a perfect case in point. At the age of thirty-five and after ten years of studying Chinese, she finally *succeeded,* landing a tenure-track professorship at a southeastern university. To give you an idea how quickly she embraced mainstream sensibilities, she hesitated to participate in this book because she was afraid it might hurt her career! She was spurred by the to-do-or-not-to-do crisis, which started when she realized her younger sister was beginning to make it in the world—and Jessica still had nothing. "I guess when I was thirty-three I began this mid-life crisis. What do I have, anyway? My only answer was, not very much. My younger sister started to be more and more successful in her career, which spooked me because it had always been the other way around. Then she bought a house, and all of a sudden I was thinking, there it is, going right by me. I'm just stagnating."

Yet even Jessica's road is by no means smooth. She frets about assuming responsibility. "I feel a lot of trepidation about my job," she confides. "It's hard to become an adult and commit one's self. I don't feel like a college professor—I feel like a fifteen-year-old. I feel like I've fooled all these people into thinking I'm an adult. I never wanted to end up in a position where I would have to take up adult responsibilities and commitments." Overworked at her first professorial assignment, she's transferred to another university where an old friend from graduate school has gained tenure. With a mentor to support her, Jessica figures she'll have an easier time gaining tenure herself.

We have great hope for Maxine, who has chosen a profession, librarianship, on the basis of heartfelt belief rather than need for the dollar. Maxine has done two very smart things. First, she's reconciled herself to a life of low income. Second, and more important, she's attacked the to-do-or-not-to-do crisis *before* it has a chance to attack her. Whereas most Hamlets wait until their mid-thirties to decide on a direction for themselves, Maxine will have her professional degree by the time she hits thirty. If she can remain content with a modest income and a profession undervalued by the mainstream, she has every chance of happily resolving the heart-or-dollar dilemma. "I would really like a computer. I would like a car. I would like to buy a house. But when I think about spending all my time earning enough money to buy these things, they become much less important. I'd rather have the time than the computer," she says, a Hamlet to the very end.

The key factor linking all Hamlets who make their way out of the syndrome is that they acknowledge the primacy of their heartfelt principles. The heart has been stronger in Hamlet all along—else he wouldn't have sought refuge on the social periphery—and it will never loosen its grip on him. *To cope with the Hamlet Syndrome, then, Hamlet has to stop looking at his heart as the greatest obstacle to success and start looking at the dollar as the greatest obstacle to contentment.* The best way for Hamlet to resolve the heart-or-dollar dilemma, in short, is *to stand by his heart and stop longing for the dollar.*

Yes, that does condemn Hamlet to permanent exile from the mainstream, and it means he can never have many of the material rewards he's always craved. But the alternative, the mainstream route, is for him a never-ending road to nowhere. The wanting never ceases: Once you have a house, you want one that's bigger or has a fireplace or swimming pool; once you make it as a corporate vice president, you want to become the chief executive officer. Jumping onto that treadmill may lead to a few brief episodes of comfort and satisfaction, but in the long run will make

Hamlet no happier than he is on the fringe. Money buys power, sex, and attention, but it doesn't buy integrity and peace of mind, the things that Hamlet needs the most.

Not only should Hamlet choose heart over dollar, but he should *follow his heart to the fullest.* To paraphrase Patrick Henry, if this be Hamlethood, make the most of it! The biggest mistake Hamlet makes is in underestimating the importance of his values—and himself. He's too deferential to mainstream sensibilities. Why should he be ashamed of his ideals and of the way he thinks? Why should he let himself be cowed by the dollar-oriented people who run the office he works in, the building he lives in, the circles he socializes in? The most they can do to him (unless they're sociopaths) is dislike him, which is better than what they do now, which is *despise* him. In their eyes he's a wimp, a loser, a failure, a fool to be laughed at and taken advantage of. Hamlet has to change that image, and the quickest way to do it is to stop feeling so apologetic about himself and his values—and to stand up for what he *knows* is right.

Once Hamlet begins to stand by his beliefs instead of apologizing for them, he'll be astounded by the results. He'll find that beneath their self-assured exteriors, most people are pitifully insecure and afraid, even more so than he is. They will, more often than not, be happy to *defer to him.* That's not to say that everyone will rally around his values and radically change their mainstream lives. But by asserting his principles he'll win respect for himself and the things he believes in. The higher he holds his head, the higher his self-esteem will rise. And who knows? He may even effect some positive changes in his workaday environment.

One caution: As he stands up for his heart, Hamlet must remember his humility. Life on the fringe has ennobled his character, and he must try to retain as much of that gentle sensibility as possible. Hamlet has to make his case without being obnoxious or persistent or vindictive. In the end, he's embracing his heart and abjuring the dollar for the sake of his sanity and long-term contentment, not to fix the world or get even with the people who make his life so difficult. His greatest strength is the knowledge that he may be wrong, and that his way of doing things isn't always right for everyone. As he goes among the dollar-craving infidel, he must hold that wisdom close.

Going for the heart and abandoning the dollar is easier said than done, of course. The tug of the dollar and the desire to conform never go away entirely, and even the most mature Hamlets sometimes feel a twinge of remorse over their decision to follow the heart. Those yearnings for a more conventional life must be endured until they pass. The first defense against them is full acceptance of the heart. But since that wall will fail every now and then, Hamlet has to build up a second line of defense. We'll talk about that second line in the following chapter.

27

When the Right Attitude Just Isn't Enough

A change in attitude—accepting that the values of his heart will always be paramount—is Hamlet's first step toward becoming contented with himself and fending off doubt. But as the American Indians who asked the spirits to make them invulnerable to the white man's bullets discovered, faith in one's beliefs isn't protection enough. A necessary second step in Hamlet's coping with the syndrome is that he learn to take positive actions that further his interests and ideals.

The most obvious positive action Hamlet can take is to seek a niche in mainstream society where he can express the values of his heart and earn a living at the same time. Such a niche may take him years to find. What he has to remember during the long search is that *the heart should always come first.* Rather than throw himself at a prestigious occupation that promises to pay well, he should discount factors like status and income and concentrate on locating work that's consistent with his values. Many Hamlets think law or some other profession will allow for a happy confluence of heart and dollar, but in general their view is naive. When they find the dollar plays a much bigger role in their chosen profession than they imagined, they're so disappointed they often wind up dropping out. Maxine's tack is wiser: Go into something you truly believe in regardless of the starting pay. Hamlet's much more likely to stick with a field that way, and in time he'll almost certainly work up to a remunerative position. The dollar often follows the heart.

But we've gotten a little bit ahead of ourselves here. Not every Hamlet has a career he believes in, and not every Hamlet has the courage to move forward when he *does* discover a career that he'd like to pursue. Over the years Hamlet has fallen into a pattern of doing nothing, of drifting and delaying and evading. Action is an alien concept. He's not about to spring out of bed and pound the pavement until he finds a job that makes him happy for the rest of his life. Before he can attempt something as vigorous as that, he has to learn to take *simple* actions on his own behalf—learn how to walk before he runs. So let's look at three ways Hamlet can start building a sense of power and possibility. If he follows through on just *one* of them, he should gain sufficient confidence to take on the world more aggressively.

The first thing Hamlet can do is address a minor frustration that's been going on too long. Perhaps he's tired of a co-worker's constant whistling, or his own habit of leaving his dirty clothes unwashed until he's practically knee-deep in them. The first example requires that Hamlet assert himself. He has to consider his right to a quiet work environment as important as his co-worker's right to whistle—and instead of just complaining about the situation, or waiting for someone else to do the dirty work, he has to confront the tootling offender. Although some Hamlets have no problem defending themselves when their interests are endangered, many allow all sorts of encroachments on their well-being. They'd rather suffer than alleviate the problem. Dealing head-on with a minor encroachment gives Hamlet practice in plotting strategy ("How do I confront the whistler? What if he starts again two hours later?") and minimizes the consequences of his failure. When his effort works, he's that much more encouraged to address larger and less tractable frustrations.

The second example, dealing with dirty laundry, requires that Hamlet summon up discipline. Many Hamlets are well-disciplined—but the great majority have discipline only for matters they enjoy or consider important. For the tangential things, Hamlet's inclined to show no discipline at all—and the number of things tangential to a Hamlet can exceed the number of cells in his body. Real discipline involves sticking to tasks one would rather not do. If Hamlet faces those unpleasant tasks straight-on and works them through, his self-esteem will rise. Again, it's important that he start with something simple and possible, like doing his laundry on a regular basis. Once he falls into the habit, he'll find that unpleasant tasks require less discipline than he imagined—you just *do* *'em,* that's all. And he'll see that large, daunting tasks can be overcome by breaking them down into smaller parts. With a steady application of time and energy, the small parts can be mastered one by one until the entire task is finished.

Asserting himself and increasing his self-discipline will help Hamlet gain a sense of power and possibility. Another way he can empower himself is to try aerobic exercising. Slow, steady, oxygen-burning exercise generates a number of positive effects on the human body, including the increased production of endorphins. Chemical compounds manufactured in the brain, endorphins promote feelings of tranquillity and contentment—they're the main cause of the "runner's high" joggers often claim to experience. But that's not the only good feeling Hamlet will get from giving his body a workout. He'll also gain a sense of accomplishment. Knowing he can run three miles without stopping, or can swim twenty laps in an Olympic-size pool, or can bicycle thirty miles a day will enhance his sense of potential. Yes, that's a hard thing to do, and I can do it, he can think proudly—and perhaps that will tempt him to try other hard things more directly connected to his place in the world.

Relatively few Hamlets exercise regularly. This is especially surprising in that Hamlets are young people who came of age during the great American fitness boom. Perhaps they were turned off by the trendiness of it all. Before you could say "Boston Marathon" it became a social crime to go jogging in anything less than a hundred-dollar pair of sneakers and a color-coordinated outfit made of form-fitting, flashy fabric. Then in the eighties the aerobics craze hit: Dozens of aspiring hardbodies paid upward of five bucks apiece to spend forty-five minutes bouncing in place to the latest FM radio hits. The whole scene stunk of *yuppie.* But trendy doesn't always equal bad, and Hamlet of all people should know better than to judge something by its appearance. Running, swimming, and dancing predate the Cro-Magnons. You don't need a fancy outfit or membership in a health club to do them. To run, just throw on some old clothes and put one foot in front of the other real fast. That's all there is to it—although once you get more involved in it, you may *want* one of those hundred-dollar pairs of sneakers.

Jessica started running and swimming during her to-do-or-not-to-do crisis. She'd broken up with a boyfriend and was getting nothing but rejections in her search for employment. "I was able to think, well, at least my body will be in good shape. It's the sort of thing people do at the end of a relationship, I guess. You think, I'm going to look so good that the next time my old boyfriend sees me, he'll be sorry he broke up with me." A wonderful thing happened on her way to a sleeker body: She felt more empowered in every aspect of her life. "I started running and swimming seriously, in a way I hadn't before, and I got back a sense of myself and control. I felt more that I could deal with things—I had a sense of power." Exercise gave her the strength to persist in her search for a professorship—and contributed to her success in landing a prestigious position.

Of course, all Hamlets, especially those nearing their fortieth birthday, should get a thorough medical checkup before they begin a regular exercise program. They should also remember that the hardest part of any new physical routine is the beginning. Sometime during that first month Hamlet will be tired, sore, and tempted to skip a session. Before long he may start excusing himself from exercise for lesser reasons, including the sure killer, "I just don't feel like it today." This is a perfect opportunity for Hamlet to develop some of the discipline we referred to earlier. The more tenacious he is in maintaining something as hard as a new exercise program, the more tenacious he's likely to be in matters more central to his existence.

The third way Hamlet can empower himself—through psychological counseling—should be undertaken only if he's troubled by an acute, immobilizing problem. The key word here is *acute*. The heart-or-dollar dilemma is a chronic problem, not an acute one—and its origin is philosophical more than psychological. As we noted in Part One, the Hamlet Syndrome is a state of mind, not a mental illness or imbalance. There is no psychotherapeutic "cure" for it, and calling in a therapist to make it go away is like hiring a plumber to roof your house. In many cases the biggest mistake Hamlet can make is to undergo prolonged therapy, for therapy plays into his tendency to substitute analysis for action. Fortunately, most Hamlets are instinctively wary of taking a long-term psychoanalytical approach to their troubles. As Martin puts it,

"Seeing a therapist is something you do when you're desperate, when you realize your friends can't help you and you're not going to make it on your own."

But brief therapy (generally defined as eighteen weeks or less) can help Hamlet deal with a specific situation that's blocking his ability to function constructively. Jessica started seeing a therapist during an especially difficult period in her life. "I was distraught—I'd been in a very bad affair and was confused about a lot of issues. My self-esteem was zero. My therapist did a lot of short-term patching up, and then she helped me sort through some of the underlying issues and see what was going on down deep. Not that she cured me or anything, but she gave me another perspective that made a lot more sense than the way I was seeing things." Jessica stayed with her therapist for two and a half years. That's longer than we've recommended, but in Jessica's case it worked, so we're not going to quibble. Our biggest concern about long-term therapy is that Hamlet will replace action and independence with psychobabble and dependence on a therapist—and Jessica didn't fall into that trap. "When I reached a point where I felt I didn't need it anymore, I stopped going," she says. "I could confront those issues on my own."

Jeff's response to therapy is more typical. Traumatized by the effects of his vitamin B_{12} deficiency, he felt he needed someone to help him cope with the situation. "About two weeks after I got the diagnosis I asked my doctor if he knew someone I could talk to about it. He sent me to this therapist, and right at the very first session the guy was concerned that I was depressed. So he put me on something, I don't remember what it was, but it lasted about three days. The things it did to me were just awful. Then he tried something else. At our sessions he wanted to bring in all this other stuff, like my family relationships, and I thought he was really getting off the track. It was a depressing time for me, true, but I wasn't clinically depressed." And so Jeff stopped the therapy after a couple of weeks, not much better off for the experience.

Hamlet must remember when he elects to see a therapist that only he can take steps to make his life more bearable. The therapist's job is to help him see his situation clearly, not to tell him which way to go. Therapy won't make the frustrations of the Hamlet Syndrome disappear. But if Hamlet needs help coping with a traumatic and paralyzing situation, such as the breakup of a relationship or a serious illness, therapy can be just the ticket. It can help him surmount his troubles by giving him a fresh perspective—and the confidence to take action.

Regardless of the strategy Hamlet uses to empower himself—addressing a minor frustration that's gone on too long, starting an exercise regimen, or seeing a therapist—he will almost certainly increase his ability to shape his life to his liking. After those simple beginnings he can tackle progressively more serious frustrations, working up to a full-blown search for a job that meets the standards of his heart. Instead of cursing the darkness of his workaday existence, he can begin to light candles.

The underlying message of this chapter (and, in many respects, of this book) is that *it's okay for Hamlet to assert himself.* It's okay for him to acknowledge his needs and take the necessary steps to fulfill them. He shouldn't feel guilty about trying to satisfy himself; although he may feel that his needs are too minor to warrant action, they're no less important than anyone else's. Nor will his self-interested actions violate his principles so long as they don't hurt others. His newfound ability to act will protect him against the occasional twinges of regret that come with the decision to follow his heart to the fullest. Even if he never finds a niche in society that satisfies his heart, by learning to take positive actions that further his interests and ideals Hamlet will greatly increase his ability to *cope* with the heart-or-dollar dilemma.

28
Finding a Niche

Oh pity the poor downtrodden Fortune 500—that's what America's been doing this past decade and longer, forgetting, it seems, the plight of the middle-class working stiff. We've linked the welfare of our sprawling corporations with our national well-being, assuming that what's good for business is what's good for America. We've lowered corporate taxes and scrapped regulations. We've lionized Lee Iacocca and Donald Trump. Our business reporters cheer Wall Street with the shamelessness of hometown sports announcers. Had we been living in Palestine three thousand years ago, we'd be firmly ensconced in Goliath's corner.

But our concern for corporations springs from a mistaken assumption. It's true that the business of America is business, but *it's not true that the business of business is America.* The business of business is keeping its stockholders happy—and the interests of the stockholders don't always match the interests of the nation at large. Take the people who own stock in cigarette companies. We all know that hundreds of thousands of people each year die prematurely as a result of tobacco addiction, and that's bad enough—but how many of us realize that cigarette smoking costs the nation $65 billion annually in health care costs and lost productivity? That represents a loss to all of us, smokers and nonsmokers alike, of $2.17 per pack of cigarettes, according to the Congressional Office of Technology Assessment. But the owners of the tobacco companies don't care—they're making a profit! They don't have to shoulder the least bit of responsibility for the burden their product inflicts on the rest of us. And this is hardly an isolated example. To maximize their shareholders' return on investment, American companies have fouled the environment, marketed unsafe or shoddy products, corrupted politicians, and exploited the American worker. Hang the consequences—it's the dollar *über Alles.*

And just who are these shareholders our companies struggle so mightily to please? The corporations would have us believe their shareholders are millions of average folks, small investors carefully building a nest egg for retirement. But less than 5 percent of the nation's population owns more than *half* the country's wealth! And as we sink further into a morass of debt, foreigners are buying into American business at an astonishing pace. Today foreign interests own more than $200 billion worth of American companies and control such well-known concerns as Allis-Chalmers, CBS Records, Doubleday, Firestone, Mack Truck, and Purina Mills. Those Middle Americans who do invest their savings generally put their money in huge retirement or mutual funds; it's ridiculous to call them shareholders when the funds are controlled by a handful of managers. Earlier Jeff noted that America is more an economic oligarchy than a true democracy—and considering the extent to which business calls the shots in this society, he's pretty much on target.

The privileged few, the major shareholders and their portfolio managers, have made out spectacularly the past decade; our M.B.A.'s have done an excellent job of keeping American companies profitable. But the cost to the average American worker has been horrendous. A study by the Joint Economic Committee of Congress discovered that between 1973 and 1985 the average weekly income of the typical American worker dropped *11 percent*—and that's adjusted for inflation. (Median family income dropped by only 3.1 percent, because so many married women went into the work force.) Blue-collar America is rapidly disappearing as corporations move production overseas. The number of permanent employees drops as companies turn more and more toward temporary hires—who generally get no benefits. New jobs in service pay rock-bottom wages. The middle class, which has been the core of American society for the last forty years, is beginning to shrink as the rich get richer and the poor get poorer.

And it's not only the wallet where the American worker's been hurting. Progressively fewer Americans enjoy the protection of a labor union—less than 20 percent now. The unions that remain find themselves in the ironic position of having inherited big business's traditional bad reputation—and of making give-backs to management. The average work week is inching *up* after an almost century-long trend downward; the typical employee now puts in almost forty-two hours per week. Benefit packages are sliding. Ronald Reagan proposed *taxing* them at one point, an idea that may come back if our national deficit continues to skyrocket. And as we make the transition to a service economy, the workplace itself becomes increasingly stifling: airless, harshly lit offices; a standard of decorum that prohibits any display of emotion; eavesdropping equipment and closed-circuit TV to monitor every employee's actions. Some zealots, despite the Fourth Amendment, even want to test all workers for drug use. The working person's lot, which had been improving decade by decade since 1900, is suddenly taking a downward turn.

Under these circumstances, how can we blame Hamlet for opting out of the bottom-line society? His voluntary removal to the fringe may be the sanest, most practical reaction to a system as harsh and dehumanized as ours. By exiling himself to the fringe he even exacts a measure of revenge. He becomes the worst of all possible things in a society where everything has a price: a *bad investment.* So much money spent to raise and teach him, and he takes a job that's designed for someone with half his qualifications. And the loss truly is society's, for it's amply clear that these days we need all the good minds we can get. All Hamlet loses is money and public esteem; he keeps what's important to him—his integrity, his principles, and his peace of mind—and he continues to eat regularly and maintain the roof over his head.

What can we do to get Hamlet to join up with the system? The workplace has to change in ways that management presently doesn't want to change it: Making the American workplace amenable to Hamlet means treating workers with respect. It means paying them a higher wage; it means offering them a flexible work schedule; it means giving them a greater voice in decision making; it means relaxing the rigid corporate hierarchy; it means humanizing the impersonal work environment. But no, the shareholders are doing well today, there's no need to make concessions to the workers or to America at large. Did you notice how fast the call to adopt Japanese management techniques petered out? That's because Japanese management requires respect for employees. In quality circles, for instance, the boss must sometimes yield to the dictates of the workers. American business doesn't *need* to respect its workers that way—and so it won't for the foreseeable future.

All this means Hamlet's search for a niche in society that dignifies his heart may go on for a long, long time. It's not always easy to find companies that care enough to provide a respectful, enlightened environment. Even the most determined Hamlet may need years to fall into, stumble upon, or otherwise find work that's both fulfilling and sufficiently remunerative. Once he does he's settled for the rest of his life; the Hamlet who's found a workaday outlet for his principles knows a sense of contentment few hotshot executives can match. But that period of searching before he discovers the niche can be terribly frustrating and painful. In hopes that we may shorten his hunt for a comfortable and personally rewarding place in society, we offer Hamlet these suggestions:

Join a Collective. Collectives are worker-owned small businesses that are democratically run. Often one doesn't even need to invest to join; one simply works a set number of hours for free to gain a stake in the enterprise equal to everyone else's. The prime advantage of a collective is that Hamlet directly participates in running the company yet shares the risks and drudgeries of being in business. Collectives also have their disadvantages: Cliques can form within the group of owners; some people lose their sense of commitment; cash flow is almost always wanting. But generally the people who start and work in collectives are a lot like Hamlet, if not Hamlets themselves. They're disillusioned with the system and are looking for an enterprise that speaks to their humanity. A great way to make peace with the free market system.

Take Part-Time Employment. This pays immediate dividends in that it allows Hamlet to spend more time pursuing the things that really matter to him: his art, his hobbies, his daydreams. It also affords him a greater sense of freedom from the workaday world, especially if he only has to report to the office two or three days a week. Many of the Hamlets we interviewed derived a great deal of satisfaction from working part-time. They loved to go grocery shopping in the middle of the day, for instance. Once Hamlet decides to search for a long-term niche, he can use the extra time to study his options. Part-time employment can also pay his way through vocational training. Jeff worked part-time while he took art classes and prepared a portfolio for architecture school. Maxine works part-time to support herself through library school. On the whole, this is a very good way to go—especially good if the concern Hamlet works for isn't entirely given over to the bottom-line mentality.

Make a Choice, Knowing It's a Direction Just for Now. Hamlet has to realize that the rest of his life is *not* one monolithic, unchangeable span. As career counselors told us in Part Three, the average American worker changes careers—not jobs, but *careers*—four times. It's silly to think that once one makes a commitment to a job or profession one has to stick with it for all time. If Hamlet has a course of action that appeals to him but he's not quite sure whether to take it, he shouldn't wait for a surge of courage or more information—he should just go out and try it! Of course, impulsiveness is not part of Hamlet's nature; he likes to look before he leaps. But so long as he allows himself to abandon the course once he realizes it's wrong for him, he's lost nothing—and *gained* a lot of valuable experience. And if it's *other* people's opinions Hamlet's worried about, he should bear in mind that to mainstream types it's better to try something and fail than to sit around and do nothing. So go back to grad school for professional training, or take that job in a field completely unrelated to anything you've done before, Hamlet; you'll never know whether it's the niche for you until you give it a shot.

Even as the stockholders of American corporations flourish, with every day the nation's position as the world's foremost economy grows more tenuous. In the next decade the economies of the Soviet Union and the People's Republic of China may develop significantly. The Pacific Rim countries, principally Japan, South Korea, Hong Kong, Singapore, and Taiwan, are expanding so fast economically they may be the primary locus of world trade by the year 2000. Meanwhile, here at home our current emphasis on short-term profits and quick fixes threatens our long-term prosperity. If we are to avoid the fate of Great Britain and other once-dominant powers, we have to start taking cues from people other than the boardroom executives and their allies in government. . . .

29

The Key to America's Future

It's hard to pity Hamlet. He's had all the advantages: a supportive family, material comfort, safety, and superior education. He is, in many ways, the very flower of American civilization. Compared to the homeless, the unemployed, and the chronically infirm, his plight is laughable in its inconsequence. So why should we concern ourselves with him and his heart-or-dollar dilemma? What's so compelling about the Hamlet Syndrome that we as a nation should take note of it and respond to it in a determined manner?

We must take heed because Hamlet tells us something very important about ourselves, something we must address if we hope to retain our freedom and prosperity: *We as a people have become so complacent that our long-term well-being is in doubt.* In terms of consciousness, we've grown so ignorant, intolerant, and gullible that we're dangerously out of touch with the world's greater realities. In terms of goals, we've put so much emphasis on the dollar that we endanger our physical survival. Never has a nation jeopardized its own future on the scale that we presently do our own. If present trends continue, a generation from now Americans could well live in a de facto dictatorship and have to pay for the very air that they breathe.

Hamlet has grown up with all the privileges of affluence and has been led by the hand to continuing prosperity. The American system was designed to work for him. Yet he's walked away from a life of security and wealth, opting to stand scorned on society's fringe. If Hamlet were alone, we could chalk up his recalcitrance to a hyperactive rebellious streak or a masochistic impulse. But there are millions of people like him, all retreated to the fringe, and there are millions of mainstreamers who feel just as alienated as he does. Hamlet is the first warning sign of a terminal cultural decay: We've created an order so completely given over to inhuman, destructive values that *even people who benefit the most from it can't stand to be part of it.*

Great nations begin to die when they answer the challenges of the present with solutions from the past. The logic goes something like this: If we only commit ourselves more vigorously to the old verities, we'll get ourselves over the hump. But that's like trying to win the next war by preparing for the last one. If the Joint Chiefs of Staff proposed to stop Soviet nuclear missiles with prop planes and ack-ack we'd bust them down to privates. A nation stays on top by keeping an eye on what the other nations are doing and by coming up with innovations of its own. Yet for at least the last ten years America has been trying to answer the challenges of the present with answers from the past. We made Ronald Reagan president precisely because he promised to restore the values of yesteryear.

But a renewed faith in the old answers won't work for us any longer. Look where our prevailing values have brought us these last ten years. We haven't fixed our country, no matter what the appearance of material prosperity suggests. We're even more out of touch with reality than we were when we ran away from it in the 1950s. We haven't kept up with the other guys, we haven't innovated—and we may soon pay the price for our inability to move with the times.

Some will counter that we as a nation don't face a crisis at all, that our system, while not perfect, is functioning just fine. Carlo Cipolla, the eminent Italian economist, notes in *The Economic Decline of Empires:*

History offers no examples of indestructible empires, yet most peoples are convinced that what happened to previous empires cannot happen to their own. In so doing they show a lack of imagination, a naive incapacity to imagine new situations for which their tastes, inclinations and institutions will grow progressively inadequate. Once the decline starts, there are still optimistic people who stubbornly deny reality.

If we are to forestall or avoid the decline of our own empire (and, fortunately, the symptoms of our decline are not yet so advanced they're incurable), we have to cease denying the signs of decay all around us, cease relying on the tried and true, and look for new solutions. The answers are close at hand. As Cipolla notes:

> It is remarkable to see how relatively numerous in declining empires are the people capable of making the right diagnosis and preaching some sensible cure. It is no less remarkable, however, that wise utterances generally remain sterile, because, as Gonzales de Cellorigo [a seventeenth-century economist] forcefully put it while watching impotently the decline of Spain, "those who can will not and those who will cannot."

Those who can will not . . . that's Hamlet! Afraid of exposing himself to even more ignominy, he keeps what he knows about society to himself. This is a national tragedy, because *Hamlet is the key to America's future.* He knows the American system inside and out—in his youth he was as much on the inside as anyone could be, and then in adulthood he took on the role of outsider. He's a well-educated but unpretentious thinker. He has no axe to grind; he's not an ideologue or quick-change artist. He sees our society from as clear, sophisticated, and sympathetic a perspective as anyone on earth. *The time has come, then, for those of us who've discounted Hamlet in the past to recognize that America has much to gain by hearing what he has to say.*

The problem is getting Hamlet to talk. From Ralph Waldo Emerson's time and probably before, the average American Hamlet has been inclined to go his own way, to seek refuge from the mainstream and shy away from dialogue concerning values. For one thing, he feels more secure keeping his own counsel. For another, by the time he's out of college he sees no use in debating values with mainstreamers. He regards people as set in their ways, and believes that even the most overwhelmingly logical argument won't convince conventional thinkers to depart from their irrational but long-standing habits. If it's no use, why even bother?

But we've gotten a clear enough picture of Hamlet by now to know what he'd tell us if we were to drag him into the national spotlight and force him to talk. He wouldn't give us answers to specific issues like abortion or defense spending—that's for the people to decide through the democratic process. He would, however, evince great concern that Americans don't know or think enough to make decisions wisely. He'd call for a revolution in the way we think—a revolution that would not only enhance our prospects for continued preeminence but would broaden and strengthen the democratic principles for which we stand. He'd offer a five-part prescription to pull us out of our decline:

1. *Tolerance.* From the very beginning we've been as much an *exclusive* as an *inclusive* culture; the Constitution, on top of legitimizing slavery, allowed only land-owning males age twenty-one or older the right to vote. The tradition of intolerance extended into the realm of the social law as well. Whereas we've made major advances toward eradicating discrimination in the written law, the social law continues to promulgate intolerance on a massive scale. It's not only a matter of racism or sexism; we have people on all sides of the political and religious spectra who would force their standards of normality on the nation as a whole.

This social intolerance has gained new impetus with the rise of television and nationwide corporations. We used to have regional differences. We'd speak differently, act differently, and buy and sell different products from one part of the nation to another. But now there's only one way for all of us to do things: the way it's done on TV. And more and more there's only a handful of competing brands for each product: those sold by the giant corporations. From Florida to Washington State our habits and holdings are more or less the same, and with this uniformity has come a mounting phobia for objects and ideas that lack the media's and corporate America's stamp of approval. If it hasn't been on TV, it's suspect or beneath us—or we don't even know it exists.

We pay a dear price for this intolerance. We lose the respect of people who can help us. We create enormous tension between ourselves and others, a tension that's palpable as we walk down a lonely city street at night. And we shut off the flow of ideas, values, and life-styles from outside, limiting our options and ultimately making us less adaptable in times of stress. Hamlet would urge us to be tolerant of foreign cultures, of different people and ideas within our own culture (including himself, naturally!), and of weakness in ourselves and others.

2. *Curiosity.* These days it seems the only Americans interested in foreigners and nonconformists are the CIA and FBI. So long as the rest of us have what we want plus a chance to get more, we don't care about anything else. Maybe this lack of curiosity is another phenomenon aggravated by TV—we've seen so many spectaculars from all over the globe that subtler things no longer enthrall us. We're easily bored, so lacking in wonder we think it a waste to learn what other cultures are like. Which is a shame, because the world offers an infinite variety of life-styles and ideas more entertaining than anything on TV.

We're inculcated with incuriosity at an early age, when our schools stress indoctrination over analysis. Learning is a process of inquiry, not merely a handing down of received wisdom. Yet we continue to insist that our schoolchildren memorize rather than figure things out. Whether the kids learn anything doesn't matter to us so long as they get good grades. The ever-curious Hamlet would first have us adults take up new interests, especially interests that show us how other people handle problems that hamper us. Then he'd insist that kids be encouraged to *pursue* learning rather than have the teacher tell them exactly what they need to know for their next exam.

3. *Critical Thought and Skepticism.* This may be the single most important antidote to decline that Hamlet has to offer. We have to stop accepting at face value whatever our leaders and media mouthpieces tell us—that much should be obvious in the aftermath of Vietnam, Watergate, the Iran-contra scandals, and the duplicities of our fundamentalist preachers—and we have to start asking questions as we never have before. Nothing should be exempt from our inquiries, not God, not business, not the two-party system or even democracy itself.

It's not enough, though, that we start asking questions. We also have to develop the patience to follow long and complicated answers. Our problems are too complex to be explained in a ninety-second news story. If we are to remain a democratic republic, we have to demand to know the whole story, and when we get it we have to have the patience to sort out the details. We can't choose wisely when we're uninformed. As a plant needs sunlight, democracy requires a steady flow of information to survive.

4. *Associative Thinking.* One of nature's timeless laws is that the more specialized a creature gets, the more trouble it has coping with change. So it is with humans. The narrower the scope of our lives, the more vulnerable we are to change in our environment. When we stake our entire well-being on just a few narrow interests, we're shattered by even minor threats. Just as corporations protect themselves by becoming conglomerates, we'd be much stronger spiritually if we diversified our interests. Not only would that help us through hard times, but it would give us a sense of the big picture.

Once we stretch intellectually and see connections instead of differences, the forest instead of trees, we'll be more receptive and adaptable to change. We'll also find out how much we depend on one another, which will help us overcome the widespread intolerance we talked about earlier. Good things happen when people see how much they have in common. As the preacher in Ecclesiastes put it:

> Two are better than one; because they have a good reward for their labour.
>
> For if they fall, the one will lift up his fellow: but woe to him that is alone when he falleth; for he hath not another to help him up.
>
> Again, if two lie together, then they have heat: but how can one be warm alone?
>
> And if one prevail against him, two shall withstand him; and a threefold cord is not quickly broken.

5. *Seeing the Consequences of Actions.* Not only in physics does every action have an equal and opposite reaction. Although it's often hard to notice in this antiseptic, disconnected, disposable society of ours, *everything* we do has consequences. More often than not, the reason our best-laid plans go haywire is that we haven't anticipated some consequence of our scheming. Humankind has never been very good at keeping an eye toward the long-term, but in the last generation we've lost even *that* minimal capacity in a frenzy of consumption and instant gratification.

Buy now, pay later: the motto of the American empire, and perhaps its epitaph as well. For *later* is getting closer every day, bringing with it the killer force of consequences built up over years of heedless action. Some of the damage is unavoidable; we could stop using chlorofluorocarbons today, for instance, but the ozone layer will continue to thin for another fifteen years. If we want to avoid further disaster, we have to start looking at our actions in terms of their consequences, not in terms of the pleasure and convenience they bring us right at the moment. We have to keep in mind a couple of important things: that consequences aren't always immediate, and that insignificant consequences become very significant when multiplied millions of times. Your driving to work by itself won't set off the Greenhouse Effect. You and *millions of other* people driving to work every day, however, *dooms* us in a few decades to a desertified Midwest and a shoreline inundated by higher ocean levels.

In one respect the Hamlet Syndrome is a paradigm for the nation as a whole. We've been secure and unchallenged for so long that we've lost our sense of initiative. Now the challenges are coming thick and fast—from demagogic leaders at home, from economic competitors abroad—and we're stuck in a mire of indecision and inaction. We want to remain free and strong, but we lack the courage to do the necessary hard things. The longer we delay, the more black and white our choice becomes: We either have to make a radical break with the past and adopt a whole new set of values, or we have to accept our imminent deterioration into an environmental disaster area run by smooth-talking dictators. Let's not make Hamlet one of those people Carlo Cipolla refers to in *The Economic Decline of Empires:* someone who watches impotently as the great nation he lives in declines. Let's instead make Hamlet's way of thinking the key to our rejuvenation. If we think more like Hamlet, we can get back in touch with one another and the larger world—and take giant steps toward ensuring the long-term well-being of our society.

Epilogue

T he dollar and the heart are eternal forces. Throughout history humankind has fought tenaciously for wealth, power, and status. The symbols of success vary by epoch and culture—from animal skins to automobiles—but their meaning stays the same. Yet humankind has from the dawn of consciousness also longed for understanding, respect, and freedom. In ancient peoples' mythology and nature worship we see the same spiritual impulse that today inspires us to follow the Golden Rule or save the environment.

The dollar's weapons are visceral and quick: competition, ruthlessness, violence. The heart's weapons are deliberate: cooperation, kindness, sagacity. The dollar has always been stronger because its weapons are readily available and incredibly destructive; a few disciples of the dollar can in minutes ruin the efforts of a million adherents of the heart. Even so, over the millennia the forces of the heart have made steady gains against the forces of the dollar. That's what we've traditionally called *progress*.

In the twentieth century, however, we redefined the word *progress* to mean technological advance. Going by the new definition we've progressed as never before; since the Depression and World War II we've invented technologies capable of completely transforming the world—or destroying it. But traditional progress continues to creep along at a glacial pace. The disparity between the rate of our technological progress and the rate of our spiritual progress is the single greatest threat to humankind. If we are to survive—in any meaningful sense of the word—we'll need the wisdom to regulate the use of our powerful new tools. That wisdom comes from only one place: our hearts. All the more reason, then, that we should listen to the Hamlets among us. They speak to the very best part of us: the part that dreams of a day when people will tolerate one another, realize their potential to the fullest, and act in a rational, mutually beneficent manner.

Sources

We supplemented hundreds of hours of interviews with Hamlets by consulting experts and books to enhance our understanding of the implications of the Hamlet Syndrome. What follows is a discussion of the sources that we found most useful. The topics addressed here include: interpretations of Shakespeare's *Hamlet*; psychiatry and psychology; sociology; the suburbs; television; health issues (vegetarianism and stress); and the workplace (job-hunting and management styles).

Hamlet's character and inaction have fascinated many great thinkers. In Hamlet's dilemma these thinkers often found reflections of their own concerns. Goethe, the German Romantic poet, was greatly influenced by Shakespeare. He thought of Hamlet as a hero struggling against a world that he must set right. Friedrich Nietzsche, the late-nineteenth-century philosopher, in *The Birth of Tragedy* (trans. Walter Kaufmann [New York: Random House, 1967]), saw Hamlet's wisdom as a transcendence of the bounds of conventional reality.

Samuel Taylor Coleridge often lectured on Shakespeare's plays. His remarks formed the most popular nineteenth-century interpretation of *Hamlet.* In the collection *Writings on Shakespeare* (ed. Terence Hawkes [New York: Capricorn Books, 1959]), he attributed Hamlet's problem to irresolution produced by excessive reflection.

Sigmund Freud, who thought only Dostoyevski could rival Shakespeare's understanding of the human condition, offered his interpretation of *Hamlet* in his seminal work, *The Interpretation of Dreams* (trans. James Strachey [New York: Basic Books, 1956]), originally published in 1900. Here, he argued that Hamlet cannot take vengeance on the uncle who killed Hamlet's father and married Hamlet's mother because the uncle's actions remind him of his own repressed oedipal wishes.

A. C. Bradley, in *Shakespearean Tragedy* (London: Macmillan and Company, 1904) dubs Hamlet the melancholy prince. This now-standard interpretation further develops the psychological perspective to elaborate on Coleridge's conclusion. Bradley points out Hamlet's inability to change, faulty excuses, and paralyzed behavior. Yet Bradley argues that the ultimate truth of Hamlet's life does not lie in his failure to act. Rather, he concludes that Hamlet, who possessed humor, a quick mind, and idealism as well as a tragic flaw, was placed in an impossible situation: He was required to act just as the moral shock brought on by the circumstances of his father's death and mother's remarriage produced an overwhelming melancholy.

Frank Kermode's analysis in *The Riverside Shakespeare* (ed. G. Blakemore Evans [Boston: Houghton Mifflin, 1974]) provides a recent perspective on Hamlet's character. For information on Shakespeare's society and life, Frank O'Connor's *The Road to Stratford* (London: Methuen and Company, 1948) and two books by A. L. Rowse, *Shakespeare the Man* (New York: Harper and Row, 1973) and *What Shakespeare Read and Thought* (New York: Coward, McCann and Geoghegan, 1981), proved especially useful.

Recently, Hamlet has been equated with lack of resolve, an echo of Coleridge's view. New York's Governor Mario Cuomo was saddled with a so-called Hamlet image because he was perceived as unwilling to face confrontations or decide whether to be a candidate for President in the 1988 election (*New York Times,* July 12, 1987). During the Hearings of the Joint Congressional Committee on the Iran-Contra Affair of 1987, Congressman Henry Hyde praised other countries who supported the contras "while Congress played Hamlet over what to do, to support or not to support" (*Taking the Stand: The Testimony of Lieutenant Colonel Oliver L. North* [New York: Pocket Books, 1987]).

Psychiatry and psychology would seem to be the obvious approach to an understanding of the Hamlet Syndrome since, as all now agree, Hamlet's interior life, his motivations and thoughts, are more significant than his actions. The

Hamlet personality also seems to have serious shortcomings according to every psychological theory's definition of the individual. S. R. Maddi's survey of these theories, *Personality Theories: A Comparative Analysis* (Homewood, Il.: Dorsey Press, 1972), illustrates this clearly. Psychiatry and psychology do provide some understanding of Hamlet's conflict with contemporary social norms. But, before accepting their characterization of Hamlet without question, we must ask if these personality theories simply want to reshape the round peg of Hamlet's personality to fit the square hole of social expectations. If so, Hamlet's criticism of the social system is dismissed without discussion. For the moment, however, we will put aside social criticism and focus on psychological interpretations of Hamlet's quandary. Freud's *Civilization and Its Discontents* (trans. James Strachey [London: Hogarth Press, 1964]) explores the conflict between the individual and society and concludes that changes in society, while certainly necessary, must be founded upon a thorough understanding of human nature.

Erik Erikson argues in *Childhood and Society* (New York: W. W. Norton, 1963) that a person goes through various stages of development as he acquires whatever characteristics he needs to fit into society. Erikson establishes, for example, that the values needed to live successfully in a Sioux Indian tribe differ from those required in an industrialized culture. Thus, he proves that adapting to a new culture demands a complex change in personality. In each stage of development, he posits, there exists a struggle between opposing values. For example, one must resolve the conflict between intimacy and isolation in young adulthood before dealing with the conflict between generativity (nurturing) and stagnation in middle adulthood. According to Erikson's theory of these stages, Hamlet is stricken by arrested development. Indeed, Erikson might claim that Hamlets never progress beyond the adolescent conflict between identity and role diffusion, in which the goal is to become an independent and effective adult.

Rather than accept Erikson's schema and tell Hamlet simply to get on with life, we must consider the recent criticism of this description of development. Carol Gilligan's *In a Different Voice* (Cambridge, Mass.: Harvard University Press, 1982) points out that women are rated lower than men according to traditional psychological measurements of moral development. She explains this by arguing that women are essentially different from men because they value interdependence rather than independence and achievement. This difference creates an alternative but unacknowledged definition of maturity. Therefore, standard psychological measurements do not accurately describe women's moral growth. The associative thinking, with its emphasis on interdependence, that characterizes Hamlet's personality suggests that Hamlet too has an unorthodox definition of maturity and explains why he falls short by orthodox standards. But as Gilligan argues, the fault may lie in the standard of measurement rather than in the person being evaluated.

In seeking a psychological theory to provide a useful foundation for our analysis of the Hamlet Syndrome, we found Erich Fromm's *Escape From Freedom* (New York: Holt, Rinehart, and Winston, 1941) extremely helpful. Fromm is more rightly called a social psychologist, for he establishes that the human psyche cannot be considered apart from its social and political context.

Robert Coles offers an interesting profile of a person doubting his choice of a career as a social activist in *The Moral Life of Children* (Boston: Atlantic Monthly Press, 1986). This young man, who abandoned his middle-class lifestyle to work for civil rights in a small southern town, was interviewed at various times in his late twenties and early thirties. He was wavering in his commitment to his cause and so found himself at a juncture very similar to Hamlet's to-do-or-not-to-do crisis. Although he felt at home in his adopted community, he realized that any opportunity to become financially secure and to find a spouse was fast fading. The contrast between himself and the friends from his past aroused both irritation and envy. This sounds very much like Hamlet's heart-or-dollar dilemma. While, as a social activist, this young man is more willing to engage the world than Hamlets are, he succumbs to Hamlet's conflict as soon as his devotion to his cause begins to waver. Therefore, although we noted that people working in public service, social activists, and professionals are immune from the Hamlet Syndrome, we must emphasize that this is true only so long as these people are more or less content with their choices. Once the fragile balance between the call of the heart and the lure of the dollar breaks down, the Hamlet Syndrome may claim another sufferer. Coles notes the young man's anguish as he struggled with the tension between his commitment to reform and the comfortable, respectable life he had grown up anticipating. From this anguish, Coles draws two conclusions. First, he makes a polite and tentative amendment to Anna Freud's view that idealism is most keenly felt in adolescence. He says that for some it continues as a moral habit throughout their lives. Second, Coles concludes that, if this young man entered psychoanalysis, he would be very hard to treat because psychoanalysis is interested in mental categories while this person describes his problem as "a moral sensibility opposed to the workings of modern corporate America." This analysis helps illuminate the Hamlet Syndrome as something other than arrested psychological development and points out the conflict between the psychological and sociological approaches to this dilemma.

Jean Piaget, like Anna Freud, sees adolescence as a time of idealism. Piaget determines why idealism should appear at this particular point in a person's development. His experiments lead him to conclude that children are unable to think in abstract terms until the age of eleven to fourteen. Until that time, their thoughts are bound to the concrete world of their observations. It is only at adolescence that children can imagine hypotheses and work out the logical consequences of these hypotheses. Adolescents, entranced by their new logical skills, become idealists. Since the ability to think abstractly is essential to

Hamlet's development, Piaget's experiments explain, in part, why the Hamlet Syndrome does not become evident until adolescence. He also feels that this idealism would be outgrown as adolescents came to realize the limits of logical analysis, a supposition we have already questioned. Jean Piaget and Barbel Inhelder give an overview of Piaget's theories in *The Psychology of the Child* (New York: Basic Books, 1969). Nathan Isaacs's *A Brief Introduction to Piaget* (New York: Schocken Books, 1974) discusses the implications of Piaget's theory for education. Margaret A. Boden gives an appreciative but more critical analysis of Piaget's work in *Jean Piaget* (New York: Viking Press, 1979). Piaget does have his critics, who claim that his findings focus on males and that the very notion of a scale of development is just as flawed in his hands as it is in Erikson's. While some have argued that children may possess the power to think abstractly at an earlier age, they seem to agree that younger children do not use this power as effectively as adolescents.

As we point out so often, Hamlets are generally viewed as failures by society. Many studies have analyzed the reasons people fail and the feelings people have about failure. Robert C. Birney, Harvey Burdick, and Richard C. Teevar provide an analysis in *Fear of Failure* (New York: Van Nostrand-Reinhold, 1969) that explains many of the reasons behind Hamlet's not-yet-begun-to-fight life-style. They assert that the fear of failure is based upon a discrepancy between "ideal" and "real" perceptions of one's self or a discrepancy between "ideal" and "real" perceptions of one's achievements. They list several avoidance strategies used to preclude a judgment of failure. Among these are: preferring very easy or very difficult tasks since neither accurately reflects ability; using imprecise or unreliable performance measures; claiming that one's performance does not reflect one's skill; rejecting responsibility for the outcome; reducing the importance of skill in the activity; refusing to try; or seeking social support in those people with similar values. They also point out that excuses are important if a failure results in lost social value. C. R. Snyder, Raymond L. Higgins, and Rita S. Stucky analyze excuse-making in *Excuses—Masquerades in Search of Grace* (New York: John Wiley and Sons, 1983). They argue that excuses are effective if they make the person feel better about falling short of a goal. In the analysis of excuses, at least in the case of Hamlets, it is very important to ask a preliminary question before assessing Hamlet's excuse: Do you really want to meet that goal? For example, a person may be late for work and offer as an excuse a faulty alarm clock. For a non-Hamlet, this excuse may be a way to preserve esteem. But for a Hamlet, it may be a way of rebelling against work conditions or work itself. Hamlets may fall short of goals because they truly do not want to meet them. Lacking the courage of their convictions, however, they make excuses to avoid performing, not to make themselves feel better.

Robert Reisfeld, Jr., M.D., is a Redwood City, California-based board-certified psychiatrist with a special interest in the Hamlet personality. In an interview, he offered some explanations for Hamlet's dilemma based on his own case studies. Rather than concentrate on definitions of failure and success, he suggests that Hamlets must understand the choices they have made. He finds that both Hamlet's adult rejection of conventional success and his uneasiness with that rebellion flow from a common source: a reliance on external authority to guide one's actions. Hamlets obeyed rules as children because if they failed to do so, they were crushed by strong negative reinforcement; they received positive reinforcement only when they fulfilled their parents' expectations. As adults, then, they continue to define themselves in terms of external authority, choosing either to rebel against or conform to various figures of authority. What the individual really wants for himself isn't clearly determined. Both the black-and-white and shades-of-gray thinking that Hamlet may use to provide excuses for inaction reflect the desire for some absolute authoritative answer. Hamlet's bad-attitude problem at work may also reflect the rebellion against authority coupled with an unwillingness to confront authority directly. Those who are more straightforward may have anarchistic views that directly question all authority. Reisfeld believes that if parents do not condition their acceptance, love, and encouragement on their children's achievement, their children will be more able to make their own independent choices. Hamlet's distaste for competition also reflects patterns learned in childhood, according to Reisfeld. Children who never feel like partners with their parents see relationships in terms of "winners versus losers." Winners are hostile and vicious while losers are simply losers—a no-win situation that Hamlet abandons so he won't be forced to either win by hurting others or lose by ruining himself. Reisfeld points out that Hamlets may find either dissatisfaction or contentment in rejecting competitive situations. They are dissatisfied if they continue to see themselves as losers, deprived of society's rewards by their decision. But, on the other hand, in their refusal to hurt others, they could consider themselves successful in their own way. With this understanding, Hamlets may be able to make one of the most profound decisions of all—to be satisfied with their choices in life.

Social forces as well as psychological patterns shape personal values. Glen H. Elder, Jr., compiled the data from a thirty-year study of Depression-era children to determine how that event affected their value system and sense of self. *Children of the Great Depression* (Chicago: University of Chicago Press, 1974) describes the parents of the Baby Boomers, including the swelling number of Hamlets. The effect of financial deprivation on the formation of attitudes was perhaps more important than the lack of money for children's clothing and entertainment during the Great Depression. These children wanted to become adults. They valued industry and admired financial responsibility. The pursuit of security embodied in Roosevelt's New Deal continued into the 1950s. When asked in 1957–58, at the age of thirty-eight, if they would prefer a secure job with a good income to a more risky job with greater rewards, 50 percent would, in early middle-age, opt for security. Adults who had been deprived as children during the 1930s generally adhered to the following values: the centrality of family and the importance of children in marriage, security, and the power of money (although Elder is hesitant to draw strong conclusions on this final point based on the evidence of this study). The Depression-era children who married in the 1950s had the highest aspirations for their children, enjoyed a rapidly advancing income, and acquired security provisions such as life insurance policies quickly. Elder concludes with a portrait of 1930s children as people who were needed and who had a sense of belonging; their contributions to the welfare of others as they took on adult responsibilities during the Great Depression provided gratification and personal growth. In contrast, Elder notes, post-World War II children were isolated from challenging situations and did not experience rewards for contributing to common endeavors.

The enhanced status of material goods in post-Depression America was not universally praised. Vance Packard wrote several books warning of the hazards associated with the increased emphasis on achievement and material well-being. In *The Waste Makers* (New York: David McKay, 1960), he discusses how planned obsolescence became a central theme in the American economy. He points out two important implications of this new mode of life: The need for two incomes to satisfy the increased demand for material goods will create a less-focused family life, and definitions of "the good life" will be materialistic, not idealistic. To solve these problems, he advocates long-term thinking that will create better patterns of consumption while preserving the economy. He notes that our faith in technology and commercialism makes it hard to acknowledge that a surplus of happiness can lead, finally, to suffering. He insists, however, that the central challenge to America is to learn to live with abundance without impoverishing the spirit.

David Riesman's extraordinary book *The Lonely Crowd: A Study of the Changing American Character* (New Haven, Conn.: Yale University Press, 1950) argues that a major shift in character—the most profound shift since the end of feudalism—transpired as a result of the prosperity of urban, middle-class, mid-twentieth-century America. Since this shift in character explains the swelling number of Hamlets during this same period, it is important to note some of the main outlines of Riesman's theory as it relates to Hamlet's heart-or-dollar dilemma. Riesman notes that all people want to conform to the acceptable norms of their times. Those norms change, however, as the growth rate of population changes. Feudal society, when population was subject to high birth and death rates, was governed by tradition. When feudalism collapsed and the death rate began to decline, the individual had greater choices and also needed greater initiative to cope with novel situations. Only by making his own way could he find some place for himself within a rapidly expanding economy and changing society. Such people were "inner-directed." This means that early in life, they would set a lifelong goal for themselves (influenced by parents and other authorities) and their individual psychological gyroscopes would keep them on course. Specific goals differed from person to person; one could decide to aim for knowledge or fame or goodness or power or possessions. Moreover, each person recognized that his particular goal might not be shared by others. But each individual remained faithful to his own goal throughout his life. Idiosyncrasy was socially acceptable. When resources became plentiful and population began a phase of incipient decline in mid-twentieth-century America, individual enterprise became less important. A new type of character was required: the "other-directed" person, who could successfully cope with the new economic abundance and with people. The "other-directed" person, doing his best to keep the economy going, is a diligent consumer who takes his cues from those around him (peers and the mass media). He is extremely sensitive to social styles and adopts as his own direction whatever will gain the approval of others. The need for approval becomes the dominant motivation for action.

This transition from inner-direction to other-direction in American society explains why the Hamlet Syndrome would explode in the 1950s and 1960s. The primacy of the heart, personal principle, defines Hamlet as inner-directed. Yet his middle-class society taught the values of other-direction, instilling in young Hamlet the need for approval, represented by the dollar. The Hamlet Syndrome is the response to this conflict. Hamlet is thus in the best position to analyze the modern American character; he acknowledges the new order of his society but also sees the value of the old. To further understand how Riesman's analysis accounts for the Hamlet Syndrome, and how inner-directed children came to be, as he puts it, "styled out of the personality market," we will briefly discuss four factors that affected the development of the Hamlets we have focused on in this book:

1. School was, for young Hamlets, a place for accomplishment rather than a place to learn peer relationships. Accomplishment, with the emphasis on grades, fosters inner-direction as the child learns his own limits and strengths. The formation of peer relationships is more important for the development of an other-directed person. Eileen's story of forgoing outstanding grades to gain friends illustrates the tension many Hamlets feel between individual accomplishment and successful peer relationships in school.

2. Both reading and mass media, especially television, were important for developing Hamlet's expectations of the world. As a reader, he comes to know models and options apart from his own life. This encourages inner-direction as the child—especially a voracious reader like Hamlet—decides what path he might want to follow. Television presents a more conventional view of life and

therefore encourages other-directed conformity. Hamlet's early television watching showed him the attractiveness of other-directed society and the acceptance it offered to him. But his final rejection of television as simplistic is also a rejection of the pressure to become other-directed.

3. Skill in craft is valued by an inner-directed person while skill in manipulating people is valued by an other-directed person. Those interested in craft want to master a process or to create something on their own. The manipulation of people makes one more effective in relationships and can hardly be done alone. Martin's pride in his ability to make decks is a good example of choosing an inner-directed craft focus. He even taught himself from books rather than seeking a teacher, which would have brought him into the other-directed realm of personal relationships.

4. Hamlet's love of solitary hobbies is another sign of his inner-direction. In an other-directed society, hobbies are valued when they are shared and so become a good subject for conversation. The solitary hobby, pursued for its own sake, is prized by the inner-directed person who gets pleasure from doing as he pleases. Martin's beer brewing is a good example of a Hamlet following his own interests.

It is appropriate to turn now to a discussion of the social institutions that are so inimical to Hamlet's values. Lewis Mumford, in his landmark book, *The City in History: Its Origins, Its Transformations, and Its Prospects* (New York: Harcourt, Brace and World, 1961), wrote of the suburbs:

> In the suburb one might live and die without marring the image of an innocent world, except when some shadow of its evil fell over a column in the newspaper. Thus the suburb served as an asylum for the preservation of illusion. Here domesticity could flourish, forgetful of the exploitation on which so much of it was based. Here individuality could prosper, oblivious of the pervasive regimentation beyond. This was not merely a child-centered environment, it was based on a childish view of the world, in which reality was sacrificed to the pleasure principle.
>
> As an attempt to recover what was missing in the city, the suburban exodus could be amply justified, for it was concerned with primary human needs. But there was another side: the temptation to retreat from unpleasant realities, to shirk public duties, and to find the whole meaning of life in the most elemental social group, the family, or even in the still more isolated and self-centered individual. . . .
>
> Even children suffered from this transformation of the whole community into a mere recreation area. For such a segregated community, composed of segregated economic strata, with little visible daily contact with

the realities of the workaday world, placed an undue burden of education on the school and family. The smallest village where people still farm and fish and hunt, the drabbest industrial town whose population still engages in essential productive enterprises, has educational possibilities that the suburb lacks. In the end, the operative differences between the contemporary suburb and the big city become increasingly minimal: for in these seemingly different environments reality has been progressively reduced to what filters through the screen of the television set. (pp. 494–496).

Mumford, while conceding that the original impulse to flee the depression and disorder of the city was valid, clearly argues that this impulse created a world in which the suburban environment, the system of education, and television combined to distort the life experienced by its inhabitants.

Suburbia has become such a part of American mythology that some authors focus on its place in the American psyche. Robert C. Wood's *Suburbia: Its People and Their Politics* (Boston: Houghton Mifflin, 1959) suggests that the growth of the suburbs in the 1950s was a response to the increasingly depersonalized society. The fear of large organizations led to the creation of these small communities that tried to re-create a Jeffersonian ideal of small-town democracies. Wood insists that this return to the past is doomed because it encourages indifference to the world and irresponsibility to one's neighbors. America, he concludes, must forgo its grass-roots customs and embrace the new ideals of the great organization. In *The Suburban Myth* (New York: Columbia University Press, 1969), Scott Donaldson challenges such a sweeping assessment of the suburbs. His review of the literature on the suburbs led him to conclude that suburbs were unfairly characterized in the 1950s and 1960s as the source of the conformity that subverted American ideals. Those who found these faults in suburban life simply had unrealistic ideals and became bitter when those ideals were not fulfilled. He notes that people do live more comfortable lives and the reality of the prosperous suburb must be accepted—not as perfect—but for its real value.

Some books attempt to provide a realistic portrayal of the suburban phenomenon by questioning the definition of *suburb*. They argue that Mumford's definition of suburbia as a white, middle-class, residential area of well-maintained single-family houses is in fact inaccurate. Bennett Berger's *Working Class Suburb* (Berkeley, Cal.: University of California Press, 1960) analyzes the values of blue-collar workers who moved into a suburban setting. He finds a wide range of home prices within American suburbia and residents varied in occupation, education levels, and outlook. Blue-collar workers may have moved to the suburbs as their rate of pay increased but they brought with them the working-class values they had always held. This research questions the belief that suburbs are a new melting pot, inculcating middle-class values in all newcomers.

In *Class in Suburbia* (Englewood Cliffs, N.J.: Prentice-Hall, 1963), William M. Dobriner agrees that ethnic and religious uniformity exert a stronger influence than suburban surroundings. Such studies lead us to insist that the Hamlet Syndrome flourishes in an environment that is comfortable financially as well as physically.

In order to avoid becoming entangled in definitions of *suburbia* according to geography, Kenneth T. Jackson defines the term by characteristics rather than by location in *Crabgrass Frontier: The Suburbanization of the United States* (New York: Oxford University Press, 1985). He defines *suburbs* as far from the workplace, composed of homes occupied by owners and surrounded by yards, and inhabited by affluent and middle-class Americans. The book gives an excellent history of such communities from the mid-nineteenth century, when the quest for privacy first led Americans to use vast tracts of open land for homes. Jackson rebuts the notion that suburbs can easily encompass a diverse population. He points out that government policy in fact discouraged diversity. Federal Housing Administration loans favored homogeneous suburbs by considering the relative economic stability of the neighborhood and the degree of protection from adverse influences. Such a policy discouraged loans if the neighborhoods were crowded, if the homes were older, or if smoke, odor, or other signs of manufacturing tainted the environment. At the same time, public housing was located in inner cities. The inner city became the province of the disadvantaged and the suburbs provided a refuge from problems of race, crime, and poverty. Although the practice of "redlining" that discriminated against blacks ended by the 1950s, FHA policies encouraged the economic and racial segregation of the suburbs as late as the 1960s. Jackson believes that the era of suburbia is ending owing to economic changes and changing attitudes about race. He also believes that changes in production and manufacturing, coupled with the need to become a more energy-efficient society, must eventually modify the suburbs.

Suburb dwellers were not only isolated from other races and economic groups but also from controversial ideas. The shopping mall is an intrinsic part of the suburban environment. For many people, it serves as a gathering place and community center as well as the main shopping facility. In this way, it is equivalent to the traditional town square. In another, important way it is quite different. The town square is owned by the city, the community. This permits anyone to exercise the right to free speech by speaking from a soapbox or distributing leaflets. The shopping mall is owned by a private developer who makes money by encouraging shoppers to patronize the mall. Based on the difference in ownership, the Supreme Court held that the private developer may prevent any exercise of free speech that makes customers uneasy so long as that speech is unrelated to the shopping center's operations. In *Food Employees* v. *Logan Valley*, 391 U.S. 308 (1968), the Supreme Court did allow a union to picket a store within a shopping center. A few years later, however, in *Lloyd*

Corporation v. *Tanner,* 407 U.S. 551 (1972), the Court prohibited anti-Vietnam War pickets from distributing leaflets in a shopping mall. The Court quoted an architectural expert's report on the purpose of a mall: "Here the shopper is isolated from the noise, fumes, confusion and distraction which he normally finds along city streets, and a controlled, carefree environment is provided." The Court concluded that receiving any offending leaflets interfered with the carefree environment and so discouraged the shopper from spending more time, or money, in the mall. As the dissenting opinion pointed out, people who do all of their shopping within the confines of the mall are effectively cut off from the exchange of ideas. This ruling illustrates not just the harmful protection one can find in the suburbs but the primacy of the dollar, even at the expense of the First Amendment.

Like *Crabgrass Frontier,* other recent books argue that the traditional suburb is undergoing a transition. As more people move to the suburbs, the demand for housing increases to the point where multiunit buildings are needed. The creation of industrial parks and office complexes has changed the suburban landscape. The suburbs have become more urban. Mark Baldassare's *Trouble in Paradise: The Suburban Transformation in America* (New York: Columbia University Press, 1986) studies a suburb in Orange County, California, to discover the various problems that have invaded the suburbs. Peter O. Muller's *Contemporary Suburban America* (Englewood Cliffs, N.J.: Prentice-Hall, 1981) provides an overview of the history of the suburbs from the early twentieth century. Both books reach similar conclusions: The growing congestion and tensions in contemporary suburbia will create a demand for even more isolated communities that will provide a refuge from suburban blight. As a result, more rigid racial and economic segregation will develop. Muller also points out that the new communities for specialized groups, such as retirement villages, will create further divisiveness in our society as people separate into microcommunities where they can protect their turf and predict the behavior of their neighbors.

Any understanding of television must begin with the work of Marshall McLuhan. *Understanding Media* (New York: McGraw-Hill, 1964) presents his discussion of various changes in technology and analyzes the way in which these changes shape our society and world-view. In *The Gutenberg Galaxy* (Toronto: University of Toronto Press, 1962), McLuhan turns his attention to the effects of print media on our modes of thought. *Media, An Introductory Analysis of American Mass Communications* by Peter M. Sandman, David M. Rubin, and David B. Sachsman (Englewood Cliffs, N.J.: Prentice-Hall, 1982) provides an excellent overview of the mass media in general.

Todd Gitlin's *Inside Prime Time* (New York: Pantheon Books, 1983) analyzes the process of developing and producing entertainment programs. He suggests that successful shows manage to discover some trend or value that reflects society's concerns. *All in the Family*, for example, reflected the contemporary concern with racial issues and the Generation Gap. This successful show did not, however, significantly change people's attitudes. Both the right-wing viewer and the left-wing viewer came away with their ideologies confirmed. Gitlin concludes that people do not realize the extent to which television could serve a social function. He notes that viewers perceive their lives in terms of their own private struggles, not as social issues, and are therefore content to be treated as consumers by the television industry. *Amusing Ourselves to Death: Public Discourse in the Age of Show Business* by Neil Postman (New York: Viking Penguin, 1985) and *Four Arguments for the Elimination of Television* by Jerry Mander (New York: William Morrow, 1978) also offer excellent critiques of television's role in society. Jonathan Kozol argues that television has encouraged illiteracy in *Death at an Early Age* (Boston: Houghton Mifflin, 1967).

   Children's Understanding of Television: Research on Attention and Comprehension (ed. Jennings Bryant and Daniel Anderson [New York: Academic Press, 1983]) presents a helpful overview of the ways in which children decipher television. It analyzes the child's inability to determine the fictional nature of situation comedies and to understand programs that do not reflect their own experience. This study suggests techniques to make television clearer to young viewers so they will not be misled. John Berger's *Ways of Seeing* (New York: Viking, 1973) argues that television advertising misleads adults. He says that advertisements are designed to make a person envy those who have purchased the particular product. Advertisements are therefore designed to create anxiety about one's place in society. Berger advocates the most extreme solution, the overthrow of capitalism, to prevent such advertising tactics. Martin Mayer, in *About Television* (New York: Harper and Row, 1972), would hardly make such a fuss. He asserts that we expect too much from television and that people have the right to live an unexamined life if they wish.

   The two health issues that most concern the Hamlets we interviewed are vegetarianism and stress. A high percentage of Hamlets practice vegetarianism, and even more endorse it in spirit. A number of Hamlets also experience crippling stress when they try to respond to their to-do-or-not-to-do crisis.

   Vegetarianism receives strong backing from current scientific research. Biologists, medical researchers, and even paleontologists have uncovered an increasing amount of evidence to suggest that the human gastrointestinal tract is designed principally for the consumption of plant matter. Our teeth resemble a grass-chomping cow's more than a flesh-tearing tiger's, and our twenty-two feet of small intestine are ideal for the digestion of grains and legumes. When we eat too much cholesterol-laden animal flesh, we increase our risk of heart disease, and many nutritional experts now suspect meat may also contribute to colon cancer and other maladies of the digestive tract. Jane Brody, in *Jane Brody's Nutrition Book* (New York: W. W. Norton, 1981), and Laurel Robertson, in *Laurel's Kitchen* (Petaluma, Cal.: Nilgiri Press, 1976), explain many of the health implications of a vegetarian diet.

Beyond the immediate considerations of health, vegetarianism is also supported by religious and political doctrines. Many religions prohibit the consumption of animal flesh because it causes suffering in sentient beings. Some Hindus and Buddhists believe that the terror an animal experiences as it is slaughtered infects the animal's meat and later causes anxiety in the consumer. There's even a case for vegetarianism in the Bible: Daniel, in order to avoid nonkosher meat, adopted a diet of pulses (peas and beans) while in Babylon and emerged from it looking "fairer and fatter in flesh than all the children which did eat the portion of the king's meat."

Politically, thanks largely to the work of nutritional researcher Frances Moore Lappé, we've become aware of the connection between meat consumption and imperialism, world hunger, and ecological deterioration. In the pioneering *Diet for a Small Planet* (New York: Ballantine Books, 1971) and subsequent tomes, Lappé points out that it takes sixteen pounds of plant protein to produce one pound of beef protein, an appallingly wasteful practice. The United States alone could reduce humanity's protein deficit by 90 percent if it halted production of livestock. From this perspective, vegetarianism becomes a political statement—and a principled effort to transform the world. Hamlets often consider vegetarianism an opportunity to extol simultaneously personal health and global well-being, a clear example of the value of Hamlet's associative thinking.

Most books on stress focus on stress management. Since life is stressful, the reasoning goes, we must find some techniques to overcome that stress. Fewer books deal with the precise causes of stress and their effects on health. Barbara B. Brown, one of the developers of biofeedback techniques, notes that stress stems from social pressure and the inability to live up to that pressure. In *Between Health and Illness* (Boston: Houghton Mifflin, 1984), she suggests that stress results from the feeling that life is unfair or that the events in one's life are undesirable. Richard Totman's *Social Causes of Illness* (New York: Pantheon Books, 1979) goes even further in defining the source of stress that is likely to lead to physical illness. He proposes a link between social disorientation (a change in the social environment that demands developing new rules of behavior) and proneness to disease. He defines a high-risk individual as one in the throes of significant social change that "leaves him socially paralyzed—unable to relate to his changed situation in a meaningful and effective manner" (p. 133). Disease, he says, is likely if one's actions do not reflect one's ideals. This certainly defines those Hamlets who are thrown into doubt by the to-do-or-not-to-do crisis. Although Totman proposes his theory as a working hypothesis, the experiences of many Hamlets support his supposition.

As we note, it's not an easy task for Hamlet to find his niche in the workplace. Books about career choices try to make this process more graceful. Most books ask, in one form or another, why people do not make appropriate decisions about their careers. In *Personal Risk* (New York: Harper and Row, 1983), Ellen Siegelman wants people to become balanced risk-takers, neither too cautious nor too impulsive in their career choices. She says that people who fear failure are not balanced risk-takers. Cautious people, certainly a group that includes some Hamlets, seek more information than necessary. Their fear of failure, she says, is clear. Impulsive people, including the shades-of-gray-thinking Hamlets who are overwhelmed by their options and make choices in exasperation, use their rash decision-making as an excuse for any failure. Siegelman suggests that if one considers the situation and the importance of the decision realistically, one can become a balanced risk-taker. Siegelman's book follows the path of John Atkinson's "Motivational Determinants of Risk-Taking Behavior" (*Psychological Review,* Vol. 64, 1957). In this article, Atkinson argues that the person who is motivated by achievement will take reasonable risks; the person motivated by shame, or the fear of failure, will take extreme risk or little risk. The extreme risk excuses failure. The slight risk guarantees success but is not an accurate evaluation of the person's ability. Eugene Burnstein's "Fear of Failure, Achievement Motivation and Aspiring to Prestigeful Occupations" (*Journal of Abnormal and Social Psychology,* Vol. 67 No. 2, 1963) confirms Atkinson's study.

Work with Passion by Nancy Anderson (New York: Carroll and Graf Publishers, 1984) suggests an approach to work that Hamlets would find attractive. She writes, "Do what you love; the money will come if you follow your heart" (p. 87). This theory, which is becoming more popular, assumes that one must enjoy one's work and that work must complement one's life-style and values. The book includes some steps to follow to discover one's passion and could be helpful to Hamlets seeking some direction. However, we would suggest a change in Anderson's statement to read: "Do what you love; the money *might* come if you follow your heart." If it does come, it provides the best possible solution to the Hamlet Syndrome. If it doesn't come, it is essential to remember that taking pleasure in one's work is the goal, not a means to reach the dollar. Anderson's approach is validated by the success of businesspeople who share her view. Elliot Hoffman is the founder of a thriving bakery, Just Desserts, and a leader of San Francisco's small-business community. He describes his philosophy this way: "Certainly, it's important to make money to provide a living but that's one piece of the whole thing. The bottom line has composites; it has pieces. The 'bottom line' to me is that I want to have the best bakery that there is, be amongst those great ones in the world, and I want to provide a model workplace, and I want to make a healthy profit. And those three go hand in hand as far as I'm concerned. . . . Be among the best and a model workplace and the money will come."

Should Hamlet decide to enter the work force seriously, he can easily become dismayed by current corporate management practices. In order for companies to be able to take advantage of Hamlet's abilities, they must reevaluate their management style. There are three basic types of styles: authoritarian, laissez faire, and democratic. The authoritarian style, requiring a firm leader in control, is exemplified by the football coach or the surgeon in the operating room. The laissez-faire style allows each person to work freely to accomplish the job. The democratic style compromises absolute freedom but gives each member of the group a voice in determining that compromise. These styles are discussed by Ralph White and Roland Lippitt in "Leader Behavior and Member Reaction in Three 'Social Climates' " (*Group Dynamics,* ed. Dorwin Cartwright and Alvin Vander [New York: Harper and Row, 1968]).

Creative Management by Norman Maier and John Hayes (New York: John Wiley and Sons, 1962) argues that traditional authoritarian management is no longer effective. They point out that those who have authority are granted absolute freedom while all other workers are required to follow orders without question. However, with an educated, well-trained work force such a management style discourages the worker and harms the company. They advocate the democratic style. They argue that if authority is delegated as much as possible, workers will be able to contribute creative solutions to corporate problems. Peter F. Drucker reaches a similar conclusion in *The Effective Executive* (New York: Harper and Row, 1966), a nuts-and-bolts book on management techniques. He insists that the executive who concentrates on the contribution of each employee will improve communication, teamwork, and performance. Giving orders in the traditional style encourages misunderstanding and discourages innovation. He also suggests that people be granted big responsibilities rather than small jobs to permit them to grow to meet the demands of the position and discover their strengths.

Twenty years later, Peter F. Drucker reiterates his advice in *The Frontiers of Management* (New York: E. P. Dutton, 1986). He writes that the need to delegate authority has become even more urgent because the Baby Boomers entering business will not find enough top management spots for all the qualified workers. In order to keep talented people challenged, or even satisfied, in lower-level positions, companies must give them increased responsibilities. In this book Drucker also advocates the management attitudes he had helped introduce to Japanese corporations. He asserts that the purpose of business is not to make money but to find and satisfy customers. He admits, however, that it is easier to teach this fundamental principle of business to the Japanese than to Americans. This principle reflects the Japanese cultural value of personal relationships. Individualistic Americans do not have a comparable tradition. The relationship between American business and the community must also be modified. Drucker insists that a business can become more successful by serving the community: learning to do good in order to do well. This same conclusion was expressed by Robert Reich in "Corporation and Nation" (*The Atlantic*, May 1988). These suggestions about business/customer and business/community relations assume that a fundamental change in American values is necessary to revitalize American business practices.

Creating Excellence: Managing Corporate Culture, Strategy, and Change in the New Age by Craig R. Hickman and Michael A. Silva (New York: New American Library, 1984) talks about the need to change the attitudes of executives in order to improve the performance of American businesses. They endorse the following agenda for executives:

1. Creative insight—adopting a variety of critical perspectives and asking the right questions;
2. Sensitivity—binding the workers together into a unified group to produce at high levels;
3. Vision—transforming data into a view of the future;
4. Versatility—anticipating changes and abandoning complacency;
5. Focus—working effectively to implement change; and
6. Patience—learning to live in the long run.

Hamlets possess all of these abilities except perhaps focus. They can therefore help make the necessary modifications to improve American business practices.

Since the qualities valued in *Creating Excellence* are the result of Hamlet's wide-ranging interests and activities, the value of Hamlet's life-style must also be acknowledged. The structure of the work day should be reconsidered in order to encourage Hamlets to participate fully in the work force. The workaholic is, in one important aspect, the mirror-image of Hamlet. They both lack a clear sense of human limitations and so fail to find satisfaction in reasonable goals at work. However, they respond to this situation in opposite ways: The workaholic, hoping to be satisfied someday, strives for constant achievement; Hamlet, accepting the inevitability of failure, embraces inaction on the job as much as possible. Workaholics have been accepted in recent years; Hamlets have been forced out of challenging jobs. Marilyn Machlowitz's *Workaholics* (Boston: Addison-Wesley Publishing Company, 1980) shows the type of work habits that have often been endorsed in the 1980s. Machlowitz implies that workaholics should not worry about making time for other activities; work is separate from the rest of living. She suggests, for example, establishing a charge account with the local cab company so the children can be driven to their appointments or hiring more help so the house will be cleaned. Such solutions are designed to provide more time to continue working without guilt or regret. It is no wonder that Hamlets feel uncomfortable in the work environment produced by such suggestions. Hamlets cannot sacrifice their variety of interests to the single-mindedness of the workaholic life-style. New forms of work time—job sharing and part-time arrangements—can be designed to meet the employee's needs and utilize Hamlet's talents. Of course, it is necessary that part-time workers receive the same respect and proportional benefits granted to full-time workers. New Ways to Work, an organization headquartered in San Francisco, helps businesses institute such alternative employment practices. Over the past fifteen years, they have worked with a variety of corporations, school districts, and law firms.

Carlo M. Cipolla's introduction to *The Economic Decline of Empires* (London: Methuen and Company, 1970) discusses the complacency of thriving economies and the need to embrace change. In a lighter mood—but with no less serious a message—Cipolla's "The Basic Laws of Human Stupidity" (*Whole Earth Review*, Spring 1987) presents the prospect of countries that decline as the intelligent portion of the population takes a more passive role in building the society.